Theology as Construction of Piety

Theology as Construction of Piety

An African Perspective

DAVID T. NGONG

RESOURCE *Publications* · Eugene, Oregon

THEOLOGY AS CONSTRUCTION OF PIETY
An African Perspective

Copyright © 2013 David T. Ngong. All rights reserved. Except for brief quotations in critical publications or reviews, no part of this book may be reproduced in any manner without prior written permission from the publisher. Write: Permissions. Wipf and Stock Publishers, 199 W. 8th Ave., Suite 3, Eugene, OR 97401.

Resource Publications
An Imprint of Wipf and Stock Publishers
199 W. 8th Ave., Suite 3
Eugene, OR 97401

www.wipfandstock.com

ISBN 13: 978-1-62032-131-7

Manufactured in the U.S.A.

To my parents:

Pa Peter Ngong Gweshomoh (late)
and
Ma Juliana Mouh

And my siblings:

Philip Ngong
Magdalene Ngong (Late)
Alexander Ngong
Martha Ngong
Celine Ngong
Regina Ngong

Their laughter and tears inform the reflections in this book.

Contents

Acknowledgements ix
Introduction xi

CHAPTER 1: What is Theology For? 1

CHAPTER 2: Providence and the Triumph of Orthodoxy 37

CHAPTER 3: God and Matter in Medieval Theology 63

CHAPTER 4: Assessing the Theology of Inculturation 91

CHAPTER 5: Constructing an Interdisciplinary Piety 128

Bibliography 155
General Index 167

Acknowledgments

THIS BOOK BEGAN LIFE as an essay of the same title submitted for publication to the *Journal of Pentecostal Theology*. One of the editors of the journal, Lee Roy Martin, pointed out that because the essay was too long, I should shorten it to a length that could be published in the journal. He then suggested that I develop the essay into a book. I took his suggestion seriously and the book you now hold in your hands is evidence of that. I would therefore like to thank Dr. Martin for his suggestion. I would like to thank Stillman College for providing me with a place of employment where I have the opportunity to think through the issues raised in this work. Finally, I would like to thank my wife, Prudencia, for the love and support she gives me and for continuously bearing my follies.

Introduction

WHAT I DO IN this book may not be adequately understood without an understanding of my socio-cultural, economic, and political location. So I will begin with a brief narrative of the place from which I write, that is, my social location. Locating myself in a particular context is not intended to justify determinism or to reduce theology to anthropology or biography; it is rather intended to acknowledge that my background has influenced who I am and how I think. It is therefore my location that leads me to carry out the kind of theological reflections which I do in this book. At the very beginning of my theological career I was taught that it is important for theologians to make explicit the place from which they write because such explicitness would help others in understanding why they say what they say.[1] That practice appears to be going out of fashion as some theologians continue to write from an omniscient perspective. It is not uncommon to find influential theological works that simply delve into the matter of doing theology without telling us who the author is, as if the author does not matter in the construction and reception of the work![2] For some theological works, we hardly know where the author is coming from and so we hardly know the story that makes the author say what they say. The claim that theology is biography, even though limited, still holds significant insight; that is why it is necessary for theologians to begin their work with their biography.[3]

---

1. See Jürgen Moltman, *Experiences in Theology*, 3–9; Laurenti Magesa, "A Theological Journey," 43–53.

2. For the importance of the author in the development of ideas, see Michel Foucault, "What is an Author?" in *The Foucault Reader*, ed. Paul Rabinow (New York: Vintage Books, 2010), 101–20.

3. See James W. McClendon, *Biography as Theology: How Life Stories Can Remake Today's Theology* (Philadelphia, PA: Trinity Press International, 1990).

Introduction

For the past thirteen years, I have lived and worked in the United States of America. However, I was born in the small village of Owe (the letters are pronounced distinctly O-w-e) in the South West Province of Cameroon. Owe is a small village about two to three miles away from Muyuka, one of the noted towns in the South West Province of Cameroon. Like other villages around Muyuka, the road from Muyuka to Owe has remained unpaved througout my lifetime. This unpaved road stretches from Owe to other villages such as Ikata, Bafia, and Muyenge, about fifty miles away from Muyuka. Growing up in Owe, I twice encountered women giving birth by the roadside because the vehicle which was carrying them to the hospital galloped in the potholes of the unpaved road so bad that the women could not reach the hospital where they were heading. This situation is not unfamiliar to many people in Cameroon. I have known pregnant women who have had to walk for at least five miles in order to get to the nearest hospital. One of my younger sisters died during childbirth in one of the most sophisticated cities in Cameroon, Limbe, because the medical care there was abysmal. The same thing happened to one of my very close friends who, at the time, was a Captain in Cameroon's military—his wife died during childbirth in what is considered to be one of the most sophisticated hospitals in the country, but which is woefully ill-equipped to deal with minute medical issues. From this brief background, one can begin to see that my social location is embedded in the story of a modern African environment. This is an environment that has come into contact with elements of modernity such as cars, hospitals, etc., elements of modernity that many expect should make the lives of people better but which have continued to elude many ordinary Africans. That Africans ought to participate in the modern world in a dignified manner is therefore a persistent vision of my theological reflection. That many Africans continue to live and die in appalling conditions, conditions that might be ameliorated by elements of modernity, such as science and technology, continues to be a major challenge to my imagination and is a central concern of this project.

My parents were originally from the village of Babungo in the North West Province of Cameroon. When they got married, they migrated about two hundred miles away from their village and settled in Owe, which is a kind of cosmopolitan village made up of people from almost every region of Cameroon and even Nigeria. In fact, while in Owe, I met people from other African countries such as Chad, Gabon, and Namibia; upon graduating from college, I did anthropological research for a European whose

Introduction

country I do not now remember. Even though Owe is a small village, it is a place where one could cross paths with people from many places around the world. Thus, Owe does not have a single language. Most people in the village speak Pidgin English, which is the lingua franca of many such villages in Cameroon. Thus, I grew up speaking Vengo, the language of Babungo, at home with my parents, English at school with my teachers, and Pidgin English while playing with my friends, some of whose parents came from Nigeria to live in Owe. The culture in Owe, even though originally made up of the Bakweri people, is not homogeneous: there are people from various cultural backgrounds who have come to live in the village and I grew up attending the traditional ceremonies of people from various ethnic groups throughout Cameroon and even Nigeria.

Owe also had many churches, including the Roman Catholic Church, Baptist, Presbyterian, Full Gospel, and many other new Pentecostal churches that came to the village. I attended a Roman Catholic primary school in the village but was a member of the Baptist Church to which I was introduced by my mother. I therefore became a Christian through my mother as my father never became a Christian. He practiced African Traditional Religion and often poured libations to our ancestors. The Christian way and the African traditional religious way were different but not contradictory for us. Whenever one of our relatives died and my father was unable to attend the funeral because he did not have enough money to travel to the village, he would conduct prayer and invoke the name of the ancestor at home in Owe. My mom would be part of all of this and on Sunday we would go to church with her. This should begin to indicate that I grew up in a context where our identity was mixed. One thing did not define us. The importance of this mixed identity to the appropriation of science and technology in African Christian theological discourse will be addressed in the final chapter of this work.

Those of us whose parents came from the North West Province and were permanently settled in the South West Province of Cameroon were often referred to using the derogatory Pidgin English expression "come no go," which means that we were settlers who have refused to return to our homeland. This was a stark reminder that we did not belong in the South West Province of Cameroon; our home was in the North West Province. Politicians often use this expression to sow discord among people residing in the South West Province but who are originally from the North West Province of the country. This is an element of the phenomenon that has

Introduction

come to be known as tribalism in many African countries. (I continue to receive similar treatment in America, as some people keep asking me if or when I will return to Cameroon.) In all this, our parents kept asking us to remember that Babungo, not Owe, was home, even though we were born in Owe and spent very little time in Babungo. Our identity was therefore made up of our Babungo background and the complex cultures of Owe. Thus, while in Cameroon, I had experienced the *mixedness and complexity of culture*. My critical evaluation of culture and my sense of seeing no culture as sacrosanct were shaped not in the United States but in Owe. My education in the United States has of course given me the language with which to express this cultural mixedness but my experience of this mixedness did not come from a reflection on the current buzzword, globalization, but from our shared life in the small village of Owe, where I interacted with people from all over the world. This mixedness and complexity of culture is a very important influence on my theological reflection and the perspective I develop in this book.

My parents were farmers and blacksmith. My father had learned blacksmithing in Babungo, one of the iron-making centers in Africa, and had carried the art to Owe where he was the only blacksmith in the village.[4] (When I expressed my yearning for the development of technology in Africa to one of my colleagues, the colleague suggested that it might well be that my father's trade as a blacksmith has influenced my thought about technology. Perhaps.) In addition to my father's blacksmithing trade, my parents had several farms on which they grew coffee, cocoa, plantain, banana, etc. These cash crops were mostly cultivated by my father. Mother took care of food crops like coco-yams, cassava, tomatoes, and other vegetables. She produced the food for the home and some that were sold in the market in Muyuka. Our parents made just enough for our upkeep.

I am the second of seven children—three boys and four girls. Only two of us have so far had the opportunity to attain higher education—the last born, who is a girl, and me. I was the only one my parents educated up to the university level. In fact, it was thanks in part to the fact that I was granted scholarship by the government of Cameroon that I could attend the University of Yaoundé in Cameroon. It was only after I graduated from the university and started working that the last born had the opportunity to obtain higher education. Mother and father, like most peasants in Owe,

---

4. See Peter R. Schmidt, *The Culture and Technology of African Iron Production* (Gainesville, FL: University Press of Florida, 1996).

Introduction

did not make enough money to send all of us to school. My three younger sisters were married off when they were still teenagers. One of the most traumatic experiences I had was the marriage of my second youngest sister, Martha. Martha is probably the most intelligent person in our home. Upon graduating from primary school, she had excellent placement to attend the secondary school. Her placement was far better than what I had when I graduated from the same primary school—that is how I know she is far more intelligent than me! However, she could not attend secondary school because she had been given into marriage when she was still in primary school. She was about thirteen years old at the time. Our parents had given her into marriage because they needed money to rescue our house from being auctioned off because of debt father owed.

The debt came about in this way: one of the things that our parents did almost every year was to take some of us to the village (Babungo) for what is called "death celebration." This event was meant to remember those who had died that year while father was away. As I indicated above, father was a traditionalist and he never became a Christian. Every year father would borrow money so that we could go to the village (Babungo) and remember one or more relatives who had died during the past year. Father often gave our home as collateral so that if he failed to pay back the money by the end of the year, our home would be sold to repay the debt. Father often successfully paid off the debt. One year, however, sometime in 1992, our father could not repay the money he had borrowed and our house was placed on the market. In order to avoid the sale of our home, father made a deal with a widow who, like my parents, had migrated from Babungo to Owe in search of a better life. The deal was that the woman would pay the money father owed and avoid the sale of our home while my younger sister would marry the widow's son (who was over twenty years old at the time) immediately after she graduated from primary school. After much resistance from me and my younger sister, she was forced into the marriage only to see the boy die two years after their marriage. After the boy died, my younger sister was given (according to our tradition) to the younger brother of the deceased, as his wife. My sister had had a son with the deceased husband. She went on to have another son with the deceased husband's brother after which the second husband immediately divorced her. I have since been supporting her.

Now, my younger sister is only one of the members of my family whom I am supporting. Some members of my family have died and left

Introduction

many kids who need to be educated. As I live in the United States, I send money to Cameroon every month to help one family member or another. This situation is not limited only to family members. It applies to close friends who constantly write to me asking for money to do one urgent task or another, tasks that often seem to have life and death implications. Sometimes it is to go to the hospital for treatment; other times it is to pay school fees for themselves or their kids. This situation, I must confess, is not peculiar to me. I have many friends from Cameroon and Nigeria who could tell the same story. These friends live in Europe or America but they have many family members to take care of back in their home countries. A burgeoning area of research now developing is on the issue of remittances, as economists call the money we send back home to our family and friends who are sometimes in dire need.[5]

The above snippet of my biography is the personal story that influences how I perceive what African theology and Christianity should be doing. In my life, I have witnessed the beautiful and harmful effects of our culture—the importance of remembering ancestors and the burden that could place on people who try to do this. I am also surrounded by people who yearn to make their lives better but whose hopes are constantly being thwarted by the nature of the economics and politics of our context. The context I know is a cosmopolitan context in which everyone is not one thing—many people come from different places to make up what we call a village. I can identify, to an extent, with Anthony Appiah's story in *In My Father's House*.[6] Even though I do not have relatives who span the globe like he does, I do have roots in different places, including my interaction with cultures that span Africa and the globe.[7] It is from this cosmopolitan context that I write.

My experiences have also led me to see that the kind of things which our people desire are quite different from some of the stories that are often told by many reflections on African theology, especially inculturation theology, which has currently morphed into African Pentecostalism. I have

---

5. Roy Richard Grinker, Stephen C. Lubkemann and Richard B. Steiner, eds., *Perspectives on Africa: A Reader in Culture, History, and Representation* (Oxford: Wiley-Blackwell, 2010), 592.

6. Kwame Anthony Appiah, *In My Father's House: Africa in the Philosophy of Culture* (Oxford: Oxford University Press, 1992).

7. For a similar cultural experience, see Ngugi wa Thiong'o, "Asia in My Life," *Chimurenga*, May 15, 2012. Accessed July 31, 2013, http://www.chimurenga.co.za/archives/2816.

come to see that our people desire to attend school, have better hospitals, and raise their kids in decent conditions. Some may think that these are negative aspirations which should be suppressed. However, I do not think so. I think these are aspirations that would enable us participate in the modern world with dignity. That is why I think that the claim that African theology of inculturation or African Pentecostalism help Africans deal with their most pressing need, a pressing need which is often said to be spiritual, is patently false. This is not to say that Africans are not concerned with the spiritual or the supernatural. However, my experience has shown me that the pressing problems for contemporary Africans is not primarily related to the spiritual world as some would want us believe; rather, it is related to the material realm—how to get money to remember the dead decently, how to educate kids, how to provide good health care for these kids, how to live in a peaceful environment in which people can flourish, how to be part of a global and globalizing world in which Africans have often been pushed to the periphery. Young people now have dreams: dreams of making their lives better than those of their parents. That is why some of them risk life and limb to move to other places around the world where they think they might find a better life. It is these aspirations that I seek to address in this book. I have come to see that Africans are tired of being different because this difference has often worked against them. Africans have often been constructed in ways that show them as other, the other who is peculiar and is not supposed to have the kind of decent life experienced by other people around the world. African cultures have often been connected to villages, against modernity, it seems. This is a narrative which is especially pushed by the elites who themselves live decent lives, some of whom spend their time between the West and their dilapidated villages in Africa. This book is a cry against the depiction of African cultures and traditions as locked in the past and pitted against modernity. It insists that Africans want to be part of a modern world in which their lives could be made better. And the theology we weave has a critical role to play in this process. Depending on how we do it, our theology may kill us or give us life. African theologians have often pointed out that the African traditional vision seeks abundant life.[8] However, theology is sometimes done in ways that may negate this abundant life if the meaning of this abundant life is not clearly spelled out. In the modern time, the abundant life should move beyond having many

---

8. Laurenti Magesa, *African Religion: The Moral Traditions of Abundant Life* (Maryknoll, NY: Orbis Books, 1997)

Introduction

kids and cattle to navigating the intricacies of modern life in decent ways. In all this, the development of science and technology is central and religion has to critically engage the development of science and technology in the continent.

The penury which many people suffer in Africa has myriad causes.[9] However, this work focuses on the issue of the development of science and technology because science and technology have helped to smooth some of the rough places in human life. The development of science and technology appear to be critical to the kind of future which young people in Africa seek. If Africa does not focus in a unique manner on the development of science and technology, I fear that our future will continue to be as precarious as our recent past has been. However, it seems to me that the theology of inculturation weaves a narrative that is inimical to this vision. Generally, it seems to have focused too much on the past, attempting to retrieve what it believes to be African culture, while ignoring the precarious lives many Africans live now. Thus, this theology has constructed concern with the spirit world as the dominant preoccupation of the African and is peddling this concern both in Africa and around the world while the people pine in penury. It has failed to see that at the heart of many spiritual problems, is material deprivation. This is the case with witchcraft accusations and so-called demonic blockages, which are now the mainstay of much Pentecostal theology in Africa. Recently, bad hygiene led to the spread of cholera in Cameroon with resultant deaths. Some of the deaths have however been attributed to witchcraft. Awful medical care has led to the death of many women at childbirth. These deaths have also been attributed to witchcraft. In the context of this seeming neglect of the material, what kind of piety are African theologians constructing, when they claim that the spiritual is central to addressing the needs of Africans? Specifically, what do inculturation theologians hope to achieve in the African context of high, and often crushed, hopes of a better life when they peddle the spiritual cosmology as the highest concern of the African in a world which is becoming increasingly scientific and technological?

---

9. For attempts at deciphering the ultimate physical causes of this, see Jared Diamond, *Guns, Germs, and Steel: The Fates of Human Society* (New York: W. W. Norton & Company, 1997) and David S. Landes, *The Wealth and the Poverty of Nations* (New York: W. W. Norton and Company, 1998, 1999). For a discussion of proximate causes, see Todd J. Moss, *African Development: Making Sense of the Issues and Actors* (Boulder, CO: Lynne Rienner Publishers, 2007).

Introduction

This book weaves a theology for a defeated people who wish to no longer remain defeated in a world that permanently marginalizes them. In a classic work of African literature entitled *Ambiguous Adventure*, the Senegalese writer, Cheikh Hamindou Kane, tells the story of the Diallobé, a peaceful, god-fearing and god-dependent African people who woke up one day to find that they had been surrounded by foreigners. When they put up a fight to repel the intruders, they are sorely defeated, largely through the superiority of the weapons of the invaders. This defeat led to deep soul searching among the Diallobé as they attempt to come to terms with the internal weakness of their society and the amoral power of the invading foreigners who have developed the "art of conquering without being in the right."[10] This soul searching leads one of the leading lights of Diallobé society, the Most Royal Lady, to insist that the people of Diallobé must insightfully study their conquerors, namely the West, so as to understand why the Diallobé had easily suffered defeat and how to prevent the possible annihilation of their society in the future. At the end of the novel we do not get any sense that the Diallobé have significantly come to grips with the internal weakness of their society or that they have learnt how not to suffer such ignominious defeat in the future. However, the call of the Most Royal Lady that the Diallobé must take seriously the internal weakness of their society and find means to ameliorate the situation has been seen as a call for Africans to find ways to overcome their marginalization in a modern world dominated by western scientific and technological knowhow.[11] In the face of the continuous weakness of many African societies, in spite of their deep religiosity, this book is offered as a contribution to the process called for by the Most Royal Lady. That is why it is a theology for a defeated people who no longer wish to remain defeated in our modern world. It is a theology for Africans who wish to reevaluate the relevance of their religiosity or faith to the reality of African weakness in the modern world.

It begins by posing the following question: what do theologians hope to achieve when they engage in the task of constructing theology? This is the central question which this book explores. Many answers could of course be given to this question.[12] It could be argued, for example, that

10. Cheikh Hamidou Kane, *Ambiguous Adventure*, trans. Katherine Woods (London: Heinemann, 1972), 37.

11. See Denis Ekpo, "Any European Around to Help me Talk About Myself? The White Man's Burden of Black Africa's Critical Practices," *Third Text* 19.2 (March 2005): 107–24.

12. See Theodore W. Jennings, Jr., *The Vocation of the Theologian* (Philadelphia, PA:

theologians aim to express their commitment to their religion or to express their love for God whenever they engage in theologizing. These are very pious and worthy endeavors. However, the answer which this book gives to that question is that theologians hope to influence piety for better or for worse each time they engage in the task of theologizing. This response is based on the simple reason that whenever theologians, both ancient and modern, write, their hope is that someone somewhere would read their work and by so doing be influenced by their work. This can be seen from the work of the Apostle Paul, the first Christian theologian, to our own day.

Focusing specifically on Christian theology, this book draws from a few critical moments in the development of the Christian faith, such as the development of the Christian doctrine of God in the early church, the rejection of materialistic Christianity of the later Middle Ages, and the contemporary trend in Christianity called postliberalism, to argue that these moments reflect the theological struggle to shape Christian piety. The idea that theology is concerned with the shaping of piety is then used to evaluate African Christian theology, focusing on the theology of inculturation, which has now flowered in the Pentecostalization of African Christianity. It will be argued that the issue for the early church was the development of the Christian doctrine of God while the issue for the Christians of the later Middle Ages was the debate about the place of material things in Christian life. Materialistic faith was faith wedded to holy people, holy places, and holy things—material objects believed to aid in the salvific process. For the postliberals, the issue appears to be the liberal corrosion of what they believe to be authentic Christianity. For African theology, however, the issue is the socio-cultural, political, and economic marginalization of African Christians and peoples in the contemporary world. If these are the central issues for African theology, then, it shall further be argued that the theology of inculturation which has flowered in the rapid Pentecostalization of African Christianity is not well equipped to construct the kind of piety which may adequately deal with these issues. This is so because the theology of inculturation uncritically appropriates the spiritualized cosmology of African traditional religious cultures in its salvific discourses. The uncritical embrace of African traditional religious cultures in its salvific discourses promotes a form of piety which is ill-equipped to deal with the marginalization of Africans in the modern world. The work draws from arguments about the complexity of African traditional religious thought and

---

Fortress, 1985).

Introduction

the early modern doctrine of revelation as involving God's two books, the Book of Nature and the Book of Scriptures, to argue that African Christians and peoples could be enabled to overcome their current marginalization in the global political economy by developing a form of piety that critically accounts for the spiritual and the material, encouraging the cultivation of science and technology in the process.

The method of this work is interdisciplinary because it hopes to evolve an *interdisciplinary piety*, a piety that probes for causes not mainly in the spiritual but also in the physical realms. This interdisciplinary piety is what Africans need in order to evolve a dignified future. This method is based on the assumption that part of the reason for our marginalization in the current global political economy is that we have not been enabled to develop the material resources that would enable us to live dignified lives and curb our dependence on outsiders. And until such dependence is curbed, we will continue to be seen as the laughing stock of the world. It is therefore part of the work of the church to enable African peoples to overcome this dependence by advocating for the development of science and technology. The development of science and technology, it shall be argued, should be taken seriously as a means of deciphering the mind of God in the world. African theologians can therefore not afford to cultivate the suspicious attitude toward science and technology that can be seen among some Western theologians who have considerably benefitted from the fruits of science and technology.

This work therefore evaluates theology not only in terms of its orthodoxy but also in terms of the consequences which particular theological constructions might have on particular churches, societies, communities, and individuals. This method of doing theology is called the *ethics of theology*, akin to the ethics of Bible reading, but different from theological ethics. It examines the ethics of theological discourses, focusing on how salutary a particular theological discourse might be to communities and individuals. It reflects on how theology might edify people and glorify God.

Chapter 1 discusses the meaning of the claim that theology is the construction of piety. It describes piety and draws from Michel Foucault to argue that constructing piety involves power play even though it is inadequate to focus only on issues of power when discussing the construction of piety. It discusses what is meant by an ethics of theology and what makes an ethics of theology different from theological ethics. It analyzes postliberal theology in terms of the ethics of theology. Chapter 2 demonstrates that

Introduction

the arguments around the development of the doctrine of God in the early church are important moments in the construction of Christian piety. It asks whether the theological positions that came to define how the triune God is to be understood in the West and East could have salutary implications. That is, what effects could belief in the God of the early Christian creeds have on societies, communities, and individuals? Chapter 3 argues that aspects of late medieval and reformation theologies were repudiation of the materialistic imagination of the Middle Ages. It was a movement away from devotion centered on material objects such as relics, shrines and even wealth and power, to one centered on the Christ who is encountered in the Bible. In fact, the rationalism which flowered in the Enlightenment had its root in this period. That modern science and technology developed from the rationalism which is rooted in the later Middle Ages, and that modern science seems to have had salutary implications for human life, should inform how rationalism should be evaluated from a Christian theological perspective.

Chapter 4 shifts to African theology. It describes the context in which the theology of inculturation developed and the central elements of this theology. Among some of the issues which African theology of inculturation has addressed are worship, ethics, and African spiritualized cosmology. It demonstrates that while the theology of inculturation has raised issues that need to be taken seriously in African Christianity, it needs to develop an interdisciplinary piety that seriously addresses the question of the development of science and technology in the continent. Chapter 5 discusses the meaning of interdisciplinary piety, giving reasons why this piety should be developed in Africa and how it should be developed. It draws from the doctrine of revelation that sees the Bible and nature as the two books by which God reveals divine life to humans, indicating that human making (*poesis*) in science and technology could be conceptualized as divine making, the scientist could be seen as a theologian and vice versa. Biblical faith and the scientific enterprise are not to be opposed to each other but are rather intricately interconnected for the edification of human beings and the exaltation of God in Christ.

CHAPTER 1

What is Theology For?

TAKING THE WRITINGS OF St. Paul in the New Testament as the genesis of Christian theological discourse, we would notice that from its very beginnings, Christian theology has been an attempt to construct piety. Among the issues which St. Paul addresses in what is believed to be the first written book of the New Testament, *First Thessalonians*, is the delayed Parousia and how Christians were to live in the meantime. During the first century of the development of the Christian faith, many Christians had heightened eschatological expectations; that is, they believed that Jesus Christ would return during their lifetimes to bring an end to the world as they knew it and usher in God's eternal reign of peace. As some of them began dying without the return of Christ, others became concerned. Paul's *First Letter to the Thessalonians* was in part intended to address the Christian unease with the fact that Christ had not yet returned, even though some of them were dying off. It was in this context that Paul wove his theology of areal paradise which speculated that, upon the return of Christ, the Christian dead would be raised and those who were alive would be taken into the clouds to be with Christ in the air (*aera* in Greek) (*First Thessalonians* 4:13–18). Paul ends this pericope by explicitly urging that the Thessalonians should encourage each other with the vision of Christ's return he had just sketched. Clearly, his goal was to help the Thessalonians deal with the exigencies of the faith they had just embraced.[1] We do not see this vision again in Paul's

---

1. See James D. G. Dunn, *The Theology of Paul the Apostle* (Grand Rapids, MI: Eerdmans, 1998), 294–316.

mature theology. Paul's attempt to influence Christian piety continued as he wrote letters to some early churches, addressing one issue or another, ranging from challenges to Paul's apostolic authority to congregational conflicts, and inaccurate beliefs about salvation.

After St. Paul, one of the landmark attempts to construct Christian piety came from the work of the Egyptian, Origen of Alexandria. At a time when Christian theological themes were still ill-defined, Origen took it upon himself to clarify some of these doctrines in what is arguably the first systematic theological treatise, *On First Principles*. In this seminal work, Origen explained how Christians ought to understand God, Jesus Christ, the soul, human beings, salvation, among other loci of constructive theology. Critical moves to construct Christian piety would characterize much of the life of the early church, as we shall see in the next chapter. Attempts to influence what Christians and even non-Christians should see as the central issues in the Christian faith continues to this day in the various theological reflections that have developed in our time.

While the awareness that theology is intended to construct piety has been explicitly recognized in much of the history of Christian theology, this awareness has also often remained unstated. Theologians hardly explicitly say that their goal of doing the work they do is to construct Christian piety, even though that is clearly why they do what they do. In their work, theologians assail or endorse one form of theologizing or another and develop new ways of thinking about the faith. However, they hardly dwell on the possible consequences which following the view proposed in their work may engender. Even those who claim that theology should be an objective academic exercise not tethered to the construction of piety, also hardly appear to recognize that this method, too, does in fact influence piety.

The present work emphasizes the point that theology constructs piety for good or ill by asking about what could be the possible outcomes of particular theological constructions. It is understood that even where one may point out the possible outcome of their work, the actual outcome may be different from the imagined one. However, the fact that one may not completely know the actual outcome of their work does not preclude the necessity of probing the possible outcome. The unwillingness to extensively engage what the possible outcome of particular theological constructions might be may demonstrate a lack of desire to be accountable to the church for which theology is done, the society with which the church interacts, and the God in whom we live, move and have our being. Thus, an attempt to probe all the possible outcomes that may ensue from a particular theological reflection should be a basic element of all theological projects. A theological project that may claim to be promoting the peace of God may actually also harbor elements that may engender strife and so undermine this very peace. Honesty and accountability in theological investigation require that these possible outcomes be probed. Trying to understand the desired outcomes or implications of particular theological constructions is what is understood in this work as the *ethics of theology*. This is different from *theological ethics*. Theological ethics is concerned with the formation of the Christian life from specific theological perspectives. The specific theological perspective that is used to form the Christian life is itself often assumed to be the right way and so is hardly critically probed for the various effects it may have on the lives of Christians, societies, and the church. The ethics of theology, on the other hand, probes the very theological ideas that are used to form the lives of Christians in terms of the kind of persons, society, and church those theological ideas may form. It does not assume that all Christian theological ideas necessarily form and inform Christian lives for the better. There are, for example, ways of looking at the Bible, the church, or God, that may not construct a helpful piety. There also are elements of the Christian faith that clearly do not form people who seek the peaceful reign of God. Thus, while all theology or theological ideas construct piety in one way or another, not all construct helpful piety. Critical reflection on the theological ideas that construct piety is central to the ethics of theology.

Drawing from this background of theology as the construction of piety, this chapter clarifies what is meant by the claim that theology is the construction of piety. It describes piety and draws from Michel Foucault and interpretations of him to argue that constructing piety involves being situated within an episteme and in power play, even though it is inadequate to focus only on issues of power in understanding the construction of piety. It discusses what is meant by an ethics of theology and what makes an ethics of theology different from theological ethics. The chapter analyzes postliberal theology, especially in its Hauerwasian manifestation, in a further attempt to clarify the difference between theological ethics and the ethics of theology.

Theology as Construction of Piety

Constructing Piety

What does it mean to speak of piety as constructed? Does describing piety as a constructed phenomenon mean that there is no surplus reality behind our beliefs and practices? That is, are our beliefs and practices just human constructs, as sociologists would have it, or is there any surplus reality behind them?[2] Is the role of theology mainly to *construct piety*? These are some of the questions which this section addresses, beginning with a description of *piety*. One understanding of piety, and perhaps the central one in Christian theology, has been given by Francis Oakley, scholar of medieval history, who describes piety as "the stance of the faithful before God as it is expressed not only in the struggle to avoid sin and to attain virtue but also in meditation, prayer, adoration, worship, and the longing for union with the divine."[3] This description implies that piety is a way of life which Christians maintain before God and the world. It acknowledges that piety is not only *part* of the Christian religion, or any religion, for that matter; it is rather the *entire* way of life of religious people. What this description also assumes is that piety is expressed in relation to supernatural force or power, what we call God. Thus, piety may also be referred to as spirituality, the recognition that life transcends just what can be seen with the eyes, the awareness of participating in the life of a "transforming and liberating power," the consciousness that there is a "hidden and transforming divine abundance" that tilts the universe towards the good, the beautiful, and the true, beckoning the world to find peace in this hidden presence.[4] Thus, constructing piety bespeaks the process of developing the awareness of participating in the life of a supernatural, hidden reality, which has an ultimate say in how the world turns. For Christians, this reality is the triune God in whom Christians participate through Christ and in the power of the Spirit. For Christians and other theists, therefore, piety involves a relationship to the divine.

Piety is however not a preserve of theistic religions as it is also found in religions that do not give a central place to divinity, such as Theravada

---

2. See Peter L. Berger and Thomas Luckmann, *The Social Construction of Reality: A Treatise in the Sociology of Knowledge* (Garden City, NY: Doubleday, 1966).

3. Francis Oakley, *The Western Church in the Later Middle Ages* (Ithaca and London: Cornell University Press, 1979), 80–81.

4. Mark A. McIntosh, "Theology and Spirituality," in *The Modern Theologians: An Introduction to Christian Theology Since 1918*, ed. David Ford, Third Edition (Oxford: Blackwell Publishing, 2005), 392–93.

What is Theology For?

Buddhism, Jainism, or classical Confucianism. It also includes the beliefs and practices of participants of all religions and even those of no religion. Thus, James McClendon is essentially correct to point out that not all piety, religions, or theologies deal with the supernatural, even though the provenance of theological discourse is rooted in meditation on the supernatural.[5]

When talking of piety, therefore, we should remember that it could refer to the cultivation of diverse forms of life. In this sense, piety could be seen as commitment, that is, how one's commitment shapes one's life. It is this commitment which the twentieth century theologian, Paul Tillich, described as ultimate concern. Construction of piety, therefore, has to do with the process of cultivating ultimate concern.[6] This broad definition of piety also implies that *theology* could be broadly described as discourses that aid in the cultivation of ultimate concern. It is in this sense that one can see the disciplines in the sciences, social sciences, and humanities as theological in character—not that they particularly deal with God or that they developed as an explicit rejection of God, as the English theologian John Milbank points out, but rather that they contribute in the process of creating ultimate concerns, ultimate commitments.[7]

While it is important to recognize this broad description of theology and piety this book, however, focuses on Christian theology and piety, insisting that Christian theology helps to construct Christian piety; that is, Christian theology helps shape Christian relationship with the triune God and the world. One way to understand the claim that theology constructs piety is to acknowledge that theology does not only form Christians to properly love God and the world; it may also lead Christians away from God and a healthy, life-giving appreciation of the world. Thus, theology is double-edged. This should not be surprising given that theologians have accused each other of leading Christians astray from the very beginnings of the Christian faith. The claim that theology's construction of piety is double-edged renders the question of whether it is the role of theology to cultivate piety moot. The question of whether or not theology's main purpose is to cultivate piety is related to the modern claim that one does not need to be a believer of a particular religion in order to do theology pertaining

---

5. James Wm. McClendon, Jr., *Ethics: Systematic Theology*, vol. 1, revised edition (Nashville, TN: Abingdon, 2002), 23–24.

6. Paul Tillich, *Dynamics of Faith* (New York, NY: Harper, 1958), chapter 1.

7. John Milbank, *Theology and Social Theory: Beyond Secular Reason* (Oxford, UK: Blackwell Publishers, 1990, 1993).

to that religion. This claim is in fact correct, especially if theology is divorced from worship and prayer. One may become an expert in the theologies of particular religions even if one is not a member of that religion. However, not belonging to a particular religion, or not being particularly religious does not mean that the theology one constructs does not have the potential to influence others. All theologies, whether from members or non-members of particular religions, have the potential to influence piety. There is therefore no objective theology whether it comes from a religious or non-religious person. All theologies are aimed at constructing piety in one way or another.

However, how should theology be understood as a *construction* of piety? Here the accent falls on *construction* rather than on *piety*. Is theological discourse wholly sociological? In other words, is there more to the Christian belief in God or is the Christian idea of God just an idea which has been fabricated and hoisted on the world, especially Africans, by the powerful in Africa and around the world? This question has to do, in the first place, with the very existence or reality of God. The question of the existence of God is important for African theology because, as one influential African theologian insightfully put it, Africans often feel forlorn because many in the continent experience life as characterized by ways of dying rather than ways of living.[8] The question then needs to be raised: if God exists, why does God allow many Africans to suffer so much? The insistence on the notorious religiousness of Africans has made this question to be a completely no-go area in African theology.[9] Some may argue that this question is not central to African contexts because African Christians are not asking the question of whether there is a God or not. In fact, the plethora of works on the growth of African Christianity all demonstrate how Africans, both inside and outside the continent, are busy worshiping God rather than questioning God's existence.[10] One African evangelical theologian put the matter bluntly: "Africans accept the fact of God's existence without these philosophical or academic arguments."[11]

---

8. Tinyiko Sam Maluleke, "Of Collapsible Coffins and Ways of Dying," *The Ecumenical Review* vol. 54 no. 3 (July 2002): 324.

9. John S. Mbiti, *African Religions and Philosophy* (New York: Praeger Publishers, 1969), 1.

10. See Afe Adogame, Roswith Gerloff and Klaus Hock, eds., *Christianity in Africa and the African Diaspora: The Appropriation of a Scattered Heritage* (London: Continuum, 2008).

11. Matthew Michael, *Christian Theology and African Traditions* (Eugene, OR:

However, the question must not be shirked. If it is true that God exists and that God is a God of life, as Christian theology teaches, the question must be raised as to why it is that many Africans experience life as ways of dying rather than ways of living. The question must be raised as to how it is that a continent in which many people are becoming Christian is arguably the most exploited and violated continent in the world. The question of belief in God in Africa is raised not mainly in the context of philosophical argument about the existence of God but rather in the context of historical praxis. The question is raised because it is an existential, not only an academic, question. This is in keeping with how Africans have traditionally interacted with their gods. Africans have traditionally interrogated the treatment which their gods accord them.[12] Ancient Israel, who, from a Christian perspective, is the original people of God, raised the question of the presence of their God with them from the perspective of historical praxis. This was not to say that ancient Israel generally had atheistic tendencies—even though such tendencies can be seen in later biblical books such as *Ecclesiastes*—but rather that this people questioned the presence of their God in crucial moments of their lives. The destruction of the Temple in Jerusalem in 586/7 ushered in despair that could be compared to that which many Africans suffer today. The biblical book of *Lamentations* properly captured the agonizing mood of many at the time. Even in our time, the question of the existence or presence of God among the Jewish people has been radically reshaped after the holocaust.[13] Considering that African peoples have suffered fates that are even worse than the holocaust should make the question of how and if God exists among us an urgent question.

Thus, the question of the existence or presence of God in Africa is not a peripheral question. Caught in a world in which the continent is continuously being preyed on by internal Christian elites and the Christian and non-Christian elites of other continents around the world, African theology needs to raise serious questions about if and how God exists in Africa. Is the God in whom African Christians believe only a construction of the theologies of the powerful or does God exist and is present in the continent?

Resource Publications, 2013), 66.

12. See Barry Hallen, "African Ethics?" in *The Blackwell Companion to Religious Ethics*, ed. William Schweiker (Oxford: Blackwell, 2006), 406–12; Segun Gbadegesin, "Origins of African Ethics," in *The Blackwell Companion to Religious Ethics*, 413–22.

13. See Steven T. Katz, Shlomo Biderman and Gershon Greenberg, eds., *Wrestling with God: Jewish Theological Response During and After the Holocaust* (Oxford: Oxford University Press, 2007).

Theology as Construction of Piety

If God exists and is present in Africa, how does God manifest the divine life in the continent? In this context, the question does not require mounting a philosophical defense of the existence of God, as the ontological argument of Anselm of Canterbury and the cosmological and teleological arguments of Thomas Aquinas were wont to do. Since David Hume declared the impossibility of corresponding the finite and the infinite and Immanuel Kant declared the impossibility of knowing that which is beyond space and time, it has become increasingly difficult to mount an abstract philosophical argument regarding the existence or non-existence of God. This is not to say that such arguments are not necessary but only that such arguments are not primarily important in contemporary Africa. One may justifiably argue that most African Christians are not asking abstract questions about the existence of God. Their question about the existence of God is rooted, rather, in their existential realities. If God exists and if God is present in Africa, how come that Africa is the laughing stock of the world? This is a question with which the Psalmist struggled and faith in God, for the Psalmist, was expressed in the context of these questions (see Psalm 89).

Contemporary missionaries who spend some time in Africa or with Africans often extoll Africans as model Christians who express strong faith in God in spite of their impoverishment. Extolling African Christians as model Christians has however done little to alleviate the various forms of indignities which Africans suffer in the world. Many of the Christians who extoll Africans as model Christians are from Europe and America, continents that have been very instrumental in the exploitation of Africa. Is the God of the European, American, and now Asian Christians who go to do mission work in Africa a living God who is also present in Africa or is this God simply a constructed idea appropriated to keep Africans in thrall? Within the framework of the perception of piety as constructed, we must take serious account of this question because it may well be that Africans are being deceived to believe in a non-existent God. It may well be that the Christian God who is being preached all over Africa is a God who has been made up by the powerful to keep the powerless in their place. African theology needs to be able to raise these questions and begin to propose some answers to the questions because the lives of our people are at stake in these questions. If our people are being deceived to believe in a God who is thought to be of no consequence by the very people who are partly responsible for bringing this God to Africa, then our people ought to know that. Clarity on how African Christians practice or fail to practice their

What is Theology For?

faith hinges on the kind of responses that are given to these questions. It has long been the practice in African theology to simply compare the Christian idea of God and the idea of God in African Traditional Religions. However, what the questions about the presence of God in Africa demands is that African theology moves beyond this practice to question the very idea of how God exists and is present in Africa.

The catholic Christian tradition teaches the objective reality of a God who is creator and sustainer of the universe. This God is known through Jesus Christ and the power of the Holy Spirit as a Trinitarian God (Father, Son, and Holy Spirit). This God is in the world and yet is more than the world. It is this God who is confessed by all the Christian churches around the world, especially in Africa. In Africa, this God is seen as a God who works all kinds of miracles. However, we also know that the church which proclaims this God has historically been on the side of the powerful in the world. From the time of Constantine to the present, the church has not stopped being on the side of the powerful. Even though Constantinian Christianity no longer obtains, it is still the case that the church is on the side of the powerful of this world. This is an insight that makes liberation theology to be continuously relevant.[14] The history of Christian missions, for example, has been one in which church and empire were often not separate. Even today we can see the example of how the Roman Catholic Church wields power on the side of the powerful when most bishops and even the Pope take the side of dictatorships in Africa. Even though the bishops of the Democratic Republic of Congo recently appeared to have been resisting dictatorship in that country, the case has been different in Cameroon where the bishops and two popes (John Paul II and Benedict XVI) have endorsed the dictatorship of Paul Biya by visiting the country and blessing his government.[15] In the eyes of many Roman Catholics in Cameroon, the president gains legitimacy when he is associated with the Pope. The association of the church with the corrupt practices of the ruling elite is not different in local Protestant congregations where favoritism is running amok, as these congregations often take the side of the rich whose

---

14. Gustavo Gutierrez, *A Theology of Liberation: History, Politics, and Salvation* (Maryknoll, NY: Orbis Books, 1973).

15. For the complex relationship between church and politics in Africa see Paul Gifford, ed. *The Christian Churches and the Democratization in Africa* (Leiden: Brill Academic Publishers, 1995); Terrence O. Ranger, ed., *Evangelical Christianity and Democracy in Africa* (Oxford: Oxford University Press, 2008); Samuel K. Elolia, ed., *Religion, Conflict, and Democracy in Modern Africa* (Eugene, Oregan: Pickwick Publications, 2012).

money pays the staff of the churches. Some influential Pentecostal preachers in many African countries have also cast their lot with the powerful, getting rich on the sweat of their congregants.[16] In our time, the church has generally fallen silent regarding the rapacious lives of the powerful in the world.

All of this goes to challenge the nature of the God the catholic tradition is preaching in Africa. If it is the case that God is creator and sustainer, how come that God appears to be sustaining the few at the expense of the many? If it is true that God cares about the weak and the dispossessed, as Jesus Christ demonstrated, how come that the weak and the dispossessed are the ones whose lives are rehearsals of various ways of dying? A decade ago I reflected on this matter in a poem, part of which reads:

> "There is a new thing," we are told,
> A new thing in the midst of the old,
> We know and do not know the new reality,
> We live in hope in paradox and incongruity,
> We worry about the now,
> Because the now does not exist for us.
> With tattered garments and flat bellies
> Our now constantly shifts into tomorrow
> A tomorrow yet deferred to another tomorrow. . . .
>
> Like cattle for the slaughter we wait . . .
> We wait to be dragged into the shambles
> There to die the death that is our lot,
> Death in the midst of Life.
> Or is our death life, as they say?
> Is death our hope? Is death our life?[17]

This sentiment, expressed a decade ago, still holds true today. In the midst of a Christian gospel that preaches life, the experience of many African people is that of death, quick, early, and painful death. Thus, the question arises: is the God being preached to us a God who is on the side of the powerful? Or could it be that it is not this God who gives life? Over and

---

16. See Asonzeh Uka, *A New Paradigm of Pentecostal Power: A Study of the Redeemed Christian Church of God in Nigeria* (Trenton, NJ: Africa World Press, 2008); Paul Gifford, *Ghana's New Christianity: Pentecostalism in a Globalizing African Economy* (Bloomington, Indiana: Indiana University Press, 2004); Ruth Marshall, *Political Spiritualities: The Pentecostal Revolution in Nigeria* (Chicago, IL: The University of Chicago Press, 2009).

17. David Tonghou Ngong, "Left Behind" *Theology Today* 59 no. 2 (July 2002): 285–86.

over Africans have been urged to rely on God only to have their lives decimated by preventable diseases and the rapacity of Western and Asian powers. Is there an objective reality behind this God who is being preached to us or are we dealing here with a constructed reality that promotes human machinations?[18]

The question of the existence and presence of God in Africa should not be limited only to the Christian faith but should also extend to African Traditional Religions (ATRs), Islam, and other religions that preach the benevolence of God in the continent. Given that ATRs were undermined by Christian missionary and colonial discourses, much of the postcolonial discourses on ATRs have been concerned with valorizing traditional religious ideas. One can detect roughly three attitudes towards traditional religions in the literature. One is the attitude of Christians who see Christianity as the true religion and so have tended to dismiss ATRs. This tendency is manifested by some evangelical Christians and scholars, such as Byang Kato,[19] and contemporary Pentecostalism. The second attitude is demonstrated by those African Christians who accommodate elements of ATRs, such as the veneration of ancestors and the incorporation of African deities into their understanding of God.[20] This attitude is represented by those who advocate the theology of inculturation, which will be discussed later in this book. These scholars tend to see ATRs as a *preparatio evangelica*, a preparation for the Christian gospel in Africa; thus, it has been superseded by Christianity. The third group is made up of advocates of ATRs who hold that ATRs are complete systems that inform the lives of many people across the continent. The religion therefore needs to be understood in its own right.[21] What all these groups have in common is that they take the religious

---

18. For the importance of raising questions such as the above in Christian theology, see Daniel L. Migliore, *Faith Seeking Understanding*, second edition (Grand Rapids, MI: Eerdmans, 1991, 2004), 1–19.

19. Byang H. Kato, *Theological Pitfalls in Africa* (Kisumu, Kenya: Evangel Publishing House, 1975).

20. See A. Okechukwu Ogbonnaya, *On Communitarian Divinity: An African Interpretation of the Trinity* (New York: Paragon House, 1994); Elochukwu Eugene Uzukwu, *God, Spirit, and Human Wholeness* (Eugene, Oregon: Pickwick Publications, 2012).

21. For an insightful discussion of African Christian responses to African traditional religious cultures, see Kwame Bediako, *Theology and Identity: The Impact of Culture Upon Christian Thought in the Second Century and in Modern Africa* (Carlisle, UK: Paternoster Publishing, 1992 and 1999). For those who see ATRs as complete systems, see Kofi Asare Opoku, "African Traditional Religion: An Enduring Heritage," in *Religious Plurality in Africa: Essays in Honor of John S. Mbiti*, ed. Jacob K. Olupona and Sulayman S. Nyang

discourses of African traditional society for granted. That is, the question of whether or not these discourses deal with objective realities or whether they are mainly discourses of power is hardly probed. The main difference, for the first and second groups, is that Christianity tends to be truer than ATRs. For the third group, ATRs tend to be truer than, or at least on the same level as, Christianity. This work introduces a fourth attitude and it is the attitude that questions the objective realities behind Christian, African traditional, and other religious discourses. Do these discourses deal with objective realities or are they constructed systems that serve particular interests and powers? If these religions deal with objective supernatural powers that care about the continent, how come that the peoples of the continent have experienced so much suffering throughout history? Are the kinds of pieties which these religions construct for our peoples pieties that promote suffering rather than health? We will discuss these questions with respect to ATRs when we address the theology of inculturation. For now, however, we only raise the questions.

Raising these questions is necessary because since Friedrich Nietzsche, Sigmund Freud, and Karl Marx, the three Western masters of suspicion, we have been taught not to take societal arrangements at face value.[22] Thus, we can no longer innocently believe that whatever is handed down to us is the truth and nothing but the truth. These scholars have taught us to be suspicious of claims people make because seemingly innocent claims may mask the play of all kinds of interests. Even though Nietzsche is mostly remembered as an atheistic destroyer of the Christian faith, he is one of those Western philosophers who have had significant impact on the way many think today and his ghost, for good or ill, is still with us. While the scientific revolution and the Enlightenment focused human gaze only on present human life, exiling the spiritual for the most part, it was Nietzsche who taught the West that ideas are human creations intended to promote particular interests. Freud introduced the idea that our religious ideas may be just illusions while Marx introduced the notion that religious (Christian) ideas were created by the powerful of the world to keep in check the aspirations of the weak. The ideas of these giants in Western philosophy have been

---

(Berlin: Mouton de Gruyter, 1993), 67–82; Ezra Chitando, "Phenomenology of Religion and the Study of African Traditional Religions," *Method and Theory in the Study of Religion* 17 (2005): 299–316.

22. See Lewis S. Mudge, "Paul Ricoeur on Biblical Interpretation," in *Paul Ricoeur: Essays on Biblical Interpretation*, ed. and trans., Lewis S. Mudge (Philadelphia: Fortress Press, 1980), 4–5.

challenged by theologians of all stripes because these ideas stab at the heart of the religious imagination. However, it appears that much of modern life, especially at a global level, follows the views expounded by these philosophers, namely that humans are in charge of how the world works and they should act accordingly. This has been the main reason behind the divinizing of science and technology in our modern world and the global surge of the military industrial complex. Even though these things seem to benefit many Christians around the world, it has not been quite so in the case of Africa. The imagination that scholars, both in and out of Africa, seem to recommend for the continent is an uncritical religious imagination even as the people are plundered by the scientific and technological machinations of the global powers.

However, the ideas of the three masters of suspicion have come to a head in the views of the French philosopher, Michel Foucault, who does not so much dwell on disputing whether there is any independent reality behind ideas and institutions; he rather probes how ideas and structures have historically been used.[23] It is in this context that his concept of *episteme* becomes significant. For Foucault, episteme is "the system of concepts that defines knowledge for a given intellectual era," it is the "intellectual subconscious" that frames what is accepted as true or false. This notion is linked to his idea of *genealogy* which Foucault sees as a means of understanding the present by questioning "the necessity of dominant categories and procedures."[24] This questioning of dominant categories and procedures challenges the socio-intellectual context in which ideas are formed and is related to the *archeological method* which interrogates the "conceptual structures subtending reality." Foucault points out that ideas that inform the present developed within particular contexts that make them possible. People think in particular ways because they live in particular times and places and under certain conditions. The circumstances that make certain ideas possible need to be probed and these ideas must themselves not be seen as ironclad. Ideas that foster specific forms of domination need to be contested.[25] This means that we have to critically evaluate the whole gamut

---

23. The following reflection is based on Paul Rabinow's discussion of Foucault's thought. See Paul Rabinow, "Introduction," in *The Foucault Reader*, ed. Paul Rabinow (New York: Vintage Books), 3–29.

24. Gary Gutting, "Introduction—Michel Foucault: A User's Manual," in *The Cambridge Companion to Foucault*, ed. Gary Gutting (Cambridge: Cambridge University Press, 1994), 9, 12.

25. Dianna Taylor, "Introduction: Power, Freedom and Subjectivity," in *Michel*

of ideas that have come to shape contemporary Africa, to interrogate why people believe certain things and the consequences which particular beliefs have or may have on the lives of the people. Rather than seeing such questioning as a sociological task usually associated with the work of Max Weber and left to sociologists, this should be a theological task for us today.[26] We should probe how theological ideas affect the lives of our people.[27]

Rather than positing or refuting grand historical abstractions such as human nature, Foucault historicizes them, showing how such ideas actually developed within particular moments in Western history and how they work in constructing present society, determining what is seen as true or false, normal or abnormal. For Foucault, therefore, "there is no external position of certainty, no universal understanding that is beyond history and society."[28] Because of this, he urged political theorists to move from an understanding of power as inherent in a sovereign or even a dominant group to an understanding of the "concrete functioning of power in society," that is, how power actually works in society as a whole. For him, no one and no place is beyond the reach of power or lacks the ability to exercise power. Everyone is implicated in how power works by giving or withholding consent, either tacitly or not. An examination of how power actually works in society will, Foucault held, alert us to the fact that ideas and institutions that appear to be neutral in character actually exercise power in a hidden way. In fact, for him, even the idea of justice is an invention that has been put at the service of power struggle. Even though the idea of justice is usually used to intimate a state of affairs where the status quo is transformed for the better, Foucault alerts us to the fact that the idea itself is not as neutral or innocent as it might first appear. It is an idea used to conjure positive images in people's minds and deployed at the service of the struggle for power in society. Knowledge production is implicated in this struggle for power so that there is a power/knowledge dynamic that contribute to how societal and individual identities have been constructed in our modern world.

Foucault: Key Concepts, ed. Dianna Taylor (Durham, UK: ACUMEN, 2011), 1–9.

26. See Samuel Zalanga, "Religion, Economic Development and Cultural Change: The Contradictory Role of Pentecostalism in Sub-Saharan Africa," *Journal of Third World Studies* vol. XXVII (2010): 43.

27. For an insightful portrayal of the relation between theology and life see Mark Lewis Taylor, *The Theological and the Political: One the Weight of the World* (Minneapolis, MN: Fortress Press, 2011).

28. Paul Rabinow, "Introduction," 4.

What is Theology For?

Foucault calls the construction of human identity in the modern world, the construction of the subject.

The construction of the subject through the interplay of knowledge and power has led to the development of discourses and techniques or practices that we tend to see today as true or normal. Thus, what is true or normal today is not a representation of a deep structure in the way things are; rather, it is the way things have been constructed to be through the use of knowledge/power regimes. These knowledge power regimes are the different modes by which people have been made subjects, the different ways by which people have been given their identity in the modern world. These different and interrelated modes of constructing the subject includes "dividing practices," which includes the practices by which one group of people are clearly demarcated from the rest of society and identified with a single characteristic, such as when those in prison are identified as criminals, even though there are many people who are criminals but who are not confined in a prison. Another means by which people are made subjects and so have their identity given to them is "scientific classification" by which disciplines in the sciences classify things as belonging to one group or another, such as the classification of living and non-living things in biology. The third way by which society or culture constructs identity is through what has been described as "subjectivisation"—the way people cooperate with their own self-formation under the tutelage of an external authority, such as when a Christian or religious person places themselves under a spiritual director.

The ability of culture to form or construct identity has especially been demonstrated in the "individualization techniques" and the "totalization procedures" of the state, engendered by "disciplinary technologies" through which societal attitudes are normalized. Some of the disciplinary technologies by which societal life is normalized include how to promote law and order and manage the economy.[29] Such normalization of elements that govern society hides the power under which people are made subjects and so makes this power invisible. Because people have been conditioned and, in some cases willingly participated in conditioning themselves, to see things in particular ways, they tend to think that such is the natural or normal way things are or how things should naturally be. Thus, Foucault sees the construction of identity as dominated by the interplay of power and knowledge. Power is not just a pernicious phenomenon used by the

---

29. Michel Foucault, "The Means of Correct Training," in *The Foucault Reader*, 188–205.

strong against the week but is also a process of cultural formation in which all sometimes willingly participate. Foucault's mission was therefore to help unearth the processes by which the contingent process of creating identities has come to be regarded as somehow natural. Drawing attention to how societal identity is constructed, he hoped, would enable people to imagine other ways of living, other ways of constructing their identity.[30]

It seems clear from the Foucauldian view of the construction of cultures and identities that what people believe and how they believe is contingent. What people believe and how they believe contribute in defining who they are in the world. Considering that people can actively participation in their subjugation or liberation through what they believe, it is critical that people be enabled to critically evaluate how their beliefs affect their lives. This should especially be the case of religious beliefs in Africa because, even though religious beliefs are not the only beliefs that shape the lives of people, religious beliefs are critical in the African context. Even though the reification of religious discourses in Africa has been challenged, the critical role which religious beliefs play in the lives of many in the continent can hardly be denied.[31] It therefore needs to be critically probed rather than just taken for granted. Foucault's views are quite helpful in showing us how we contribute both to our empowerment and our enslavement. We therefore need to figure out how our religious imagination contributes in liberating or enslaving us.

However, was Foucault right in holding that societal and individual identities are constructed through the interplay of power/knowledge dynamics so that there is no remainder? Foucault's position commits him to a materialism that leaves no remainder, no objective reality outside the material interaction of knowledge/power dynamics. Such a position may not be supported from a Christian theological perspective which has historically argued, to use the language associated with the renowned Swiss theologian, Karl Barth, that God is wholly Other.[32] The wholly Otherness of God means that God is an objective reality different from created reality and historical processes. Theologians such as the American Gordon Kaufman has seemingly taken the route of Michel Foucault to argue that, apart from

---

30. Gary Gutting, "Foucault, Michel," in *The Cambridge Dictionary of Philosophy*, ed. Robert Audi (New York, NY: Cambridge University Press, 1995, 1999), 320–21.

31. See Maia Green, "Confronting Categorical Assumptions About the Power of Religion in Africa," *Review of African Political Economy*, 33.110 (2006): 635–50.

32. Daniel W Hardy, "Karl Barth," in *The Modern Theologians*, 24.

What is Theology For?

an immanent "mystery" of life, there is no remainder behind the realities of Christian doctrines because Christians inhabit a constructed story that needs to be reconstructed for the modern, scientific age.[33] However, it is worth point out that disputes in metaphysical discourses, such as theology, can hardly be adjudicated by argument, whether philosophical or otherwise. This means that there is no way to prove whether Foucault is right or wrong. We can only appeal to our commitment to a particular way of life at this point. Appealing to a particular commitment or way of life may go against the grain of Foucault's vision given that he insisted on the contingency of the reality we experience and urged that we constantly labor to find alternative, especially when the history of the present is a pernicious one. Foucault's commitment to materialism and contingency notwithstanding, Christians need to maintain their commitment in the historical tradition of the Church while critically examining this historical tradition. This historical tradition is anchored in a reality that encompasses but also moves beyond the historical. The historical tradition of the Christian church has taught that the mystery of life is not just immanent or material, as Kaufman seems to have it, but is also transcendent and supernatural. This mystery is named as the triune God. Christians need to realize that it is within this historical tradition that their imagination is formed and they need to be aware of how their imagination is formed within this framework.

Acknowledging that the historical Christian tradition posits a surplus to reality does not mean that Christians have nothing to learn from Foucault. Recently, theologians have increasingly come to the realization that there is much they can learn from Foucault, such as "the need to take the ethical responsibility to examine their utterances in terms of the regimes of power knowledge they propagate and be willing to suspend such judgment in the face of critique within the Christian community."[34] One may immediately add that such critique may not only come from within the Christian community; it may also come from without the Christian community. A community that is not open to critique from both within and without may suffer from an insufferable myopia, as seems to be the case

---

33. Gordon Kaufman, *In Face of Mystery: A Constructive Theology* (Cambridge, MA: Harvard University Press, 1993), ix-xv.

34. James Bernauer and Jeremy Carrette, "Introduction—The Enduring Problem: Foucault, Theology and Culture," in *Michel Foucault and Theology: The Politics of Religious Experience*, ed. James Bernauer and Jeremy Carrette (Hampshire, England: Ashgate, 2002), 4.

with those forms of theological discourses that limit divine presence within the Judeo-Christian tradition.

The Vietnamese-American theologian, Jonathan Tran, has argued that Christians could appropriate some of Foucault's ideas, especially his ideas on the role of power in the formation of identity, to resist or renegotiate the identity which capitalism is constructing for contemporary Christians.[35] Tran's position notwithstanding, we appropriate Foucault in this work not to resist capitalism, which seems to be the enemy of Christianity in the contemporary Western world, but to empower those who have not yet had the opportunity to participate in some of the benefits of the modern world. Granted that modernity and capitalism have their dark sides, they also have benefits which only the few, including those who condemn modernity, are currently enjoying. Thus, capitalism does not simply come off as an enemy to us but as a potential good. In fact, it seems that discourses against capitalism conceal the fact that most of those who rail against it today are beneficiaries of the system. One of the things we learn from Foucault is how the power/knowledge dynamic interacts in such a way that power is not neatly separated from knowledge and vice versa. The power regime of capitalism is therefore not separated from the intellectual context in which theological discourse is carried out. Thus, while it is important to insist that Christians should not be formed by the wiles of capitalism, we must not lose sight of how those who are involved in this discourse have been empowered by capitalistic practices to rail against capitalism. Thus, those who have not significantly benefited from capitalism need to be wary of the provenance of the discourses against capitalism. This does not mean that capitalism should not be critiqued for its anomalies, central to which is the exploitation of the Two-Thirds World for the benefit of the One-Third World; rather, it means that the critique of capitalism that comes from the Two-Thirds World should not simply mimic the views of those who have extensively benefited from, and are even experiencing a kind of fatigue with, the process.

Questioning the critique of capitalism that comes from theologians in the dominant world falls within the ambit of the Foucauldian call to question seemingly innocent or neutral ideas and institutions for the interests which they may be serving. This applies not only to the Christian theology that emanates from the West but also to those that are propagated in Africa today. Whose interests are being served by the dominant forms

---

35. Jonathan Tran, *Foucault and Theology* (London: T & T Clark, 2011).

of Christianity in Africa today? How do the central elements of Christian doctrine preached in much of Africa today affect African Christians? It is now common for some scholars of world Christianity to lift up African Christianity as holding important lessons for the West.[36] However, the question has to be asked about the interests which African Christianity, as it stands, serve? Are the scholars who are lifting up African Christianity as holding critical lessons for the West themselves ready to practice the kind of Christianity which they see in Africa or are they involved in the power/knowledge dynamic that seeks to grant African Christians a sense of importance even as they are being marginalized in almost every other aspect of global interaction? How do African theologians themselves, especially those who promote the theology of inculturation, contribute in marginalizing their own people in the modern world? These questions fall squarely within the framework of what the former Archbishop of Canterbury, Rowan Williams, talks about when he calls for the cultivation of theological integrity. According to Williams, theological discourse has to acknowledge its political character and endeavor to be as clear and forthcoming (honest) about its subject matter as possible. Thus, theological integrity calls for the acknowledgement of the interests served by theological constructions.[37] The recognition of the interests which theological constructions serve and the questioning of the kind of piety which theologies attempt to construct, is what is referred to in this work as the ethics of theology.

The idea of the ethics of theology has been borrowed from the idea of the ethics of reading the Bible. The ethics of reading the Bible has recently been brought to the fore by the feminist biblical scholar Elizabeth Schüssler Fiorenza. She draws from critical theory to argue for the recovery of the "political context of biblical scholarship and its public responsibility." She calls our attention to the fact that Bible reading has consequences—it does things to people—and scholars must be aware of the consequences that their reading of the Bible may have on people. They must be aware of the vision of the world that their reading creates. Bible reading must therefore be accountable to the people whose lives are at stake in the activity of biblical interpretation. Biblical scholars should therefore ask themselves questions about the kind of society which particular readings of the Bible may

---

36. Mark R. Gornick, *Word Made Global: Stories of African Christianity in New York City* (Grand Rapids, MI: Eerdmans, 2011), 5; Andrew F. Walls, "The Cost of Discipleship: The Witness of the African Church," *Word and World* 25.4 (Fall 2005): 433–43.

37. Rowan Williams, *On Christian Theology* (Oxford, UK: Blackwell Publishing, 2000), 3–9.

engender: is it a society of justice and human flourishing or one of injustice and the diminishment of human well-being? For her, biblical scholars should read the Bible in ways that seek "justice and the well-being of all."[38] It is in this light that other scholars advocate that the Bible should be read as if lives depended on it because lives do, in fact, depend on how the Bible is read.[39] Applied to theology, the ethics of theology requires theologians to work for the promotion of the well-being of all because God is concerned about the well-being of all (John 3:16). Christian theologians need to inquire into the potential outcomes of their theological visions and whether this outcome may lead to the well-being of all. How then is this work different from theological ethics?

Ethics of Theology, Theological Ethics, and Postliberalism

Perhaps the place to situate a discussion of the nature of Christian ethics is the recent debate dealing with how the discipline of Christian ethics should be understood. In an important, edited book, which is a culmination of years of reflecting on the matter, Duke Divinity School theologian, Stanley Hauerwas, and Dean of Chapel at Duke Divinity School, Samuel Wells, have called into question the very existence of the discipline of Christian ethics.[40] For them, the discipline of Christian ethics is a modern creation that obfuscates the nature of a distinctly Christian life. The introductory chapters that set the tone for the other contributions in the book portray Christian ethics as a modern creation based on the views of Immanuel Kant who placed Christian ethics within the context of universal reason rather than in the context of how Christians have historically understood the nature of the Christian life. Hauerwas and Wells argue that modern

---

38. Elizabeth Schüssler Fiorenza, "The Ethics of Biblical Interpretation: Decentering Biblical Scholarship," *Journal of Biblical Literature* 107 no. 1 (1988): 3–17.

39. Garry A. Phillips and Danna Nolan Fewell, "Ethics, Bible, Reading As If" in *Bible and Ethics of Reading, Semea 77*, ed, Danna Nolan Fewell and Garry A. Phillips (Atlanta: Scholars Press, 1997), 1–21.

40. Stanley Hauerwas and Samuel Wells, eds., *The Blackwell Companion to Christian Ethics* (Oxford: Blackwell, 2004, 2006). Although this book is edited by Hauerwas and Wells and contains contributions from many scholars, the book may be described as Hauerwas's book because the organizing principles of the book is Hauerwasian, that is, it is based on ideas Hauerwas has been putting forward throughout his academic career. That is why the editor describe the book as "Hauerwas's 'big book'" (p. xiii). Also see Stanley Hauerwas, *A Community of Character: Toward a Constructive Christian Social Ethic* (Notre Dame, IN: University of Notre Dame Press, 1981).

What is Theology For?

Christian ethics was created in Germany through Kant and Ernst Troeltsch and blossomed in America in the twentieth century as a result of the social gospel movement and the influential work of H. Richard Niebhur, *Christ and Culture*. Before the emergence of the modern view of Christian ethics, Hauerwas and Wells argue, Christians had basically construed their lives theologically as designed to fulfill the righteousness of the God of Jesus Christ through the power of the Holy Spirit. Thus, before modern Christian ethics was invented, Christians based their understanding of the Christian life on the fact that they were followers of the Christ who called Christians to be friends of God. The central context for the formation of Christian character was worship or Eucharist. In this context, theology and ethics were not separate disciplines because in worship Christians understood themselves theologically and acted from a specifically Christian theological perspective rather than on the postulates of universal reason which Kant developed and on which modern Christian ethics was built. It was for this reason that early Christians read the Gospels as a manual of Christian formation, seeing themselves as people who were to be imitators of Christ.

According to Hauerwas and Wells, even though the coming to power of Emperor Constantine vitiated the courage that it took to maintain the Christian difference, Christians still attempted to maintain this difference by, in some cases, becoming ascetics and by insisting on the worship of the true God detailed in St. Augustine's *City of God*. On the centrality of the worship of the true God in the moral formation of Christians, Hauerwas and Wells cite book XIX of Augustine's *City of God*, which states that a people cannot be just if they do not worship the true God:

> Justice is found where God, the one supreme God, rules an obedient City according to his grace, forbidding sacrifice to any being save himself alone; and where in consequence the soul rules the body in all men who belong to this city and obey God, and the reason faithfully rules the vices in a lawful system of subordination; so that just as the individual righteous man lives on the basis of faith which is active in love, so the association, or people, of righteous men lives on the same basis of faith, active in love, the love with which a man loves God as God ought to be loved, and loves his neighbor as himself. But where this justice does not exist, there is certainly no "association of men united by a common sense of right and by a community of interest." Therefore there

Theology as Construction of Piety

> is no commonwealth; for where there is no "people," there is no "weal of the people."[41]

Hauerwas and Wells observe that the text from Augustine cited above could be seen as a blueprint for Christian ethics because it shows the Christian life as shaped by the virtues that are in turn shaped by love for God. The cited text also shows that the Christian love for God determines the relation of the church to the social order and in this relation the church should understand itself as "the only true political community."[42] This emphasis on the cultivation of Christian virtue, they argue, could also be seen in the *Summa Theologiae* of St. Thomas Aquinas and the stories of the lives of Christian saints who were seen as moral examples by medieval Christians. During the Middle Ages, the cultivation of the Christian life was so central that, Hauerwas and Wells point out, Christian participation in the Crusades and the Spanish Inquisition should be read within the context of Christian moral formation.

> It is important to remember that the Crusades and the Inquisition, so habitually derided in modernity, both gained general support from their ability to transform elitist spirituality into popular practices. The Crusades captured the imagination of the medieval church, not so much because Islam presented a mortal threat, but more because here was a chance for ordinary people to find salvation. Those who were not spiritual or material aristocrats, and especially those whose sins strained their confessors' ears, found in the Crusades a pilgrimage that could reincorporate them into the body of the faithful. Likewise the Spanish Inquisition, while it promoted disturbing degrees of hostility to Jews and Muslims, gained its strength from the revival of Catholic piety in Spain and Italy in the late fifteenth century through oratories devoted to works of charity—a revival that led to the establishment of the Capuchins and Jesuits. It is not far from the discovery that everyone *could* be holy to the insistence that everyone *should* be.[43]

This medieval Christian life took place within the framework of what has been described as the medieval synthesis in which church and state were intimately connected. This synthesis was however undermined by the

---

41. Cited in Stanley Hauerwas and Samuel Wells, "Why Christian Ethics Was Invented," in *The Blackwell Companion to Christian Ethics*, 43.

42. Cited in Hauerwas and Wells, "Why Christian Ethics was Invented," 44.

43. Hauerwas and Wells, "Why Christian Ethics was Invented," 47. Emphasis in original.

Reformation. Hauerwas and Wells point out that even though the Reformation undermined this synthesis, the ethical vision of the reformers, such as Martin Luther and the Anabaptists, was not severed from the biblical and theological framework in which it had been tethered since the emergence of the faith—Jesus Christ and the Bible were still central to these reformers. The Anabaptists are especially significant for Hauerwas and Wells because they (the Anabaptists) saw church and state as coterminous and called for the non-violent ethic of Jesus Christ.

The story so far, as Hauerwas and Wells tell it, describes a time before the invention of what is described today as Christian ethics, a time when there was no severance between ethics and theology, a time when worship of the true God was seen as the context for the formation of Christian habits, a time when Christians relied on the resources of the church to "fulfill all righteousness."[44] Although Hauerwas and Wells hold that fulfilling all righteousness is "the purpose of Christian ethics," they are also clear that even though the time stretching from the early church to the breakdown of the medieval synthesis could be seen as somehow ideal, at no time have Christians ever gotten it right and it does not appear that, safe for God's total eschatological reign, Christians will ever get it right. However, it appears that the conception of the Christian life was more substantive before the emergence of the modern period. With the emergence of modernity, several things went wrong and so made modernity bad for the flourishing of Christian piety—there was a severance of the centrality of the church for the Christian life and Christians came to be seen as people who needed to appropriate the Christian faith to fund other forms of life, such as the democratic state; Christian ethics came to be founded not on the formation of Christian virtues/habits through the worship of the true God in Christ but on Kantian universal reason; the Kantian separation of the noumenal from the phenomenal, which declared that the noumenal is unknowable, came to separate theology from ethics, thus leading to the development of Christian ethics. The edited book by Hauerwas and Wells intended, therefore, to do two things: to locate Christian formation in worship and the Eucharist and to problematize and eliminate the distinction between ethics and theology. Thus, they raise the question not only of what Christian ethics is but also about whether Christian ethics and theology should be

---

44. Hauerwas and Wells, "The Gift of the Church and the Gifts God Gives It," in *The Blackwell Companion to Christian Ethics*, 14.

separate, as is presently the case in the academy. After Hauerwas and Wells, is it still possible to speak of Christian ethics?[45]

Hauerwas and Wells have done well to draw attention to the fact that Christian ethics and theology should not be regarded as separate disciplines. How Christians should live is not to be separated from what Christians believe. The early church saw that it was critical to carefully craft what Christians should believe because Christian beliefs have implications for Christian living. What Christians believe about God, for example, contributes in shaping the Christian life. This was the understanding of the relation between Christian belief and practice that animated the debates about the Christian idea of God in the early church. However, to say that theology and ethics should not be separated does not mean that it is no longer necessary to speak of Christian ethics. In spite of their attempt to not separate theology from ethics it is still clear that Hauerwas and Wells see the formation of Christian habits or character, using the resources of the liturgy, as central to this discourse. This formation may not be separated from Christian theology but it also does not mean that it can simply be identified with theology. Even though theology has ethical implications, this does not mean that theology should be collapsed into ethics or vice versa. Theology is more than ethics. It speaks of the triune God's freely established relationship with, and providential care of, the whole of creation. Because Christian theology is more than ethics, it will always be useful to speak of Christian ethics even though the two should not be rigidly separated.

It is indisputable that Christian worship or liturgy has significant potential to form Christian habits. An *ethics of theology*, however, only recognizes the *potential* of Christian worship to form Christian character in a salutary way rather than simply assuming a priori that "Christians believe that the set of rules they practice and embody in worship is a *good* set of rules, a set by which they may identify and judge other sets."[46] Through such a priori assumptions, Christian practices in worship are already accounted good and they become the only lens by which other views may be judged. In this scheme of things, Christian practices have the upper hand over all other forms of life and can judge but cannot be judged by other ways of life. Thus, the church can only judge others but cannot be judged by

---

45. For more on the debates and history of Christian ethics, see the section on "Christian Ethics" in William Schweiker, ed., *The Blackwell Companion to Religious Ethics* (Oxford: Blackwell, 2006), 197–236.

46. Stanley Hauerwas and Samuel Wells, "Christian Ethics as Informed Prayer," in *The Blackwell Companion to Christian Ethics*, 4. Emphasis in original.

others. Or even where it is granted that others can judge the church, it does not appear that the church may learn from others to improve how it forms the character of Christians.

The Hauerwasian understanding of ethics above is different from the Greek foundational understanding of ethics as "the rational analysis and justification of norms, practices, forms of character, and ways of life believed to secure human happiness or well-being (*eudaimonia*)."[47] The classical view of ethics does not assume that the way tradition forms people is necessarily good or that traditions can declare a priori that they are good even before they are put to the test. That is why the critique of every tradition is a critical part of ethics, Christian ethics included. It is true that the Christian faith proposes a particular way by which *eudaimonia* might be achieved and forms people to live according to that vision. However, limiting Christian formation only to Christian worship or even only to the church may blind Christians to other ways of life that might inform or critique the Christian faith. Nicholas Healy succinctly makes this point in his review of the book under consideration when he stated that Christian ethical reflections do not only happen in the church but also "in a family or a university setting, with Christian and non-Christian friends."[48] Acknowledging this fact means that Christian ethical reflection appropriates more resources than only those available through worship. By rejecting the fact that Christians may make use of universal reason in ethical refection, Hauerwas and Wells deprive Christians of other resources that may prove beneficial. This is theologically problematic because of its strict division of the church and the non-church. Such a division neglects the value of the doctrine of creation and providence to Christian ethics and undermines the bridge which Hauerwas and Wells claim they want to build between theology and ethics. All this states a central difference between *Christian ethics*, at least as conceived by Hauerwas and Wells and other likeminded theologians, and the *ethics of theology*: the ethics of theology assesses the possible outcomes of the theological ideas that form Christians, while theological ethics, at least in the Hauerwasian mold, begins from the point that Christian ideas are already good ideas. Also, the ethics of theology does not

---

47. William Schweiker, "On Religious Ethics," in *The Blackwell Companion to Religious Ethics*, ed., William Schweiker (Oxford: Blackwell), 1.

48. Nicholas Healy, "Review of *The Blackwell Companion to Christian Ethics*, eds. Stanley Hauerwas and Samuel Wells," *Studies in Christian Ethics* 19 (April 2006): 122.

despise universal truths given that Christians do not hold a monopoly on truth.

Further, let us focus on the central claim in this work, namely that theology is the construction of piety. Hauerwas and Wells seem to have, on the one hand taken seriously the fact that theology constructs piety but have, on the other hand, not taken that fact seriously enough. They have taken seriously the fact that theology is the construction of piety inasmuch as they have insisted that Christian moral habits are formed in the context of Christian worship. Thus, they have seen that the Christian character would not be formed by central Christian beliefs if it is not formed within the context of worship. They are clear that they do not want Christians to be formed by universal truth claims that seem to be accessible to everybody or by the democratic capitalist state. However, they have neglected to point out that their proposal that Christian virtue should be formed only by worship is just one way of constructing Christian piety. Even during the early church, Christian formation did not take place only within the context of worship. There were those, as Hauerwas and Wells point out above, who moved away from society to live as lone hermits. Also, it is true that Christian habits may be formed through worship but that is not quite obvious, given that the actions performed in worship are not transparent.[49] In fact, the book by Hauerwas and Wells was written in order to draw attention to the centrality of worship. This does not mean that those who applied universal reason to Christian ethical issues did not attend church; they did, but interpreted the worship experience differently as something that was not incompatible with the appropriation of universal reason in the construction of Christian ethics. Even more, people might regularly participate in Christian worship and might want their ethical actions to be informed only by worship practices; however, they might end up being formed in ways that might be objected to by Christians and non-Christians alike. The church in America is a good example of this. For a very long time, many Christians attended many churches in America that taught them that racism is the will of God. That racism is the will of God was read from the Bible during worship services and so people believed it. In America, many churches are still divided on racial lines. One wonders the kind of formation which Christians who attend a dominantly white or a dominantly black church

---

49. See Michael Banner, "Review of *The Blackwell Companion to Christian Ethics*, eds., Stanley Hauerwas and Samuel Wells," *International Journal of Systematic Theology* (January 2007): 108.

may reap from worship or the Eucharist. This is not to say that worship may not inculcate good values or habits in Christians; in fact, it does. It does not also mean that the Christian faith does not bring out good vision of life; it does. The argument here is, first, that the significance of Christian worship to Christian ethical formation is ambivalent and, second, that Christians need to be formed in particular ways if they are to live up to the vision of the Christian life which Hauerwas and his sympathizers are advocating. This argument makes the point that theology is the construction of piety intended to promote particular visions. We need to be aware of the kind of vision that is being inculcated even through Christian worship.

While Christian ethics, as seen by Hauerwas and Wells, simply seem to draw from Christian beliefs and practices to form the Christian life, one of the points this book is making is that these beliefs and practices should themselves be interrogated as to the kind of habits or character they may form in an individual or group of people. What kind of person or group of people, for example, is formed by the view that only the Christian vision of life is correct and all other visions of life must be judged only from their point of view? A central claim of the Hauerwasian view of Christian ethics is that Christians should be formed using only Christian beliefs and practices and that Christians can and should judge others only from the context of their particular beliefs and practices. That is one of the reasons why Hauerwas has been unsatisfied with Christians who have drawn from other sources to inform their Christian life. According to Hauerwas, Christians who borrow from other sources, especially from the Kantian perspective of universal reason, fail to do Christian ethics because they do not sufficiently focus on Christian particularity. These Christians do not sufficiently acknowledge that the church is the only true political community and have thus sold out to other political communities, such as the democratic state. So the question becomes: what kind of person is formed by the idea that the church is the only true political community while all other political communities are illegitimate?

Having been born and raised in a village in Cameroon, I can appreciate the centrality of village life in our upbringing. Even though there were many Christians and many churches in our village, we did not so much relate to each other based on the fact that we were Christians as on the fact that we all belonged to the same village. Some of the villagers who became what is called "born-again" Christians instead became deeply antisocial because they believed that they were the children of God while other

Theology as Construction of Piety

Christians and villagers who were not Christians were going to hell. To this day, Christians who believe that they are the children of God while non-Christians are doomed continue to disrupt communal life in the villages. Is it not burdensome for someone to always think that only they have the right answers to critical questions of life? What kind of relationship might people who believe that they have the only true answers to central questions of life have with other people in their community? Healy has posed this question in terms of the kind of mindset that is at work when the church and the world are seen as "two opposing, monolithic camps, the one right, the other wrong."[50] And the church is often seen as having the right answers while the world does not.

Also, what kind of habit or character is constructed by a faith which sees the Crusades or the Spanish Inquisition as somehow a legitimate way to express the faith? Is it therefore legitimate, as Hauerwas and Wells seem to think, for ordinary Christians to participate in violence, such as the Crusades, as a means of achieving salvation? The intimation that the Crusades and the Inquisition might have been ways of expressing a revival of the Christian faith seems to go against the non-violence which Hauerwas and Wells see as critical to the Christian moral life. Thus, unlike the view of ethics which sees Christian beliefs and practices as inherently good, the ethics of theology questions the salutary character of the theological beliefs and practices that inform the Christian life. Christian beliefs and practices may be good but their goodness is not always obvious, especially to those who have been on the receiving end of some of the unsalutary effects of Christian formation.

Christian beliefs and practices are not always transparent and so have to be explained in particular ways for them to make sense. That is why the church has often needed teachers and theologians. As pointed out earlier, that is why Hauerwas and Wells needed to put together the book we have so far been critiquing. The book takes particular items in the practice of Christian worship and discusses how the Christian character might be formed by them. Some reviewers of the book have argued that some of the interpretations are forced. It is not clear, for example, that the Greeting in the liturgy should bring about racial harmony that moves beyond racial reconciliation, as one article in the book argues. Churches composed of a single race, as is the case in America (in spite of its multiracial context) will hardly see the Greeting in the worship service as necessitating a form of life

---

50. Healy, "Review of *The Blackwell Companion to Christian Ethics*," 123.

that moves beyond racial reconciliation.[51] It is also not clear that Christians gathered around the Eucharist represent "an alternative to the bodies that incorporate systemic sin," such as transnational corporations, as another article in the book argues. In fact, among the Christians gathered around the Eucharistic table are owners of or investors in transnational corporations who live by the very capitalistic tendencies that Hauerwas decries. In this instance, the church is already so entangled in the world that the Hauerwasian attempt to separate the two is at serious risk of becoming futile. Because the elements of the liturgy have to be interpreted, we need to evaluate how they are being interpreted in order to determine whether or not they may have salutary outcomes. The current project thus goes beyond the conception of Christian ethics that assumes the a priori salutarity of Christian doctrines and practices but maintains the classical understanding of ethics as reflection on beliefs and practices that may enhance *eudaimonia*.

Through engaging the edited book by Hauerwas and Wells, have already been assessing postliberal theology because the Hauerwasian vision of Christian ethics is situated within the context of postliberal theology to which he is a significant figure. The shift which Hauerwas attempts to generate in Christian ethics is similar to the shift which other significant representatives of the movement, such and Hans Frei and George Lindbeck, have generated for biblical hermeneutics and the study of theological doctrines, respectively.

So, what is postliberal theology? Postliberal theology attempts to overcome what it sees as the corrosive effect which modernity has had on Christian thought and practices. These corrosive effects have manifested themselves especially in the Western Christian espousal of universal reason (the possibility of accessing truth that is available to all), individualism, and democratic capitalism. The stance against individualism, for example, is one of the reasons why communal practices are stressed, as we see in Hauerwas' stress on the place of Christian worship in Christian formation. George Lindbeck also proposes that religion or faith does not have to do with individual rational assents to some beliefs or with feeling but with communal formation. For him, therefore, religion or faith is learned just as people learn a language. Just as one can learn a language only within the context of a community, so too is the Christian faith learned only by being

---

51. Emmanuel Katongole, "Greeting: Beyond Racial Reconciliation," in *The Blackwell Companion to Christian Ethics*, 68–81. Also see, Healy, "Review of *The Blackwell Companion to Christian Ethics*," 122; Banner, Review of *The Blackwell Companion to Christian Ethics*," 108.

immersed in the community in which Christian narrative is rehearsed. Lindbeck's position has been described as the "cultural-linguistic" model of understanding Christian doctrine.[52]

Postliberal theology also intends to regain premodern sensibilities in its engagement with the Christian life, especially in relation to its approach to the Bible and Christian tradition. It emphasizes "the peculiar grammar of the Christian faith" as discerned from the biblical narrative and the premodern Christian tradition. Also, for postliberal theology, theology serves "a primarily corrective rather than a constitutive function." That is, theology does not make the faith, rather, it helps Christians to live out the faith well within the parameters of the Christian grammar or language. Like linguists who only describe how a language works rather than prescribing how it should work, theologians do not create the faith but rather describe how it works best. Since theology does not make the faith but rather describes it, postliberal theology "sees its primary task as descriptive rather than apologetic."[53]

This last point—postliberal theology's understanding of the task of theology as corrective rather than constitutive, as descriptive, rather than apologetic—obfuscates the extent to which theology actually creates the faith rather than just describing it. As proponents of postliberal theology know fully well, the Christian faith is not static; rather, it is dynamic. The recognition that the Christian faith is dynamic rather than static has led Healy to suggest that the elements of Christian worship should not be regarded as no longer in need of reform as appeared to be the case in the Hauerwasian vision of Christian worship.[54] Because the Christian faith changes over time and space, different elements that have not always been part of the faith, emerge. These different elements do not usually fall within the parameters or grammar of the faith, but sometimes even contradict the faith. The grammar of the Christian faith is therefore like the grammar of any language—it has the potential to both expand and contract. And these expansion and contraction are sometimes occasioned not only by the native speakers of the language but also by linguists (read theologians). Thus, theologians are not innocent people who simply describe how the Chris-

---

52. James Fodor, "Postliberal Theology," in *The Modern Theologians: An Introduction to Christian Theology Since 1918*, ed. David Ford (Oxford: Blackwell, 2006), 232; George Lindbeck, *The Nature of Doctrine: Religion and Theology in a Postliberal Age* (Loiusville, KY: Westminster John Knox Press, 1984)

53. Fodor, "Postliberal Theology," 229–31.

54. Healy, "Review of *The Blackwell Companion to Christian Ethics*," 123.

tian faith works best; they also bring in new elements that give direction regarding how the Christian faith should work. Thus it is that someone like St. Augustine of Hippo, a theologian by the way, has come to have a huge influence on the Christian understanding of just war. Jesus Christ did not teach anything about a just war; however, it has come to be part of the Christian language through the influence of St. Augustine and later theological developments. It is debatable whether the just war theory is a legitimate expression of the Christian faith. However, it is not debatable that the just war theory is now part of the Christian tradition. It is perhaps the realization that Jesus taught nothing about the just war that has led someone like Hauerwas to opt for non-violence. But not all in the postliberal theological movement agree with his stance. Thus, portraying theologians as people who simply help Christians understand how to live the Christian life within the framework of Christian grammar is to obfuscate the fact that theologians sometimes actually create the faith, rather than work only within the grammar of the faith.

Further, one of the significant leaders of the movement, Hans Frei, proposed that the biblical narrative needs to be recovered for theology. By calling for the recovery of the biblical narrative for Christian theology, Frei was decrying a tendency in modern liberal and conservative theology that seems to appropriate the Christian story to fit another story. Thus, rather than entering the world of the Bible and letting the contemporary world be informed by the biblical world, modern Christian theologians appropriated the biblical story to fund the modern vision of life. According to Frei, "[a]ccommodating the Bible to a more determinative framework robs scripture of its own reality-constituting powers, either by transforming it into a source for historical reconstruction of past events or reducing it to simply one more instantiation of timeless, universal symbols or general quality of human experience."[55] According to Frei, therefore, instead of letting our world interpret the Bible, we should rather let the Bible interpret our world. Christians need to enter the scriptural narrative and live it out as their narrative. This method of biblical appropriation obviously takes the Bible quite seriously by seeing it as the sole determinant of contemporary Christian life. It seems to be similar to the understanding of the Bible which the American historian, Philip Jenkins, sees as characteristic of Bible reading by Christians of the global South (especially Africa and Asia). According to Jenkins, most Christians in the global South tend to

---

55. Fodor, "Postliberal Theology," 235.

take the Bible very seriously because they tend to inhabit the biblical world. Because to many in the global South life is still very much as was the case during biblical times, it has not been difficult for these Christians to enter the world of the Bible and appropriate it as their own. For example, because the lives of many Christians in the global South are still animated by the presence of spiritual reality, they tend to take the spiritualized cosmology of the Bible seriously. Thus, belief in miracles, for example, is dominant in the global South. Jenkins laments that through the development of science and technology (critical elements in modernity), the churches of the global North (America and Europe) have lost touch with the background that leads Christians to take the Bible seriously.[56] Jenkins seems to suggest that to take the Bible seriously, Christians in the global North need to learn from their counterpart in the global South. It is however not clear if Jenkins' description of how the Bible is appropriated in the global South falls within the narrative framework which Frei called for, given that Western Christian theologians and biblical scholars, especially postliberal theologians, hardly engage the views of global South Christians. Engaging the views of global South Christians may, perhaps, lead postliberal theologians to see that they have much in common with these Christians. The emphasis on the appropriation of the biblical world and the stress on communal formation in opposition to individualism, are among interests that postliberal and global South Christians may share. However, it must be pointed out that while entering the biblical world may lead Christians to appropriate elements of the faith that may otherwise be ignored, the method raises some questions.

The first question it raises has to do with the nature of physical life in the premodern world, as found in the biblical narratives and the Middle Ages. Postliberals say that they want to reclaim premodern religious sensibilities but they hardly address issues dealing with the physical life which people lived during premodern times. During premodern times life, for many, was hard and short because much of the technology which has contributed to easing physical life for many today had not been developed. These technologies, such as those that led to the development of modern medicine, were developed in modern times. This is not to suggest that modern science and technology are unproblematic; rather, it is to suggest that modern technology has done much to improve human life. Think of the reduction in maternal and infant mortalities as a result of developments

---

56. Philip Jenkins, *The New Faces of Christianity: Believing the Bible in the Global South* (Oxford: Oxford University Press, 2006).

What is Theology For?

in modern medicine. Jenkins has suggested that one of the reasons why Christians in the global South easily dwell in the biblical narrative is the fact that life in many societies in the global South is just as precarious as it was for many in biblical times. It appears that such precarious life is the soil in which premodern sensibilities grow; thus, advocating premodern sensibilities is not only about calling for the appropriation of premodern religion or philosophy in our time, but also the appropriation of premodern life as a whole, including the hardships and shortness of life that comes with that. Given that the ideal setting for the flourishing of premodern sensibilities is the premodern world, which can partly be experienced in parts of the global South today it appears that postliberalism would thrive in parts of the global South. Postliberal scholars however hardly engage the difficulty of life in some areas of the global South. They hardly even spend time in the regions of the global South which could serve as testing ground for the theological imagination they advocate.

The global South, however, does not need to indwell the biblical narrative, as it currently does with apparent applause from Western Christians. They should rather critically indwell the biblical narrative with an eye to how modernity may improve their standard of living. To say that Christians have to indwell the biblical world and have their lives be shaped by that world rather than the modern world does not sufficiently address the precariousness of life for many in Africa, Asia, and Latin America. It appears that the dominant accent in postliberal theology is that Christians should be wary of modern technology. Thus, an essay that attempts to discuss how Christians should engage the issue of hunger in the contemporary world seems to endorse fair trade, fasting, almsgiving, and the Jubilee Debt Campaign but called on Christians to remain very suspicious of the technology that leads to the development of Genetically Modified Foods. This suspicion of technology is further manifested by the rather problematic claim that "hunger is often the result of inequitable distribution, not of inadequate production" of food.[57] Given that the essay began with a graphic description of how hunger led to slow and painful deaths in Ethiopia, one would be justified to wonder how the rejection of Genetically Modified food might apply to the people who were dying of hunger in that country. If they had the technology to produce their own food, even their own genetically modified food, would they have died of hunger? Where was the

---

57. Robert Song, "Sharing Communion: Hunger, Food, and Genetically Modified Foods," in *The Blackwell Companion to Christian Ethics*, 388–400.

33

food that had already been produced when those people were dying—with the hungry people in Ethiopia or in Europe and America? The point here is that the claim that hunger is often caused by inequitable distribution rather than inadequate production is simply not correct. In Africa, hunger has often been caused by limited production sometimes caused by premodern farming methods. The farming technology is often inadequate and so people cannot often weather famines engendered by droughts. Most farmers in Africa still engage in subsistence farming that is at the mercy of the elements of the weather. There might be more food produced in America or Europe during the same time that Africans lack food but Europe and America are not Africa. Casting the distribution, rather than the production, of food as the problem ignores the fact that much of the food in the world is not being produced in Africa. Implying that Africans should rely on foods produced outside the continent casts Africans as victims who simply need food that have been produced elsewhere rather than as agents who should be producing their own food in great quantity. Africans should rather be encouraged to develop the technology that could enable them to produce their own food rather than be told to be wary of this technology, expecting food to be distributed from elsewhere to them.

Another question which the postliberal desire to inhabit the biblical world raises is that of the complexity of the biblical narrative. Given that the nature of the biblical narrative is complex, how should Christians enter the biblical narrative? Should Christians appropriate the whole biblical narrative for modern living or should they selectively read this narrative? Given that the biblical narrative is often selectively read and that the Bible does not interpret itself (it is interpreted by people), who decides which elements of the biblical narrative should be emphasized? The magisterium? Biblical and theological scholars? Preachers? Given that the role of the theologian in postliberal theology is to help Christians live faithfully within the framework of the Christian faith, it would probably fall to the theologian to interpret how the biblical narrative should be understood. This leads to the question about how those who would interpret the Bible actually interpret it. Whose interest shall it serve?

Further, the Bible tells the story of God's engagement with humanity and creation as a whole through Israel and the church. However, there are elements of this narrative that raise significant problems. One such element of the biblical story has to do with the issue of land, especially with the appropriation of the land of the Canaanites as Promised Land.

The question of land is connected to the doctrine of election which is central to the biblical narrative. As an elect people, Israel is believed to have been given the Promised Land by God. One of the questions this narrative raises is the kind of person a story like this is supposed to form. Historically, we have seen that the claim that God gave the Promised Land to the Israelites has been appropriated by Western Christians to claim land all over the world, ranging from America to South Africa. Could it be that imperialism is built into the Christian narrative? This would especially be so if the doctrine of election is coupled with the view that the church is the only true political community. Thus, Christians may see it as incumbent upon them to save others from themselves by converting them, using all means possible, to the Christian faith. This has sometimes led to violence. The struggle over divinely granted land appears to be part of the impetus behind the Crusades which was fought in part to reclaim Jerusalem, the Holy Land. This same story animates one of the most contentious disputes in our time, the Israeli-Palestinian conflict. If the biblical narrative is to be the sole source that shapes the life of Christians, it is conceivable that the Bible itself would form a person of violence who follows the voice of God to take other people's land by violence, if need be. The history of Christian missions is not unconnected to such violence. Thus, even though a postliberal theologian like Hauerwas opts for non-violence he raises little objection to the Crusades and the Inquisition, events that have been rightly condemned by many. Rather, he sees it as a legitimate framework in which premodern Christians sought to achieve salvation. Such uncritical attitude to the Christian narrative is to be questioned and the ethics of theology promotes such questioning.

Conclusion

This chapter has discussed the meaning of piety and what it means for theology to construct piety. The chapter has sought to show the difference between the ethics of theology and theological ethics, arguing that the ethics of theology seeks to ensure that theological ideas and practices that are used to form Christians should be wholesome ideas so that Christians may not be formed in ways that are detrimental to themselves and others. The ethics of theology is different from theological ethics inasmuch as theological ethics simply seeks to appropriate Christian theological ideas to form Christians without evaluating the possible outcomes, both positive and negative, of such theological ideas. It has used the notion of the ethics of theology to evaluate postliberal theology and has found elements of postliberal theology wanting in the African context. Drawing from Foucault, we have seen that it is needful to critically investigate the ideas that form people, especially the religious ideas that form Africans. In the next chapter, we shall discuss and raise questions about how the early church appropriated theology to construct piety.

CHAPTER 2

Providence and the Triumph of Orthodoxy

A BOOK THAT DESCRIBES theology as the construction of piety begs the question not only of the objective reality of God and how a theological movement may conceive its task, as we discussed in chapter 1, but also about the role of providence in the construction of piety and the development of doctrine. The question about providence being raised here is not just about God's sustenance of the universe but more specifically about the possibility of identifying the triumph of God in the world, especially in the formulation of Christian doctrine. Is it possible to point to particular events in the world and say that they are the work of God? If so, can we see the development of Christian doctrine not only as human attempts to construct piety but also as divine activity? This question is especially pertinent when it comes to the development of the Christian doctrine of God. As historians of Christian thought are aware, the process leading to the development of the Christian doctrine of God in the early church was quite messy. It was a process that led to exiles, violence, deaths, and splits in the church.[1] In the end, however, it has become possible to speak not only of the triumph of Christianity in the broader sense of an obscure

---

1. Averil Cameron, *The Later Roman Empire, AD 284–430* (Cambridge, MA: Harvard University Press, 1993), 66–112; Philip Jenkins, *Jesus Wars* (New York, NY: HarperOne, 2010).

Jewish sect which has become a dominant world religion today,[2] but also in the specific sense of the triumph of a particular brand of Christianity, the brand of Christianity known as the Nicene faith, which is arguably the dominant form of Christianity today.[3] First, we will raise the question of the possibility of deciphering providence in the messiness of ecclesiastical life within which the Nicene faith developed. We shall see that the complexity of talking about providence in this context calls for theological reserve on the matter. It will then be argued that, in spite of the various players who had roles in the development of Christian doctrine, theologians played a significant role in crafting what was to be believed and how what was to be believed was to influence the Christian life. In doing this, questions about the consequences of the triumphant doctrines will be raised. The period to be covered in this discussion begins in the fourth century and ends with what has been described as the Triumph of Orthodoxy in ninth century Eastern Orthodox Church.

Providence and Doctrine

"If the doctrine of providence is to have any significance for theologians today, it should make a difference to how we understand Nicaea. If it is useless there, then there really is no such thing as *historical* theology" (emphasis in original).[4] This claim is taken from a scathing critique of an otherwise well received book on the development and importance of the Christian doctrine of God rooted in the Council of Nicaea, that was held in 325 C.E. and validated by subsequent councils of the early church. Lewis Ayres, author of this book, is recognized as one of the leading voices in the reconstruction of the Trinitarian theology that emerged from Nicaea. However, the above critique leveled against Ayres' book is based on the fact that Ayres acknowledges what many historians of Christian thought now recognize—the precarious nature of the development of Christian doctrine. The recognition of the precariousness that characterizes the de-

2. Rodney Stark, *The Triumph of Christianity* (New York, NY: HarperOne, 2011).

3. The idea of the Nicene faith originates from the Creed of the Council of Nicaea in 325 and validated by subsequent creeds in the early church. See Lewis Ayres, *Nicaea and Its Legacy: An Approach to Fourth-Century Trinitarian Theology* (Oxford: Oxford University Press, 2004); John Behr, *The Nicene Faith*, volumes 1 and 2 (Crestwood, NY: St. Vladimir's Seminary Press, 2004).

4. Stephen H. Webb, "Review of *Nicaea and Its Legacy* by Lewis Ayres," *Conversations in Religion and Theology* 6.2 (2008): 139.

velopment of Christian doctrine means that it is difficult to see the hand of God in the development of Christian doctrine. This is especially so in the development of early Christian doctrine where political and other motives played a considerable role in the way events unfolded.⁵ However, for critic of Ayres' book, it seems that historical theology stands or falls with the recognition of God's providential hand guiding the process. The critic has not been alone in calling for the recognition of providence in the development of Christian thought. The British theologian, Sarah Coakley, has suggested that "the remarkable collapse of the secularization thesis" should be interpreted "as a sign of divine 'power.'"⁶ Some sociologists and theologians of the last century had claimed that religion would be eclipsed by secularism. This prognosis, however, has not occurred as there has instead been a steady revival in world religions.⁷ For Coakley, therefore, this revival should be interpreted as a sign of divine power. In reviewing the work of the recently deceased Nigerian church historian, Ogbu Kalu, Clifton Clark of Regent University suggests that one of the weaknesses of Kalu's history of Pentecostalism is that Kalu does not describe African Pentecostalism as occasioned by the universal movement of the Spirit of God.⁸ This critique suggests that Kalu does not sufficiently identify providence in his historical analysis.

The claim that evaluations of developments in Christian history or historical theology somehow fall short because they fail to explicitly acknowledge divine providence seems to undermine the difficulty involved in laying specific claims to divine providence. While it is theologically apposite to insist on divine providence in all creaturely affairs, it is however quite another issue to point to particular developments this side of the eschaton and say "there is the work of God." This is not to say that it is impossible to identify such events in human history. We can point to salutary events in

---

5. D. H. Williams, *Ambrose of Milan and the End of the "Arian"-Nicene Conflicts* (Oxford: Clarendon Press, 1995). See Michel René Barnes, "Review of Ambrose of Milan and the End of the "Arian"-Nicene Conflicts," by D. H. Williams, *Journal of Religion* (April 1997): 293-95.

6. Sarah Coakley, *Powers and Submissions: Spirituality, Philosophy and Gender* (Oxford: Blackwell, 2002).

7. Harvey Cox, *Fire from Heaven: The Rise of Pentecostal Spirituality and the Reshaping of Religion in the Twenty-First Century* (Cambridge, MA: Da Capo Press, 2001), xv. For different conceptions of the relation between religion and secularism, see Harvey Cox, "Response to Professor Nimi Wariboko," Pneuma 33 (2011): 409-16.

8. Clifton R. Clark, "Ogbu Kalu and Africa's Christianity: A Tribute," *Pneuma* 32 (2010): 115-16.

human and ecclesial life and say that we do detect the working of God in those events. However, theologians need to be careful not to simply point to the victors of disputes as those on whose side God stands. Doing this would mean that we have missed a key insight of liberation and prophetic theologies, namely that God is deeply concerned for the defeated of the world. Further, doing so would lead us to a situation where providence is unequivocally cited as the reason for the triumph of particular theological doctrines. This would then imply that the opposing sides did not succeed because providence was not on their side. If we have learned anything from liberation and prophetic theologies, it is that God should hardly be seen to be on the side of the victors of history.

To not explicitly cite providence as the reason for particular developments in Christian doctrine is not to be historically agnostic, as Webb seems to suggest in the critique above; it is rather to recognize that there are events about which we cannot unequivocally pass judgment. Christians obviously believe that God is creator and sustainer of the universe. This confession does not, however, commit Christians to seeing certain events in the world or even in Christian history as particularly providential. There are events that defy our adequate description of the nature of divine providence expressed in them. Perhaps the development of Christian doctrine should be among those events. This side of the eschaton, we see through a glass darkly and what we celebrate as triumph or success may actually not be the case. There are those for whom the "rise" of the church since Constantine (and this includes the development of Trinitarian theology) actually marks the beginnings of the fall of the church. For these people, the development of doctrine during this period does not so much mark an expression of divine providence as it demonstrates the evils of human machinations. Historical theology or theology in general therefore does not stand or fall on the confession of specific events as providential. It is based on confessing the triune God, even if we sometimes cannot quite understand why certain things happen the way they do. We receive what has been given to us, in this case the various Christians doctrines emanating from the early church, and make the best Christian use we can make of them. Claiming providence to support the development of doctrine would be, in most cases, to baptize the triumph of the powerful or those who survive messy processes. Those who perish would accordingly be seen as belonging to the wrong side of providence. This would be a theologically problematic claim, given that we know that the wicked often prosper (Ps. 73).

Providence and the Triumph of Orthodoxy

The view of providence described above places historical theology and theology itself on very shaky grounds—and rightly so. Theology, especially as understood in this book, is not so much divine activity as is an element of human making. True, we can say that God inspires theologians as God did some of those we find in the pages of the Bible. However, that does not mean that humans do not meddle in theological construction. The very reason to stress that theology is *construction* is to point to the human side of the endeavor. We can see the human product of theology but we cannot clearly ascribe this product to God. This, however, does not mean that the divine side is not present; it only means that we cannot clearly see it and we must carefully discern its presence. This is where we have been placed ever since David Hume's and Immanuel Kant's critique of natural theology. They pointed out the difficulty of detecting divine presence in creaturely affairs. While this may drive some into fideism, a kind of faith in the presence of God in the world that does not entertain interrogation, we should not simply call faith to the rescue but must wrestle with the question of providence, even when it comes to the development of theological doctrines.

The Development of Nicene Faith

Perhaps the place to start our story of the development of Christian doctrine in the fourth century is with Constantine's defeat of Maxentius at the Battle of the Milvian Bridge in 312. This event, which Constantine is believed to have interpreted as occasioned by the Christian God, later led to Constantine becoming the sole ruler of the Roman Empire. As sole ruler of the Roman Empire, Constantine became critically aware that peace in the church was important to the peace of the empire. Seeing himself as the thirteenth apostle of Jesus Christ, he took it upon himself to work for the peace of the church. Under Constantine's rule, therefore, the church became increasingly privileged. The clergy became exempt from some civic duties and the construction of churches, such as St. Peter's in the Vatican and the church of the Holy Sepulcher in Jerusalem, are credited both to Constantine and his mother, Helena, respectively. With Constantine and succeeding emperors in the fourth and fifth centuries, Christianity was on its way to becoming a dominant religion in the Roman Empire and thereafter. The church historian, Eusebius of Caesarea, who wrote in the fourth century, saw the rise of Constantine and the increasing clout of Christianity as an unambiguous sign of the in-breaking of the reign of God. This unambiguous recognition

Theology as Construction of Piety

of divine providence was however to be corrected by St. Augustine in the fifth century. For St. Augustine, history is mixed even for Christians.[9]

From this brief story we already see the danger of attributing the apparent success of Christianity to divine providence. An important contribution of St. Augustine to the Christian understanding of history is the view that Christians should not unambiguously see divine hand in history, not even in the history of the church. To do so would be to miss an important element of how things work this side of the eschaton, namely, that the hand of God cannot be clearly seen in history.

Even though the reign of Constantine did not necessarily coincide with the explosive growth of Christianity, his reign was critically important in the development of the Christian doctrine of God. Probably seeing himself as particularly favored by the Christian God, he saw it as his duty to bring peace among the often quarrelsome Christians. The direction that the Christian doctrine of God was to take later was therefore to be significantly influenced by Constantine. This is especially seen in the fact that he called what is referred to as the First Ecumenical Council, the Council of Nicaea, in 325, and is even believed to have suggested the word which was to be central in the debate about the relation among the persons of the Trinity—*homoousios*.[10]

The battle for the Christian doctrine of God began in the early fourth century in Alexandria, Egypt, when Arius, a Presbyter from Libya, objected to the preaching of his bishop, Alexander of Alexandria, who argued in a discourse on the Trinity that Jesus Christ the Son of God was of the same status or substance as God the Father.[11] Arius' rejection of the preaching of his bishop was based on the apparently unproblematic Christian claim that God the Son was born (begotten) by God the Father (the unbegotten). Arius reasoned that if God the Son is begotten and God the Father is unbegotten, then the begotten obviously has a beginning by virtue of being begotten. God the Father who is unbegotten and so without beginning is higher in status than God the Son who is begotten. This is because the one without a beginning is obviously of higher status than the one with a beginning. For Arius, therefore, because there was a time when the Son did not exist,

---

9. The preceding discussion has been drawn from Cameron, *The Later Roman Empire*, 47–65.

10. *Ibid.*

11. J. Stevenson, *A New Eusebius*, revised by W. H. C. Frend, New Edition (London: SPCK, 1987), 321.

Providence and the Triumph of Orthodoxy

the Son derived his being from the Father—the begotten derived his being from the unbegotten. Even though Arius's position seems logical—and Arius was a very logical person—its implications for the Christian doctrine of God were immense and decades were to be expended hammering out what was proper for Christians to say and believe about their God.

One of the implications of Arius' view for the Christian doctrine of God was that it directly questioned how Christians were to say that they worshiped one God. Even more important, it questioned the identification of Jesus with God, an identification which had been made at the very beginnings of Christianity (Jn 1:1–14). The identification of the Son with the Father, notwithstanding, Arius also recognized that there are parts of the Christian scriptures which implied that the Son was somehow less than the Father (Pr. 8:22). We therefore have here not only a philosophical, but also a biblical and theological, conundrum. Philosophical inconsistencies, biblical contradictions, and theological opacity about the relation of the persons of the Trinity would henceforth have to be carefully straightened out. The fact that Christianity had recently been tolerated in the Empire and Christians could therefore speak freely under Constantine meant that their contradictory positions and quarrels could not be ignored for long. In fact, with this debate, the necessity of sustained theological reflection on the nature of the Christian doctrine of God was born. In about 318 when this controversy started, it was not clear which direction the Christian doctrine of God was to take because these matters had not been clearly defined. That is why a seminal work on this controversy describes the process that led to a definition of how Christians were to speak of God as three in one and one in three as "the search for the Christian doctrine of God."[12] That it was a process in which Christians were engaged in a search of how to speak of their God does not mean that Christians did not generally know how to think and speak about their God. Christians had a good idea of who their God was but these ideas had not been clearly and coherently articulated. In fact, to this day, these issues are still debated, especially when one considers the recent interest in Trinitarian theology.[13]

---

12. R. P. C. Hanson, *The Search for the Christian Doctrine of God: The Arian Controversy 318 -381* (Edinburgh: T & T Clark, 1988). Gregg and Groh have argued that the debates be understood not as being about the Christian doctrine of God but rather as being about the Christian doctrine of salvation. See Robert C. Gregg and Dennis E. Groh, "The Centrality of Soteriology in Early Arianism," *Anglican Theological Review* 59 no. 3 (1977): 260–78.

13. Giulio Maspero and Robert J. Woźniak, eds., *Rethinking Trinitarian Theology:*

Theology as Construction of Piety

From the beginning of the Christian faith, Christians had held that God is made up of Father, Son, and Holy Spirit. However, how exactly the three are one God had not been dogmatized.[14] Arius raised the issue in such a way that Christian leaders saw that they had to clearly and coherently state how it is that the Christian God could be said to be one in three and three in one. The process of articulating the Christian doctrine of God should be understood as motivated by the desire to construct Christian piety rather than just a debate about how God should be understood, as has often been portrayed.[15] There were well-meaning Christians on all sides of the dispute, struggling to understand their God in ways that made sense to them and the churches which they led. Those involved in this dispute probably honestly believed that having clarity about the nature of the Christian God would place the piety of Christians on a sure footing. However, reading about the aspersions that the various sides in the debate threw at each other, one may come away with the impression that one side or the other was consciously in the employ of Satan, intent on undoing the church. That reading of the situation would however miss the point that these were possibly well-meaning Christians struggling and even dying for their faith.[16]

Rowan Williams has convincingly argued that the dispute about the doctrine of God in the fourth century could also be understood as a dispute about biblical hermeneutics, the authority of the bishop, and the very nature of theology itself. As a dispute about biblical hermeneutics, Williams portrays the dispute as based in how the Bible was to be interpreted, especially with regards to how Christians were to understand God. Probably influenced by theological and philosophical backgrounds that stress the singularity, transcendence and incomprehensibility of God, Arius read the Bible in ways that aimed at preserving this view of God. Arius' view of God was therefore not merely abstract but rooted in his reading of the Christian Scriptures.[17] Thus, it would not be proper to accuse Arius of deriving

---

Disputed Questions and Contemporary Issues in Trinitarian Theology (London: T & T Clark, 2012).

14. John Behr, *Formation of Christian Theology: The Way to Nicaea*, vol. 1 (Crestwood, New York: St. Vladimir's Seminary Press, 2001).

15. This insight has been aided by Lewis Ayres, "The Trinity and the Life of the Christian: A Liturgical Catechism," *New Blackfriars* (2010): 3–17.

16. J. Rebecca Lyman, "Heresiology: The Invention of 'heresy' and 'schism,'" in *The Cambridge History of Christianity*, vol. 2: Constantine to c. 600, eds. Augustine Casiday and Frederick W. Norris (Cambridge: Cambridge University Press, 2007), 299–313.

17. Rowan Williams, *Arius: Heresy and Tradition*, revised edition (Grand Rapids, MI/

his doctrine of God from elsewhere and then imposing it on scripture, as Widdicombe seems to do.[18]

One of the important biblical texts that animated early Christian exegesis and which may not seem that important to Christians today is Proverbs 8:22. In this text, Wisdom is speaking about the importance of Wisdom in the divine scheme of things and in the process of doing this, Wisdom declares: "The Lord created me at the beginning of his work, the first of his acts of long ago" (NRSV). In early Christian exegesis, Wisdom was equated with the Son and so when it is declared that Wisdom was created at the beginning of God's work, it meant, for Arius, that Wisdom could not have been eternal or unbegotten. That which is unbegotten, Arius held, cannot be said to have been created. The reverse is therefore also true. Interpreting Proverbs 8:22 as saying that the Son or Christ was created, leads to the belief that the Son is a creature or, at least, not equal to God the Father. While for Arius this would preserve the unity or monarchy of the Godhead, that is, that God is ineffably one or single, for those who have come to be seen today as supporting the orthodox position or the Nicene faith, seeing the Son or Christ as a creature contradicted a proper understanding of Christ.

As Williams further points out, the issue here was not just the interpretation of scripture but also the ecclesial authority by which to interpret scripture. Arius's interpretation of scripture was not ecclesially acceptable because it was apparently based on Arius's own authority rather than the authority of the church represented by his bishop. As a presbyter, Arius was under the bishop. Given that the bishop was the head of the church and responsible for defining Christian doctrine, Arius' interpretation of the Bible could not take precedence over that of the bishop. Arius's biblical interpretation was therefore academic or private and did not represent how the church wanted the scriptures to be interpreted. The point was not that there had been any established way by which the controversial biblical passages should be interpreted; rather, the point was that the way Arius interpreted the Bible did not support the views of the church on the matter at hand, that is, how to understand the relation among the members of the Trinity.[19] The point being made here is one that has been crucial in the

---

Cambridge, UK, 1987, 2001), 108–09.

18. Peter Widdicombe, "Athanasius and the Making of the Doctrine of the Trinity," *Pro Ecclesia* VI.4 (Fall 1997): 459.

19. Williams, *Arius*, 110.

development of Christian doctrine—anyone may interpret the Bible as they see fit; however, interpretations that are acceptable to the church are those that help in building the faith experience of Christians and support Christian doctrines. Readings that seem to undermine Christian doctrines and possibly the faith of individual Christians are strenuously opposed. Arius' interpretation of scripture, his opponents held, was not conducive to the faith of the church. It strained the equal divinity among the members of the Trinity.

The strenuous opposition mounted against Arius led to acrimonious and raucous debates that occasioned the intervention of Emperor Constantine as mediator. Constantine called the First Ecumenical Council, the Council of Nicaea in 325 CE, in order that Christian leaders may come up with a proper way of speaking about God that would engender peace in the empire. It was at this council that the first faltering attempts were made to clearly define how Christians were to understand the relationship among the three members of divine life. The formula that was constructed at this gathering read as follows:

> We believe in One God, the Father, Almighty, Maker of all things, visible and invisible:
> And in One Lord Jesus Christ, the Son of God, begotten of the Father, Only-begotten,
> that is, from the substance of the Father;
> God from God, Light from Light, very God from very God, begotten not made,
> Consubstantial (*homoousios*) with the Father, by whom all things were made, both things in heaven and things on earth;
> who for us men [sic] and for our salvation came down and was incarnate, was made man, suffered, and rose again the third day, ascended into heaven, and is coming to judge living and dead.
> And in the Holy Ghost.[20]

One issue that should immediately be clear from this short statement of faith (creed) is that it does not say very much about God the Father apart from the fact that the Father is the source of the Son. It focuses on stating how the Son should be understood as related to the Father and barely acknowledges the presence of the Holy Spirit. The reason for structure of this creed should be immediately clear: the point of the creed was not so much to argue for belief in God the Father—that was not in dispute. Thus

20. Stevenson, *A New Eusebius*, 345.

Providence and the Triumph of Orthodoxy

the confession about the Father was brief. The area of dispute was how the relation of the Son to the Father was to be understood. Significant space is therefore given to this matter. Further, even though Christians had worshiped the deity as Father, Son, and Holy Spirit, the issue of the relation of the Spirit to the Father and the Son had not yet been seriously raised. This was to come later in the 350s and 360s. Thus, we have only an acknowledgement of the Holy Spirit as a member of the Godhead in this creed.

Even though the short statement of faith above gave much space to discussing how the relation of the Son and the Father should be understood, the matter was very far from settled. One sticking point had to do with the word "consubstantial" or "same substance" (*homoousios*). Now, to say that the Son was of the same substance with the Father was to make a claim that was eerily similar to the claims that had been designated heretical and associated with the name of a Christian leader called Sabellius. To say that the Father and the Son were of the same substance, as Sabellius did, was to say that the Father and the Son were not distinct or that they were the same "individual" who merely appeared in different forms. In fact, at this time it was not clear in the minds of many Christian leaders, both those who supported the Nicene settlement and those who did not, that the word *homoousios* was the proper word to use in describing the relation between the Father and the Son. The question as to exactly how the relation of the Father and the Son should be understood was to rage on right into the waning decades of the fourth century and even into the fifth century. During this time, theologians put forth various proposals as to how the relation among the members of the Trinity should be understood.

It was during the period after the Council of Nicaea that bishop Athanasius of Alexandria emerged as an important figure in the formulation of the Christian doctrine of God. Athanasius eventually came to see *homoousios* as central to how the relationship in the Godhead should be understood.[21] First, Athanasius argued that the Son should be understood as of the same being (substance) with the Father rather than as having originated from the will of the Father, as Arius taught. According to Athanasius, the Son should not be understood as born of the Father after the Father had already been in existence, as is the case with human beings, but rather as eternally begotten of the Father. Drawing from the foundation laid by Origen, Athanasius

---

21. Thomas F. Torrance, "The Doctrine of the Holy Trinity According to St. Athanasius," *Anglican Theological Review* LXX1.4 (1989): 397.

Theology as Construction of Piety

argued that Father and Son are correlative rather than temporal terms.[22] That is, Father and Son should be understood as eternally defining each other, as Origen said, rather than as having developed over time, as is the case with human beings. With human beings fathers are older than their sons or children but that is not so with God. The understanding of how God is Father should be removed from the temporal realm and placed in the eternal realm where time does not exist. If the Father had eternally been Father, it stands to reason that he Son had always been Son. The conclusion is based on the belief, common in early Christianity, that God does not change, that is, that God is impassible. If God is not always Father, it means that God is passible or changeable. Divine changeability was abhorred in early Christianity because it brought uncertainty into divine life. If God could not be trusted to be today what God was yesterday, it may not be possible to tell what God might become tomorrow. Arius' view that there was a time when the Son did not exist brought changeability into divine life and so made God untrustworthy. Thus the issue here was not just how to describe God but rather how to describe God in such a way that Christians could trust God. If piety is to be based on the fact that Christians trust God to be today and tomorrow what God was yesterday, then describing God in ways that shake this assurance was regarded as dangerous for the development of Christian faith. Thus, much about how the Christian life was lived depended on how Christians understood who their God is.

Second, Athanasius taught that, in describing the relation between the Father and the Son, it would be proper to refer to them as Father and Son rather than as unoriginate and originate.[23] Referring to Father and Son as unoriginate and originate, respectively, may give the impression that their relationship is sequential, rather that simultaneous. Even though Athanasius acknowledges that the Father is the source or fount of the Son, he insists that this should not be understood as intimating that the Father is prior or superior to the Son. Father and Son are ontologically united in being and activity even though they should also be recognized as distinct. His main reason for insisting that we should speak of Father and Son rather than unoriginate and originate is that the former correctly describes the biblical portrayal of God—Jesus refers to God as Father and Christians are called upon to address God as Father (Abba). Understanding God as Father, Son, and Holy Spirit would not only be biblically apposite

---

22. Widdicombe, "Athanasius," 457.
23. Widdicombe, "Athanasius," 461.

Providence and the Triumph of Orthodoxy

but would also describe Christian worship of God, especially as found in the baptismal formula of Matthew 28:19. In this text, Christians are called upon to baptize in the name of the Father, Son, and Holy Spirit, not in the name of unoriginate, originate, and the Holy Spirit.

At this point, it is important to point out that the description of God as Father, Son, and Holy Spirit has been challenged by contemporary feminist theology, which has argued that the notion that God is Father, Son, and Holy Spirit is a sexist notion of God.[24] We are not quite sure how Athanasius would have reacted to this development if he were alive today. However, it is important to be theologically sensitive to the feminist critique of the conception of the Trinity in our time and try to think about the Trinity in ways that do not give the impression that God is ontologically male. As Jesus himself pointed out, "God is Spirit, and those who worship God must worship in Spirit and truth" (John 4:24, NRSV, modified). This statement demonstrates that God is not ontologically human or male, even though we may claim that God has become human through the incarnation. We should therefore learn to use both feminine and masculine images when we talk about God as Trinity. If theology is the construction of piety, it means that by continuing to describe God in masculine terms, we are encouraging Christians to think of God as male. Talking about the Trinity in feminine terms will begin to change this masculine imagination that has come to characterize discourse on the Trinity. How this is to be properly done is still under negotiation and is an important debate in Christian theology.

Third, for Athanasius, the views of Arius were not only based on an erroneous reading of the Bible but, more especially, raised questions about the nature of Christian salvation itself.[25] As Greg and Groh have argued, Arius was critically concerned about the nature of Christian salvation and that is why he saw the Son as a creature, even though an elevated creature. For Arius, because the Son was passible, his incorporation into divine life was not a given. It was his tenacity in focusing on divine things that finally gave him access into the eternal divine life which he now enjoys. This description of the Son assumes that, like all other human beings, the Son is passible. By uniquely focusing on divine things and so gaining access into divine life, the Son teaches us what we are to do in order to gain access into

---

24. Rosemay Radford Reuther, *Sexism and God-talk: Toward a Feminist Theology* (Boston, MA: Beacon Press, 1983, 1993).

25. Khaled Anatalios, *Athanasius* (London: Routledge, 2004), pp. 31–69.

divine life—be singularly focused on divine things.[26] Here the Son is seen as an example rather than as the divine One whose life, death, and resurrection miraculously reconciles humans and the rest of creation to God. For Athanasius, however, if the Son is a creature, it implies that Christian salvation is based on creaturely act. However, as far as Athanasius could see it, Christians did not claim that they were saved by a creature—Christians believed that they were saved by God. Assuming that the Son was created, even if such createdness is elevated, as Arius did, was to jeopardize the Christian view of salvation. It was in this light that Athanasius insisted that Christians must understand their salvation as orchestrated by God rather than by a creaturely being. All creatures, Athanasius held, are in need of salvation and so could not save themselves. Because only God could save, God became human so that humans might become divine. The Son is therefore the one whose incarnated life, death, and resurrection miraculously reconciles and unites human life with divine life. It is because the Son is fully divine that he could do this. When the idea of the divinity of the Spirit was challenge in the 350s and 360s, Athanasius included the Holy Spirit in his argument and insisted that humans are saved through the activity of Father, Son, and Holy Spirit who are equally (consubstantially) divine.

It is important to note that the argument of Athanasius is not based on "a precise definition of the relation" among the three members of the Trinity but rather on the revelation of God in Christ as expressed in the beliefs and practices of the church. Thus, we see that even though Athanasius insisted on the unity of the three he is not quite clear about how they are distinct. Such clarity would be brought to the argument by later theologians such as Gregory of Nyssa and Gregory of Nazianzen. Because some apparently began to imagine that by talking of the unity of the Father, Son, and Holy Spirit Christians might have been talking about three different Gods, someone like Gregory of Nyssa sought to address the issue of the distinction and unity of the three by moving away from the language of *ousia* and *hypostasis* and emphasizing divine power, activity and causality.[27] Rather than stressing the language of *ousia* and *hypostasis*, as Athanasius had done, Nyssa appropriated what Ayres has called the grammar of Trinitarian theology that began from the perspective that true divinity was simple

26. Gregg and Groh, "The Centrality of Soteriology."

27. Lewis Ayres, "On Not Three People: The Fundamental Themes of Gregory of Nyssa's Trinitarian Theology as seen in *To Ablabius: On Not Three Gods*," *Modern Theology* 18.4 (October 2002): 446. The following discussion draws from this text.

Providence and the Triumph of Orthodoxy

and indivisible and should form the context for all talk of differentiation in divine life.[28] In addition, the absolute distinction between Creator and creature, an idea Athanasius had insisted upon, was also emphasized. In dealing with the distinction between God and human beings (creature), Nyssa pointed out that human language should not be seen as capable of completely describing divine life. For him, therefore, names for the divine nature should not be seen as describing God directly but rather as describing the actions of God—divine nature remains unknown. Thus, describing God as three in one should not be misconstrued as saying that God is made up of three different members but rather as human means of describing the activity of the one God. For him, therefore, the action of the members of the Trinity is one, the power is one, and the nature is one.[29] The members of the Trinity may be differentiated only in terms of origin or causal relationship. In this case, the Father is seen as the origin or source of the Son and the Spirit. That the Father is seen as origin, source, or cause of the Son and the Spirit should not be construed in a temporal manner, as Athanasius warned, because speaking about origins in divine life is not a temporal category. Theological reflections like Nyssa's that argued for how the three members of divine life are one and yet separate led to the formulation of the Niceno-Constantinopolitan Creed or, simply, the Nicene Creed of 381, which forms the basis of the Trinitarian faith of many Christians today. This Creed, which is a modification of the Creed of 325 because of its inclusion of the Holy Spirit as truly God, reads:

> We believe in one God the Father
> almight, maker of heaven and
> earth, of all things visible and
> invisible;
>
> And in one Lord Jesus Christ, the
> only begotten Son of God,
> begotten from the Father before
> all ages, light from light, true God
> from true God, begotten not
> made, of one substance with the
> Father, through whom all things,

---

28. Ayres, "On Not Three People," 150–51.

29. For more on the use of the idea of divine power in the Trinitarian debates of the fourth century, see Michel René Barnes, *The Power of God: δυναμίς in Gregory of Nyssa's Trinitarian Theology* (Washington, DC: Catholic University of America Press, 2001).

Theology as Construction of Piety

> came into existence, Who
> because of us men and because of
> our salvation came down from the
> heavens, and was incarnate from
> the Holy Spirit and the Virgin Mary
> and became man, and was
> crucified for us under Pontius
> Pilate, and suffered and was
> buried, and rose again on the third
> day according to the Scripture and
> ascended to heaven, and sits on
> the right hand of the Father, and
> will come again with glory to judge
> living and dead, of Whose kingdom
> there will be no end;
>
> And in the Holy Spirit, the Lord
> and life-giver, Who proceeds from
> the Father, Who with the Father and
> the Son is together worshiped and
> together glorified, Who spoke through
> the prophets; in one holy Catholic
> and apostolic Church. We confess one
> baptism for the remission of sins; we
> look forward to the resurrection of the
> dead and the life of the world to
> come. Amen.[30]

Because the notion of the divinity of the Spirit had also become debatable after the Council of Nicaea, it had to be clearly stated, both in individual theological reflections (beginning with Athanasius and increasingly clarified by the Cappadocians) and important documents of the church, such as the Creed from the Council of Constantinople in 381, that the Holy Spirit is God.

The idea that the Spirit proceeds from the Father would later erupt in what is described as the *filioque* controversy that contributed to the division between Western and Eastern churches. In this controversy, the Western church insisted that the Spirit proceeds from both the Father and the Son while the Eastern churches insisted upon the formulation of the Creed of

---

30. J. Stevenson, *Creeds, Councils and Controversies: Documents Illustrating the History of the Church, AD 337–461*, New Edition (London: SPCK, 1989), 114–15. Italics have not been maintained.

Providence and the Triumph of Orthodoxy

Constantinople, that the Spirit proceeds from the Father. Dialog is still being conducted today between Western and Eastern theologians with the aim of overcoming this division.[31]

The *filioque* controversy was a later development in the history of Christian doctrine but during the fourth century the agreement arrived at during the Council of Constantinople, namely, the Niceno-Constantinopolitan Creed, needed to be shored up because not every influential Christian in the Roman Empire agreed with that formulation. Those who favored an "Arian" understanding of the Christian God had not gone away. In order to shore up the Trinitarian faith emanating from Nicaea and Constantinople, two important events took place, one legislative and the other miraculous. First, in his struggle against "Arians" in Milan, Ambrose of Milan discovered the bodies of two Christian martyrs, Prostasius and Gervasius, in 386 CE. At a time when the relics of saints mattered much in the building of churches, this discovery proved Ambrose to be a veritable man of God and drew many to his side. Ambrose of Milan was one of the most ardent defenders of the Nicene faith and his victory over the "Arians" solidified the Nicene faith. Second, Emperor Theodosius I, had decreed in 380 CE that only those who adhered to the Nicene faith were to be considered as legitimate Christians. In a decree dated 380 CE, Theodosius I wrote:

> We command that those persons who follow this rule [the creed of Nicaea and later Constantinople] shall embrace the name of Catholic Christians. The rest, however, whom We adjudge demented and insane, shall sustain the infamy of heretical dogmas, their meeting places shall not receive the name of churches, and they shall be smitten first by divine vengeance and secondly by the retribution of Our own initiative, which We shall assume in accordance with divine judgment.[32]

Seeing imperial action as divine action, Theodosius I therefore made Nicene Christianity to be the only valid form of Christianity and, in fact religion, in the empire and so began the process by which the Nicene understanding of God would become the dominant understanding of God.[33] This

---

31. Mary B. Cunningham and Elizabeth Theokritoff, "Who are the Orthodox Christians? A Historical Introduction," *The Cambridge Companion to Orthodox Christian Theology*, eds. Mary B. Cunningham and Elizabeth Theokritoff (Cambridge: Cambridge University Press, 2008), 4.

32. Stevenson, *Creeds*, 150.

33. For more on the role of Ambrose and Theodosius I in bringing about the "end" of the Trinitarian controversy of the fourth century, see Daniel H. Williams, *Ambrose of*

understanding of God became mainstream especially with the extinction of "Arian" Christianity. And so the Trinitarian understand of God held by many Christians today is one that came from a messy process that included significant theological constructions.

The Nicene Faith after the Fourth Century

A question that began to gain increasing attention after Constantinople 381 was how to understand Jesus Christ as both divine and human. This was a continuation of the Trinitarian controversy but the focus was placed on how it could be said that Jesus Christ was both human and divine rather than how the Son fits in the divine economy. If Jesus Christ the Son is God, as the Nicene creeds seem to have settled, how could he be human at the same time? Some, such as Apollinaris of Laodicia (d. c 390), argued that Jesus Christ was fully God but not fully human because he did not possess a rational soul. This lack of a rational soul meant that Jesus Christ did not have human understanding. But Appolinaris' understanding of Jesus Christ flew in the face of an understanding of salvation that became standard in the fourth century, namely that Jesus Christ could not save human beings if he was himself not completely human.[34] It was acknowledged by proponents of the Nicene faith in the fourth century that Jesus Christ could not save humans if he were not fully God, on the one hand, and not fully human, on the other. However, the question arose as to how it is that Jesus Christ could be seen as fully God and fully human.

The matter about the divinity and humanity of Christ came to a head when a theologian from Antioch called Nestorius (d. 451) was made bishop of Constantinople.[35] A person with the zeal for sniffing heretics, by which he meant the "Arians," he became a victim of his own theological zealousness. His reasoning about the relationship between the humanity and divinity of Christ went something like this: Given that the Son of God, the Logos, is coeternal with God, as we saw in the argument for the Nicene

---

Milan, chapter 8.

34. Elias Tsonievsky, "The Union of the Two Natures in Christ According to the Non-Chalcedonian Churches and Orthodoxy," *Greek Orthodox Theological Review* (September 1968): 171.

35. For more on Nestorius, see Frances M. Young, *From Nicaea to Chalcedon: A Guide to the Literature and its Background*, second edition (Grand Rapids, MI: Baker Academic, 2010), 288–97.

faith above, it is not possible for this same Son to have been born of a human being like Mary. This would mean that the Son of God was born twice, the first being the origination from the eternal divine life and the second being the birth from a human source. Because it is impossible for the Son of God, the Logos, to be born twice, Nestorius thought, it is therefore not appropriate to describe Mary as the Mother of God (*Theotokos*), as was commonly done at the time. Mary should rather be called Mother of Christ (*Christotokos*), the human being. The implication of this reasoning was that it separated the divinity and humanity of Christ in ways that some thought went against what Christians had historically believed about Christ. A leading opponent of Nestorius, who was critical in developing what is now seen as the orthodox understanding of Christ, was the brash and fearful bishop of Alexandria, Cyril.[36] Cyril's zeal was a match for Nestorius' as he used theological savvy and ecclesiastical machinations to make sure that Nestorius' views did not stand.

The basic argument Cyril made was that Jesus Christ should be understood as a single person in whom divinity and humanity was united. For him, therefore, the incarnation of the Son of God, the Logos, meant that the Word took on human flesh without diminishing divinity and without undermining humanity. Even though the human and the divine in Jesus Christ were complete, Jesus Christ should not be spoken of as being two persons because the human and the divine were united in one person. It was in this light that he used the haunted expression that the Son was *mia phusis* (one hypostasis) after the incarnation. When Cyril talked of *mia phusis*, he was not stating that Jesus Christ had only one nature (*ousia*) but rather that through hypostatic union, the Son of God could be seen as one person after the incarnation. That is, after the incarnation, the Son of God was one person in whom is united divinity and humanity. The unity here should not be understood as a merger or a union in which the two natures (*ousia*) of Christ, divinity and humanity, are not separate. The unity therefore was not unity of nature (*ousia*) but unity of two natures in a single person (hypostatic union). Jesus Christ is therefore not two persons, human and divine, but one person in whom divinity and humanity are united.

Cyril supported his view by drawing from how Jesus Christ is presented in the Gospels. In the Gospels, Jesus Christ is presented as equal to

---

36. Cyril's tenure as bishop of Alexandria saw some of his opponents flee the city and others even murdered. It is said that when he was alive he was feared and when he died some people were happy that he was gone. For more on Cyril, see Frances M. Young, *From Nicaea to Chalcedon*, 298–321.

God but also as less than God. Borrowing from a method of reading the Bible that had been used by Athanasius, Cyril insisted that where Jesus is presented as being less than divine, we should understand that as referring to his humanity and where he is presented as equal to God, we should understand it as referring to his divinity. It is by reading the Gospels in this way that we would understand the nature of the hypostatic union.[37] This way of understanding the notion of the hypostatic union, however, left unanswered how to deal with the issue of the passion or suffering and death of Christ. As we saw above, ancient Christians generally held that divinity is impassible, that is, God does not suffer or change like creatures do. Now, if Jesus Christ was God, how come that he suffered and died when God does not suffer? Was it then possible to say that God suffered and died, as some modern theologians seem to be saying?[38] According to Cyril, divinity does not suffer and so we can say that the Logos suffered and died only by means of what has been described as *communicatio idiomatum* (communication of idioms or attributes). This means that we can associate elements of the humanity of the Son to his divinity by virtue of the fact that both natures inhere in the same person. Thus, when we say that Jesus Christ suffered and died, we are not saying that the divinity in him suffered and died, given that it is not possible for divinity to suffer and die. However, when we say that the Son of God suffered and died we are saying that the divinity suffered and died by virtue of the fact that this divinity has been clothed in the human, the imperishable in the perishable.

A third argument which Cyril uses is the argument from worship. He points out that Christians worship Jesus Christ not as two persons, divine and human, or as a human being who has been adopted into divine life but rather as one in whom inheres both divinity and humanity. This is especially manifested, he points out, in the "bloodless sacrifice" of the Eucharist in which Christians received the body and blood of Christ not as the body and blood of an "ordinary person" but rather as the body and blood of the Word.[39] Finally, in the incarnation the Word took on the flesh of Mary and was born as a human being. Because the Word took on the flesh of Mary and was born, it is therefore legitimate to describe Mary as the mother of

---

37. Stevenson, *Creeds*, 305.

38. Jurgen Moltman, *The Crucified God: The Cross of Christ as the Foundation and Criticism of Christian Theology*, trans. R. A. Wilson and John Bowden (Minneapolis, MN: Fortress Press, 1993).

39. Stevenson, *Creeds*, 304. Ellen Concannon, "The Eucharist as Source of St. Cyril of Alexandria's Christology," *Pro Ecclesia* 18 no. 3 (2009): 318–36.

Providence and the Triumph of Orthodoxy

God rather than just the mother of Christ, as Nestorius taught. Mary was not just the mother of a human being but also the mother of God, given that God condescended to be born as a human being.

Cyril's theology was to form one of the main frameworks for the crafting of the Creed of Chalcedon (451), which outlined what it is that Christians were to believe about the nature of Jesus Christ as human and divine. It rejected the teaching of Nestorius on this matter. At the Council of Chalcedon, which was called to address this Christological dispute, the following formula was crafted:

> Wherefore, following the holy Fathers, we all with one voice confess our Lord Jesus Christ one and the same Son, the same perfect in Godhead, the same perfect in manhood, truly God and truly man, the same consisting of a reasonable soul and body, of one substance with the Father as touching the Godhead, the same of one substance with us as touching the manhood, like us in all things apart from sin; begotten of the Father before the ages as touching the Godhead, the same in the last days, for us and for our salvation, born from the Virgin Mary, the Theotokos, as touching the manhood, one and the same Christ, Son, Lord, Only-begotten, to be acknowledged in two natures, without confusion, without change, without division, without separation; the distinction of the natures being in no way abolished because of the union, but rather the characteristic property of each nature being preserved, and concurring into one Person and one subsistence (ὑπόστασις), not as if Christ were parted or divided into two persons, but one and the same Son and only-begotten God, Word, Jesus Christ; even as the Prophets from the very beginning spoke concerning him, and our Lord Jesus Christ instructed us, and the Creed of the Fathers has handed down to us.[40]

Through this formula, the Council of Chalcedon was propounding as tradition an understanding of Jesus Christ that had been arrived at through a long, laborious process and so was setting the boundaries concerning how Christians should understand Jesus Christ. The main points of Cyril's Christology, especially the idea of the hypostatic union, were found in the Creed. However, not all were happy with the understanding of Christ enunciated in this creed.

After the Council of Chalcedon, there emerged what has been described as non-Chalcedonian churches, including the Coptic, Ethiopian,

---

40. Stevenson, *Creeds*, 352–53.

Armenian, Syrian, and Malabarite churches. These churches rejected the Creed of Chalcedon for being a betrayal of the theology of Cyril of Alexandria. Interestingly, both the churches that accepted the Creed of Chalcedon and those that did not, claim Cyril as their representative theologian. The non-Chalcedonian churches have erroneously been called monophysite churches because they were thought to hold that Jesus Christ has only one nature (the divine), as Eutychus taught. However, they insist that, like Cyril, they hold that humanity and divinity were united in Christ, so that after the incarnation, we may speak of Christ as one person. This does not mean that they hold that Christ has only one nature (*ousia*) but rather that Christ is one person (*phusis*). The non-Chalcedonian churches therefore see the formula arrived at in Chalcedon as a betrayal of Cyril's teaching and Nestorian in character because it says that Christ is one person in two natures. Thus, when the Creed of Chalcedon says that Christ was to be acknowledged in two natures, the non-Chalcedonians take this to mean that the Creed is saying that Christ is to be understood as two distinct persons (hypostasis) rather than as one person composed of two distinct substances (*ousia*), human and divine. What is going on here, as some have suggested, seems to be a confusion of terminology rather than profound disagreement. That is why moves are currently being made to orchestrate dialogue between the non-Chalcedonian and Chalcedonian churches, so as to repair the difference that brought about this painful division in the church.[41]

Even though the attempts to define Christ as human and divine at Chalcedon is seen as the end point of the development of Christian doctrine in the early church by the West, disputes about the nature of Christ did not come to an end. It continued in the Eastern Church with the convening of three further councils to address different elements of the nature of Christ. One of the councils held after Chalcedon (the Second Council of Constantinople in 553 or the Fifth Ecumenical Council) condemned Nestorian understanding of Christ, which had not gone away in spite of the Creed of Chalcedon. However, this council was apparently intended to bolster a monophysite, rather than a Cyrillian, understanding of Christ. The dispute about the nature of Christ would continue in what has been described as the monothelitic controversy. This dispute centered on whether Christ was to be understood as having one or two wills. The dispute was a

---

41. Tsonievsky, "The Union of the Two Natures in Christ." Mary B. Cunningham and Elizabeth Theokritoff, "Who are the Orthodox Christians: A Historical Introduction," 3–4.

Providence and the Triumph of Orthodoxy

replay of the question of how to understand the humanity and divinity of Christ. The question arose as to whether Christ was to be understood as having only one, divine will or two wills, divine and human. Those who saw him as having only one nature (divine) insisted that he had only one, divine will. However, accepting this view would imply accepting the earlier monophysite position that had been rejected at the Council of Chalcedon. Thus, at the Third Council of Constantinople or the Sixth Ecumenical Council (680–681), the monothelitic position was rejected in favor of the view that Christ has two wills, human and divine. One final dogmatic council was to be held in order to bring this period of formulating the Christian doctrine of God in the East to a close. This council, the Second Council of Nicaea or the Seventh Ecumenical Council, dealt with the weighty issue of icons.

As Greek Orthodox theologian Kallistos Ware has shown, an icon is "an image or visual representation of Christ, the Virgin Mary, the angels, or the saints" and it may "take the form of a painted panel of wood, but could be equally a mosaic or fresco on the wall of the church wall, an embroidery, a portrait in metal" or in very rare cases, a statue.[42] Icons were used in Christian worship because they aid the worshiper contemplate the divine and they were also used to teach the Christian story to converts. They were like books of images that tell the Christian story and so made it possible for Christians who could not read to learn the Christian story easily. Thus, icons had both pedagogical and liturgical functions.[43] However, for reasons that scholars are still debating, including the Islamic rejection of images, the thought that God might bring judgment on people who worship idols, and the desire to return the church to what is believed to be its earliest period when images were not allowed, there emerged some Christians called iconoclasts, who strongly objected to the use of icons in the Orthodox Church.[44] However various the reasons for the rise of iconoclasm in the Orthodox Church, the use of these images were especially objected to on theological grounds. One such grounds was that icons were idols, something that was prohibited with the commandment that "You shall not make for yourself an idol, whether in form of anything that is in the heaven

---

42. Kallistos Ware, "Eastern Christendom," in *The Oxford History of Christianity*, ed., John McManners (Oxford: Oxford University Press, 1990), 148. Also see Mariamna Fortounatto and Mary B Cunningham, "Theology of Icon" in *The Cambridge Companion to Orthodox Christian Theology*, 136–37.

43. Fortounatto and Cunningham, "Theology of Icon," 136–37.

44. See Leslie Brubaker, *Inventing Byzantium Iconoclasm* (London, UK: Bristol Classical Press, 2012).

above, or that is on the earth beneath, or that is in the water under the earth. You shall not bow down to them or worship them" (Exod. 20:4, NRSV). Another theological ground on which icons were rejected was drawn from the debate about the humanity and divinity of Christ. Iconoclasts argued that making an image of Christ was inaccurate because it failed to represent the two natures of Christ. Given that Christ is divine and human, icons show only the human side of Christ because it is not possible to represent his divine side in icons. Those who made icons were, therefore, guilty of Nestorianism because they divided the natures of Christ, showing only his human side and not showing his divine side.

Responding to the charge that icons were idols, supporters of icons (iconophiles) suggested that icons were not idols because an idol was a false god. Icons depicted the story of the true God with human beings and so cannot be said to be idols. Even an icon of Christ was not an idol because Christ was truly God. Supporters also pointed out that these images were not being worshiped but were rather venerated and so the claim of idolatry did not hold. Responding to the charge that creating an icon of Christ made one guilty of creating only the humanity of Christ and so dividing his humanity from his divinity, iconophiles argued that claiming that icons created only the humanity of Christ was itself the heretical position because the Creed of Chalcedon had held that Christians should understand Christ as one person composed of two natures. In the incarnated Christ divinity and humanity inhered and so representing Christ in icons was intended to depict both his humanity and divinity. Iconography was therefore in agreement with the Creed of Chalcedon rather than against it. As Ware notes, the debates about icons were seen as Christological debates because they had to do with whether or not Christ could be represented in images. Banning the representation of Christ in images, supporters of the practice claimed, is tantamount to denying the physicality of Christ and thus succumbing to the heretical, docetic, idea that Christ only appeared to be physical but was not actually so. Even more, it was argued that the incarnation itself made iconography possible because in the incarnation the immaterial God became material. In Christ the immaterial God had become material and so representing this God in material terms did not violate the nature of God but instead glorified it. Also, the icon itself was not meant to be the object which it represented; rather, it was intended to help Christians participate in the prototype through meditation on the image. These images, proponents argued, aid in worship by reminding Christians, especially those who were illiterate (and there were many at this time), of God.[45] Thus, rather than being a bulwark to the proper worship of God, icons actually helped Christians worship God properly. These theological arguments were, with the help of imperial power, codified during the Seventh Ecumenical Council, also known as the Second Council of Nicaea, held in 787. The defeat of iconoclasm and the triumph of iconography came to be known and celebrated as the Triumph of Orthodoxy in the Orthodox churches of the East.

Conclusion

Is the process that led up to the Triumph of Orthodoxy the triumph of God or the triumph of particular human attempts at constructing Christian piety? The doctrine of the unity of the divine and the human in Jesus Christ, as enunciated in Chalcedon for example, might lead Christians to hold that we should not make a sharp distinction between the human and the divine in the development of doctrine. That is, this doctrine may lead to the view that God and humans collaborate in development of Christian doctrine just as divinity and humanity coincide in Christ. Those who hold this view may believe that God and humans closely work together to ensure the outcome of what Christians are to believe. However, we must not forget that the nature of the unity between humanity and divinity in Christ is unique and so applies only to Christ and not to all humans. This means that our thoughts and actions are not always in sync with God's as Christ's was. Thus, what we do does not always represent what God would like us to do. Thus, Christians should be circumspect about their perception of the hand of God in their theological, or other, activities. Christians should therefore not be in a hurry to see the hand of God as guaranteeing the triumph of one or more of the positions in the process of defining key elements of the faith. God may be present in this process but, again, God may not be. What seems clear is that the whole process is characterized by moves to determine what Christians are to legitimately think and do. In the process, some positions are rejected and even outlawed while others are upheld. It may well be that some positions that are outlawed may contain salutary elements that are lost to us in their rejection. For example, Arius' view that the Son is less than the father and so procured salvation (became divine) through a single-minded focus on divine things may hold significant promise for Christian ethics

---

45. For a challenge to this position, however, see John H. Arnold, *Belief and Unbelief in Medieval Europe* (London: Hodder Arnold, 2005), 51–52.

with its insistence that humans are divinized through doing divine things; but that vision is now suspect because it has been declared unorthodox. However, Christians are called upon to imitate Christ in their daily living. The question that needs to be raised here is how it is that Christians can adequately imitate Christ when it is clear that Christ is qualitatively different from humans because he is of the same substance as God? Could it be the case that Christ was able to do what he did because he was God so that it is impossible for ordinary Christians to imitate him? On the other hand, if Christ were less than God but became divine through a single-minded focus on divine things, does that not make it possible for humans to also be divinized through single-minded focus on divine things? Would the call for Christians to imitate Christ not make more sense if Christ were less than God? Further, it may also be that some of the views that are upheld in the process of defining the doctrine of God may be unsalutary.[46] It may actually be that the focus on icons in worship impedes rather than help human communication with God, as iconoclasts argued. The danger of focusing on the icon rather than on that which the icon represents is therefore real. We need to think carefully about the process of theological construction of the faith in order not to throw out the proverbial baby with the bathwater. In all this we need to be acutely aware that theology constructs piety and so continuously ask ourselves the kind of piety that we are enabling. This should even be more so for contemporary African theology because the piety this theology constructs does not only affect human relation with the divine but determines the quality of their lives in this world.

---

46. On the salutarity of Christian doctrines, see Ellen Charry, *By the Renewing of Your Minds: The Pastoral Function of Christian Doctrine* (Oxford: Oxford University Press, 1997).

CHAPTER 3

God and Matter in Medieval Theology

ALTHOUGH IT HAS BEEN much problematized, the claim that the European Middle Ages was an age of faith can hardly be completely rejected.[1] Given that the Christian faith defined the lives of most people in Europe during this time, it is perhaps not possible to reject the characterization of the period as an age of faith. The emphasis on faith in the Middle Ages seems to be echoed in contemporary Africa, which has recently been described as characterized by "competing claims to faith."[2] The competing claims to faith in contemporary Africa involve many different religions, such as African Traditional Religions, Islam, and Christianity, which live side by side in many countries in the continent. As an age of faith, the European Middle Ages can be said to have experienced some religious competition, even though the competition was only to a lesser extent about different religions, such as Christianity, Judaism, and Islam, and to a greater extent about differences within Christianity itself.[3] One can say that the faith of the Middle Ages was largely the Christian faith because the Christian faith suppressed, or worked to suppress, all other competing faiths. More

---

1. See Andrea Martignoni, "Unbelief in the 'Age of Faith': Atheism and Skepticism in the Middle Ages," *Revue de l'histoire des religions* vol. 229 no. 3 (2012): 432–56; John H. Arnold, *Belief and Unbelief in Medieval Europe*.

2. Philip Jenkins, *The New Faces of Christianity*, 5.

3. Jaroslav Pelikan, *A History of the Development of Christian Doctrine*, vol. 3: *The Growth of Medieval Theology* (600–1300) (Chicago and London: The University of Chicago Press, 1978), 242–55.

Theology as Construction of Piety

precisely, what was regarded as catholic Christian faith suppressed other forms of Christian faith and tried to suppress even non-Christian faiths. In fact, even within what was seen as the catholic Christian faith, there existed intense competition to define what should count as correct beliefs and practices. Thus, the attempt to construct Christian piety in the European Middle Ages led Christian theologians to engage both Christian and non-Christian religions. The *Summa Contra Gentes* of Thomas Aquinas, which was directed against non-Christian religions, could be seen as a good example of the Christian engagement with other religions. This notwithstanding, the dominance of faith in medieval Europe can, in some ways, be likened to the dominance of faith in contemporary Africa and some of the issues which medieval European Christians debated could be said to be relevant to contemporary African Christianity. We will however be addressing the relevance of developments in medieval European Christianity to contemporary African Christianity in the next chapter. In this chapter, we will focus on discussing the debates about the perception of matter in the construction of medieval Christianity piety.

The major claim of this chapter is that the construction of Christian piety in medieval Europe was centered on what the medievalist Catherine Bynum has described as "holy matter."[4] This holy matter included relics, sacramentals, the Eucharist and devotional images such as statues and prayer cards. To this list, we should also add the wealth and power which the institutional church sought in order to enhance its position in medieval society. The Christian relationship to material things, including objects of Christian worship and material possessions, was therefore the locus of the construction of Christian piety during this period.

This Christian materiality therefore focused on the importance of holy people, holy places and holy things in the communication of the Christian understanding of salvation or the good life, conceptualized as living well in this life and uniting with God in the hereafter. Thus, a central theological concern was how to conceptualize the manifestation of God in material things such as relics, icons, statues, the Eucharist, grave sites, indulgences, and even wealth. This was a time when the power of God was believed to be accessed through these material things, thus making them sources through which God sometimes miraculously manifested to communicate salvation to people through healing, forgiveness, protest, and other acts

---

4. Catherine Walker Bynum, *Christian Materiality: An Essay on Religion in Late Medieval Europe* (Brooklyn, NY: Zone Books, 2011), 25–33.

that demonstrated that God was in control of the world, was taking care of the people, and bringing the world to its ultimate end in God. How material things were supposed to make salvation possible became a topic of heated debates so that by the end of the Middle Ages, some of these material things had been dethroned from the important places they held in the life of the catholic church. By the end of the Middle Ages, pilgrimages, for example, would no longer be seen as activities that necessarily demanded the physical movement of people from unholy to holy sites, as we see in Chaucer's *The Canterbury Tales*, but rather as metaphorical journeys that brought about the transformation of the believer, as we see in John Bunyan's *The Pilgrim's Progress*. Thus, pilgrimage would change from being a literal journey across time and space to an allegory about the "Christian journey and the way to glory," as Bunyan puts it.[5]

This chapter presents the decline of materialistic religion in medieval Europe as resulting from the theological construction of Christian piety. This view is, however, not intended to make extravagant claims about the importance of theological reflection in determining the outcome of Christian faith. Thus, it should be remembered that there were other reasons that could be given to account for this decline in materialistic Christianity. Also, it should be noted that those who sometimes challenged Christian materiality were not themselves seasoned theologians. Nevertheless, theological construction should be seen as one of the significant reasons for the decline in materialistic religions because theological reasons were sometimes stressed, even by the laity, to justify why these material things were not to be considered central to Christian piety; the alternatives that were often presented were believed to be forms of Christian piety that were pleasing to God. The use of statues of Mary in Christian piety, for example, was seen as idolatry because some interpreted it as worshiping something other than God. Thus, in medieval Europe, we begin to see Christians moving away from faith that is informed by connection to material objects to faith that is interiorized. The journey from the interiorized faith of the later Middle Ages to the faith that relies on reason, as we find during the Enlightenment and even our own time, would not be a long one.

---

5. John Bunyan, *The Pilgrim's Progress* (Wheaton, IL: Tyndale House Publishers, 1991), xvii.

Debates on Christian Materiality

Among the important doctrinal bases for the debates on Christian materiality in medieval Europe were the doctrines of the incarnation and creation.[6] The doctrine of the incarnation deals with the Christian belief that in Jesus Christ, the Son of God, God became human. The doctrine of creation, on the other hand, holds that all reality that is not God has been created by God and is thus distinct from and not equal to God. Put together, the question arises as to how material reality could be seen as related to God. How is it, for example, that God could be said to have become human, a created reality? Also, if God is qualitatively distinct from creation, how is it that God could be manifested in creation? In short, should creation be seen as manifesting the power and presence of God or is God radically distinct from created reality so that God's power and salvation could be communicated even without the use of material things?

The question about the incarnation is, in many ways, similar to the debate in the early church about how the Son of God could be equal to the Father. In the early church, the debate was also anchored in the doctrine of the incarnation and creation since Arianism claimed that the Son could not be equal to the Father by virtue of the incarnation and creation. Created reality, Arius claimed, could not be of the same metaphysical order as uncreated reality (God). Given that the Son was created reality he could not be said to be of the same status as God the Father who is an uncreated reality. Many of the arguments against Arius distinguished between the humanity and divinity of the Son and then insisted, first, that the Son is not a creation, and second, that the Son is equal to the Father. The question of the humanity and divinity of the Son was hardly settled even with the waning of the Arian controversy. When Nestorius argued that Mary could not be viewed as the Mother of God but rather should be called the Mother of Christ, his claim was based on the doctrines of the incarnation and creation. Created reality, he seemed to claim, should not be understand as giving birth to the divine or even containing the divine. His argument could be seen as an early argument that was intended to place a clear distinction between materiality and divinity. In his view, therefore, divinity was more than materiality and materiality should not be said to encapsulate divinity. We fail to see this point when we call Mary the Mother of God

---

6. Bynum, *Christian Materiality*, 33–36, 285; Jaroslav Pelikan, *The Growth of Medieval Theology (600–1300)*, 158.

rather than the mother of Christ. The intricate, official settlement of this question was crafted at the Council of Chalcedon in 451 and this settlement held together the materiality and divinity of the Son in a creative tension. In short, one could read the Creed of Chalcedon as saying that when one conceives of divinity, one should hold materiality and immateriality together. We therefore fail to make an adequate conception of God when we do not hold together materiality and immateriality. Just how we should understand the divine as manifested in the material, though, continues to be debated up to our time. However, from the early church, Christians had seen the presence of God as manifested not only in the incarnation but also in material things such as relics that worked miracles.[7] However, it was also understood that perceiving God as subsisting in material things could lead to confusing these material things for God. This was especially evident in the iconoclastic controversy in the Eastern Church and would also be part of the debates in medieval Western Church.

While the iconoclastic controversy in the Eastern Church centered on how Christians were to relate to images of holy people, in the medieval Western Church there emerged a whole regime in which the grace of God (salvation) was understood to be communicated through Christian materiality. The medieval church saw itself as the authentic arbiter of this salvific materiality. Thus, a central question that arose was whether or not salvation could be communicated through the materiality of the sacraments of the church or even without them. That is, are the sacraments of the church, which came to a total of seven in the Middle Ages, the only means by which God could save sinners or could God save sinners even without them?

The seven sacraments through which salvation was believed to be mediated and which are still central to Roman Catholic doctrine today are baptism, confirmation, penance, the Eucharist, extreme unction, marriage, and ordination. These all deal with material things that beg the question of how the divine is manifested in or through each of them. A tendency toward undermining these material things as locus of divine manifestation began with the blanket question of whether or not God needs them to effect salvation and moved on to the question of how God might be present in each of them. As the historian of Christian thought, Steven Ozment, has argued, debates on the significance of the sacraments stemmed from an Augustinian perception of salvation and damnation.[8] According to Au-

---

7. Bynum, *Christian Materiality*, 20.
8. The discussion in this section draws from Steven Ozment, *The Age of Reform,*

gustine, the fall of Adam and Eve resulted in human damnation and human beings could only be rescued from this damnation through the healing power of salvation in Christ through the sacraments of the church. The sacraments, according to Augustine, were especially efficacious in repairing the human will, which is the central element that was damaged in the fall. The power of the church to heal broken human will through the sacraments and so save humankind from eternal damnation was based on the fact that the church, as a continuation of the incarnation, had been endowed with these sacraments, "the medicine of immortality." "Sacramental grace," for Augustine and the later scholastics, "became the equivalent in the present life of the lost supernatural aid that had specially assisted Adam [and Eve] in living a life ordered to God in Paradise."[9]

One of the earliest challenges to this sacramental theology came during the Donatist controversy which developed in Augustine's lifetime. The fact that the sacraments were thus critical in the salvific process led to the question of whether or not an immoral or apparently illegitimate priest (stemming from the irregularity of his ordination) could preside over an efficacious sacrament. The Donatist controversy could be seen as an attempt to define the real church from the false and so determine which of the two churches' sacraments could be seen as salvifically efficacious.[10] For the Donatists, the true church was the church that held high moral standards, especially represented by the high morality of its priests. Thus, Donatists argued that sacraments presided over by immoral priests were not salvifically efficacious. Augustine, however, disagreed. For him, to say that the salvific relevance of the sacraments depends on the righteousness of the officiating priests was to make salvation dependent on human rather than divine action. This argument was in line with Augustine's other arguments about the nature of salvation. Against Pelagius and his followers who argued that humans could work out their salvation through their actions, Augustine argued that human salvation had been decided even before the fall of Adam and Eve. Here we find an apparent inconsistency in Augustine's argument with regards to the salvific significance of the sacraments and this inconsistency would be exploited later in the Middle Ages to

---

1250–1550: *An Intellectual and Religious History of Late Medieval and Reformation Europe* (New Haven, CT: Yale University Press, 1980).

9. Ozment, *The Age of Reform*, 28.

10. For a recent reconstruction of Donatism, see Maureen A Tilley, *The Bible in Christian North Africa: The Donatist World* (Minneapolis, MN: Fortress Press, 1997).

God and Matter in Medieval Theology

undermine the argument for the salvific necessity of the sacraments. This inconsistency has to do with how it is that the sacraments are necessary for salvation if who is to be saved had already been decided by God even before the fall of Adam and Eve. Be that as it may, Augustine's argument against the Donatists, that the salvific significance of the sacraments does not depend on the morality of the officiating priest, came to be standard in the medieval church. Scholastic theologians referred to the idea that the efficacy of the sacrament does not depend on the morality of the officiating priest by using the Latin expression *ex opere operato*: that the efficacy of the sacraments occurs "simply by virtue of their sheer objective performance." The expression *ex opere operantis* was used to describe the Donatist view that the efficacy of the sacraments is based on "the personal character of the agent who performed them."[11]

The Augustinian emphasis on the centrality of the sacraments in the salvific process was, however, challenged in the later Middle Ages. This challenge came in an indirect way through the scholastic debate about how the grace that orchestrates human salvation is present within the human soul. This question developed because of the perception, among the scholastics, that salvation is obtained when God confers grace in the human soul and so enable humans to love God in the proper way. However, given that the human soul is created and grace is divine, the question was raised about "how something divine could be within human nature."[12] This is a classic Christological question that was broadly applied to all human beings. It is also a question about the doctrine of creation, given that it is vital to clarify the Christian belief that the created is not the creator. If the created (humans) is not the creator (divine), how can the creator be said to inhere in the created? Given that some human beings love God more than others and are thus saved while others are not, could the love with which humans love God and so merit salvation be seen as divine or human? This question animated late medieval theology with some scholars, such as Peter Lombard, arguing that such love is orchestrated by the Spirit of God dwelling in the human soul rather than through human volition or will. However, a scholar such as Thomas Aquinas held that such love should be understood as at least partly emerging from human volition. For Aquinas, therefore, God supplies the grace but humans needed to constantly work to keep the grace active or alive in the soul. Even though this grace cannot be

---

11. Ozment, *The Age of Reform*, 28.
12. Ibid., 31.

lost once it has been given by God, it can be dormant or inactive if a person does not work to keep it alive. It is for this reason that the sacraments of the church were critical—they were the means that help Christians keep the grace of God alive in their souls.

Influenced by the Augustinian doctrine of predestination, the Franciscan scholar, Duns Scotus (1266–1308), taught that Aquinas' view on how the grace of God worked in the human soul tied divinity too closely to the sacraments of the church. Appropriating the view that God had already decided those who would be saved and those who would be damned, Scotus pointed out that it is divine will rather than the condition of the human soul that is responsible for salvation. That is, God saves not through human action, not even through the sacraments of the church, but rather through the fact that God has freely chosen whom to save. Scotus said this not because he was against the sacraments of the church but rather because, following Augustine, he did not think that divine action should be dependent upon human action. Scotus, therefore, did not reject the sacraments but rather defined the nature of their efficacy and necessity differently from Aquinas. While for Aquinas God works through the sacraments to keep grace alive in the human soul, for Scotus the sacraments were efficacious because God had willed to be present through them. Even though God does not need them for salvation, Scotus taught, God wills to make use of them in the salvific scheme. The sacraments were therefore subordinate to the divine will. From this position one would not need to travel far to encounter the argument that the sacraments were actually not needed for salvation.

The argument for the contingency of the sacraments was actually picked up by William Ockham (1288–1347) when he argued for the subordination of God's ordained power, that is, what God has chosen to do in time (such as the use of sacraments in the salvific scheme) to God's absolute power, that is, the "infinite possibilities" that are eternally opened to God (such as the fact that God may not need the sacraments to bring about salvation). The fact that God uses the sacraments to effect salvation should therefore not be understood to mean that God needs the sacraments to effect salvation. Because of God's absolute power God could effect salvation in whatever way God chooses. Thus, even though Ockham seemed to argue that human actions may earn them salvation he, like Scotus, saw divine will as having the final say in the matter. For Ockham, therefore, even the church itself was a creature and so divine action should not be seen as dependent upon creaturely action (the sacraments of the church).

God and Matter in Medieval Theology

Arguments from scholars such as Scotus and Ockham demonstrated the precariousness of materiality or the creaturely as locus for the manifestation of divinity. The arguments of the scholars, however, did not stop many in the Middle Ages from continuing to see holy people, holy places, and holy things as media of divine manifestation in the world. In fact, the debates were taking place in the midst of the perception of these things as media of divine manifestation.

One holy person in whom divine life was seen to be manifest was Mary, the Mother of our Lord. As we saw in the previous chapter, Mary had been declared to be the Mother of God at the Council of Ephesus in 431. This was against the view, espoused by Nestorius and his followers, that Mary should be understood mainly as the mother of the human being, Jesus Christ. By declaring Mary to be the Mother of God, the church was giving her a very critical place in the salvific scheme, a place that did not appear to be apparent at the time, but which would be clearly revealed in the Middle Ages, as Mary and Christ came to share almost the same status. In fact, in the Middle Ages, Mary came to be seen as an agent through whom the grace of God was conferred on human beings, the very person who made possible the incarnation and universal salvation. Thus, the high position which Mary was to occupy in medieval theology and which she still occupies in Roman Catholic theology today, was grounded in a theological understanding of her position in divine life and the economy of salvation.

Theological understanding of Mary, as Pelikan has demonstrated, may partly be seen from the honorific titles that were bestowed on her. Among these titles were "city of God" and "the Virgin Mother." These two titles were interconnected in that they conjured the image of Mary as the place (city) where God dwelled, albeit in a miraculous way. As city of God, she could be conceived as the very dwelling place of God, the one in whom the fullness of God was pleased to dwell, a language that is used of Christ himself. As the virgin mother, she is unlike other mothers in that the method by which she conceived was unlike that of other mothers. While other mothers conceived through the sexual act that clearly eliminated their virginity, Mary, as a special vessel chosen by God to birth God into the world, did not experience elimination of her virginity, even with the birth of Christ. As Virgin Mother, she was the incorruptible dwelling place of God and the standard bearer of Christian piety. She was standard bearer of Christian piety because she proved that virginity was central to proper Christian piety.

Thus, the recommendation of virginity to the clergy would stem in part from the virginity of Mary and her son, Jesus Christ.

The reflection on the centrality of virginity in Mary's conception of God not only underscored the importance of virginity to the Christian life but also raised questions about the birth of Mary herself. Some realized that if virginity is the means to be born if one is not to be sullied with original sin, it was also needful that Mary should have been born by a virgin. This led to the postulation of the idea of Mary's Immaculate Conception, the idea that Mary, like her son, was born without sin. The many difficulties this position raised was recognized in the Middle Ages, one of which was the fact that if Mary was to be understood as having been conceived immaculately, this should not apply only to her—there had to be a continuous regress in which her ancestors, up to Adam and Eve, had been conceived immaculately. This realization made this view to be tenuous throughout the Middle Ages and was only made into a dogma by the Roman Catholic Church in the nineteenth century. The high position which Mary commanded in the Middle Ages also led to speculations about the nature of her death. Given that she was so intricately connected to the divine economy, could she have suffered an ordinary death like everyone else or did she not experience death? These questions led to the dogma about the Assumption of Mary, the belief that upon her death, Mary was bodily taken into heaven. This belief was not made a dogma until the Roman Catholic Church did so in the twentieth century.

The high status of Mary in the Middle Ages was also demonstrated in the understanding of her as *mediatrix*, as the one who played a central role not only in bringing divinity to humanity but also in enabling humanity ascend to divinity. In this, Mary had a position that was similar though not equal to that of Christ himself. As *mediatrix*, Mary was imaged as the second Eve, whose humility and obedience led to the overturning of the disobedience of the first Eve. In this, Mary was placed alongside Christ who is seen as the second Adam, the one whose humility and obedience overturned the trespasses of the first Adam. If Mary had not been obedient to God as the Son was, the possibility of human salvation, it was held, would have been jeopardized. In her obedience, therefore, Mary was not only seen as having set an excellent example for Christians but was also understood as intimately connected to divine life itself in that she was the bearer of God. This connection, as Medieval Christians imaged it, made it possible for her to command the attention of her son, Jesus Christ. She could therefore intercede for others because she had this close proximity to her son. Indeed, she was imaged as participating in divine life itself. Thus, even though Mary was not imaged as God, she came very close to being divine. This perception of Mary still influences how the Roman Catholic Church views her to this day and Protestants would do well to carefully meditate on her place in the salvific process. The oblivion to which some Protestant Christians have consigned Mary today is a demonstration of lack of theological sophistication.

Even though Mary was intimately connected to divine life through being the Mother of God, she came to be associated with the saints rather than with God. Although the word "saints" could be understood to include Christians who are both dead and alive, the word was especially applied to those dead Christians who had manifested Christian excellence in life and in death. The saints, like Mary, had closer access to God even though Mary's access is closer by virtue of her being the Mother of God. Because of the closeness to God which the saints were believed to have, living Christians saw them as a means by which divine grace could be communicated to the world. Such saints included early Christians such as Matthew, Peter, and Paul, important leaders in the early church and important medieval saints such as Benedict of Nursia and Martin of Tours. Among the saints were martyrs who had died bearing witness to Jesus Christ. The saints were therefore those whose virtues made them to be especially close to God in death and who could thus be called upon to intercede on behalf of living Christians as they go through the trials of life—and there were many trials which medieval Christians had to undergo thus making reliance on the mediation of the saints critical.

Saints were thus especially associated with miracles. Miracles could be obtained through direct appeal to them in prayer or through contacts with objects that were connected to them. Such objects could be relics (body parts of the saints or objects they had touched, such as their clothing, or their statue or painting). Paintings and statues of Mary, for example, were believed to possess supernatural powers that made them come to life and sometimes effect healings. A painting of Mary in fifteenth century Prato was believed to have leaped from a wall and cleaned an abandoned prison. An Italian Franciscan friar who visited Damascus in the fourteenth century reported of an image of Mary that had supernatural powers found at a monastery in Damascus. The image, he reported, exuded holy oil that healed illnesses and protected travelers against storms at sea. In an iconoclastic

Theology as Construction of Piety

episode in fifteenth century Bavaria, a statue of Mary that was struck in the head with a lance is believed to have spewed forth blood in protest against its ill-treatment. In some cases, when an image of a saint was placed on a woman who was undergoing difficult labor, her travail eased and she gave birth without trouble.[13]

Saints' bodies and objects that had come into contact with their bodies were especially prized. The French medievalist, Jacques le Goff, calls these forms of relics *"reliques corporelles"* (corporeal relics), pointing out that they consisted of clothing and everything that had come into contact with the saints when they were alive and their corpses or tombs when they died.[14] The bodies of saints, which were most precious and in high demand (because of their miraculous power), led to quarrels between peoples who wanted to keep these bodies. Gregory of Tours tells of one such quarrel between the people of Poitiers and the people of Tours (in France) who were gathered at Candes to claim the body of St. Martin of Tour. Each of them claimed that the bishop belonged to them and quarreled until nightfall when each of the groups decided to guard the corpse, waiting to continue the struggle the next day. But under cover of night, the people of Tours stole the body and the people of Poitiers were only alerted to this by the hymn which the people of Tours sang as they rowed off toward Tours. The people of Poitiers returned home "without acquiring the treasure which they were guarding."[15]

Another story of this nature is seen in the case of Lupicinus, a saint who lived in Lipidiacum. When he died, a wealthy woman came to claim his body but the peasants of the village resisted her attempt because they wanted to bury him in their village so that he could help them miraculously. When they started digging a grave to bury him the woman went and sought help and a group of people came, "put the peasants to flight and took away the holy body by force."[16] The need for the saints' bodies

---

13. Bynum, *Christian Materiality*, 106-12.

14. Jacques Le Goff, *Le Dieu du Moyen Âge* (Paris: Bayard, 2003), 26. Le Goff says that these were considered to be the most precious (les plus précieuses) relics. Also see G. J. C. Snoek, *Medieval Piety from Relics to the Eucharist: A Process of Mutual Interaction* (Leiden: Brill, 1995), 11–12.

15. This story is taken from Aron Gurevich, *Medieval Popular Culture: Problems of Belief and Perception*, trans., János M. Bak and Paul A. Hollingsworth (Cambridge: Cambridge University Press, 1988), 39.

16. Gregory of Tours, *Life of the Fathers*, trans., Edward James (Liverpool: Liverpool University Press, 1991), 88–89.

God and Matter in Medieval Theology

is further exemplified by the fact that some priests from France went to Italy and smuggled the bones of St. Benedict and his sister, St. Scholastica, to France. The importance of relics in God's providence is explained thus: the relics are used by God to bring people to an awareness of their need for religion and holiness. The relics "confer benefits upon all who pray unto the Father through Jesus Christ, the Son of God who liveth and reigneth in the unity of the Holy Ghost, world without end. Amen."[17] Thus, the relics are presented as means by which the presence and power of God are made manifest in the world.

These relics which people fought over usually served as public relics and the tombs of the saints whose relics were venerated served as shrines and churches were built on some of them. Regular pilgrimages were made to some of the churches with important relics. In fact, churches could hardly be seen as authentic if they did not have a relic of a saint. Churches therefore had to collect relics and put them in a reliquary or enclosed in an altar stone. One of the most important pilgrimages that took place in the Middle Ages was called in 1300 by Pope Boniface VIII. Forgiveness of sins was granted to those who made the pilgrimage to Rome, believed to be the death place of two very important leaders of the early church, Peter and Paul.[18]

Having been on pilgrimages to places like Rome and Jerusalem, some groups began to claim that they were in possession of relics of Christ himself. Known as *arma Christi*, these relics had to do with elements that were used in the crucifixion of Christ, such as the spear that was used in piercing him, the crown of thorns that was placed on his head, ropes that were used to bound him, the sponge that was used to soak the vinegar that was dipped into his mouth, the clothes he wore on the way to be crucified, and pieces of the cross on which he was crucified.[19] As time went on, others started claiming that they were in possession of body parts of Christ, such as his childhood teeth and the foreskin that was discarded when he was circumcised.[20] These relics were believed to be far more powerful than the relics of the saints but some of these claims stretched credulity and led to arguments

---

17. G. G. Coulton, *Life in the Middle Ages* (Cambridge: Cambridge University Press, 1954), 29–31.

18. David Chidester, *Christianity: A Global History* (New York, NY: HarperSanFrancisco, 2000), 215.

19. See Bynum, *Christian Materiality*, 64.

20. Pelikan, *The Growth of Medieval Theology*, 183.

on the importance of relics and other material objects in Christian piety. These arguments animated Christian theology in the Middle Ages, leading into the Reformation.

One of the arguments that were made with respect to Christian reliance on the relics of the saints was that Christians should see the saints as moral icons rather than mainly as sources of miracles. They were urged to see the virtues which the saints manifested as being just as important as, if not even more important than, the miracles they performed. Moral transformation, in this scheme of things, was put forward as just as important as miraculous healing. In fact, moral transformation could itself be seen as the very locus of the miraculous. Saints could perform miracles because of their moral rectitude. By stressing the importance of virtues vis-à-vis miracles, we begin to see a tendency toward undermining the Christian materiality of the Middle Ages. Intangible virtues were put forward as similar to tangible relics that worked miracles.

Another important issue for the medieval debates on Christian materiality was that important symbol of Christian unity—the Eucharist. Medieval Eucharistic theology was essentially about how it is that grace could be communicated through matter, specifically through the matter of bread and wine. This Eucharistic theology was based on the doctrine that Jesus was crucified for the salvation of the world. On the night before he was crucified, however, Jesus had a meal with his twelve disciples, during which he described the bread and wine which they ate and drank as his body and blood. By eating the bread and drinking the wine, therefore, his disciples were eating his body and drinking his blood. The elements of bread and wine, which came to be central in the Eucharistic celebration, were therefore believed to be Christ himself. But how was it that the bread and wine, ordinary material elements, could be said to be the body and blood of Christ through which grace is transmitted to human beings for their salvation? In order to understand how this was so, it is important to begin with the understanding of the Mass or the Eucharist in medieval theology.

In medieval theology, the Mass was understood to be a dramatic re-enactment of the sacrifice of Christ on the cross. Christ's sacrifice was a bloody sacrifice orchestrated by his enemies but the sacrifice of the Mass was a bloodless sacrifice orchestrated by his friends. Because the sacrifice on the cross was a real sacrifice carried out by Christ himself, the sacrifice of the Mass was also perceived as real because it was about the real Christ who was crucified on the cross, nay, the Christ who was in fact born o the

Virgin Mary. But how was this Christ present in the sacrifice of the Mass? He was present through the bread and wine that became his real body and blood. However, everyone could see that the bread and wine in the Eucharist were clearly bread and wine and did not become the human body and blood of Christ. Even when Christians received the Eucharist, what they chewed was bread not the flesh of Christ (because medieval Christians often received only the bread that stood in for both the bread and the wine). So how was the bread the body of Christ and the wine his blood, as Christ himself had described these elements: "this is my body... this is my blood" (Mk 14:22–24)? Does saying that the bread and wine were the body and blood of Christ mean that the bread and wine were actually the body and blood of Christ or did they rather represent his body and blood? How were the body and blood of Christ actually present in the elements of bread and wine? The arguments that purported to deal with these questions is known as the argument about the *real presence*, that is, the argument about how the real body and blood of Christ were present in the bread and wine of the Eucharist, even though these elements ostensibly remained bread and wine in the Eucharistic celebration?[21]

The debate about the real presence animated medieval theology with one side, represented by theologians such as Radbertus and Lafranc, insisting that the real presence should be understood literally, that is, that the bread and wine of the Eucharist became the actual body and blood of Christ, and the other side, represented by theologians such as Ratramus and Berengar of Tours, insisting that the bread and wine of the Eucharist should be understood as the body and blood of Christ in a non-literal way. Those who held that Christ was present in the Eucharistic bread and wine in a literal manner insisted that this position was viable in part because the sacrifice of Christ in the Mass was a real sacrifice and so his bodily presence in this event had to be real just as it was real on the cross. If the presence of Christ was real on the cross, it would be remiss of Christians to think that the same body was not present in the sacrifice of the Mass, which carries as much import for salvation as the sacrifice on the cross. The argument that the sacrifice which Christ made on the cross is non-repeatable did not quite hold water in a system where the conduct of each sacrifice in the Mass carried salvific import for both the living and the dead. Even though one of the important understanding of a sacrament in the Middle Ages

---

21. The discussion in this section has benefited from Pelikan, *The Growth of Medieval Theology (600–1300)*, 184–204.

was its perception as a sign of grace, those who interpreted the presence of Christ in the Eucharist in a literal manner thought that the sacrament of the Eucharist should be more than a sign of the presence of Christ—it depicted the very presence of Christ himself in his capacity as Savior of humankind.

One question which the insistence that the bread and wine were actually the body and blood of Christ raised, was how Christ could be present in the Eucharistic elements if he were, at the same time, seated at the right hand of God the Father. In response to this question, proponents of a literal understanding of real presence argued that because Christ was also divine, he could be anywhere at any time. It was pointed out that Christ's sitting at the right hand of the Father should not be understood to mean that Christ was confined to one place, given that he could be wherever he wanted to be at any time. This argument was also applied to concerns that eating pieces of the Eucharistic bread may imply eating only a part of Christ rather than the whole Christ. To this concern, it was pointed out that each piece of the Eucharistic elements should be understood as containing the whole of Christ so that just as it was the whole of Christ who was sacrificed on the cross and in each Mass, so too was it the whole Christ who was present in every piece of the Eucharistic elements of bread and wine. In fact, those who received only the bread without receiving the wine, as it was common in the Middle Ages, should not fear that they were receiving only a part of Christ because each piece of the consecrated bread contains the whole of Christ.

It was further recognized that the Eucharistic bread could decay. If this occurred, would it not mean that, on a literal reading of the presence of Christ in the bread, the incorruptible body of Christ should have suffered corruption? This question was simple but striking in that it dealt with the complex relation between created and corruptible matter and uncreated and incorruptible divinity. Concerns about the incorruptible body of Christ suffering corruption sometimes acted as an argument against why the presence of Christ in the bread and wine should not be understood in a literally. However, Christians were also urged to consume the Eucharistic elements immediately so that they may not decay.

A significant issue in medieval Eucharistic theology was just how it was that the ordinary matter of bread and wine became the body and blood of Christ. The response to this question was that the bread and wine became the body and blood of Christ when the priest consecrated them. Upon their consecration, the bread and wine became the actual body and blood of Christ. But how could this be, given that what the faithful received still tasted as bread and wine? To answer this question, it was posited that even though the faithful still tasted bread and wine when they received the elements, the substance of the bread and wine had changed into the body and blood of Christ. Thus, the faithful were to believe that they were no longer eating just ordinary bread or drinking just ordinary wine but the actual flesh and blood of Jesus Christ. The argument about the change in the substance of the bread and wine was in fact influenced by the Aristotlelian idea of substance and accident. Part of this idea had been appropriated in the early church in the debate about how the Father, Son and Holy Spirit could be said to be one God rather than three gods. There it was argued, as we saw in the last chapter, that the three persons in the divine life should be understood as *homoousios* (of the same substance).[22] A substance, according to Aristotle, was the essence of a thing, what actually makes a thing what it is. An accident, however, was the appearance of a thing. The way a thing appears or looks like is not what is essential about that thing. Thus, what is essential in a person is that the person is human rather than whether they are short, tall or thin, black, white, or brown. One's height or color is an accident. Applied to the argument about how the elements of the Eucharist became the actual body and blood of Christ, Christians were urged to believe that after the bread and wine had been consecrated, the essence of the bread and wine changed to the body and blood of Christ but the accidents remained the same. Thus, what the faithful ate and drank still tasted as bread and wine but, through faith, they were to understand that those were no longer bread and wine but the body and blood of Christ. What they tasted as they ate the elements were the accidents; the change of the essence of the elements was to be apprehended by faith. It was this understanding of the Eucharist that came to be described as transubstantiation and, through the Council of Trent, became the official doctrine of the Eucharist of the Roman Catholic Church.

Those who argued against the literal interpretation of the presence of Christ in the Eucharistic elements had an uphill task because many already held to the view that the bread and wine became the actual body and blood of Christ. Opponents of the literal interpretation of the presence of Christ in the Eucharist argued that the presence of Christ should be understood in a spiritual sense. For them, Christ was present in the elements but the

---

22. Diogenes Allen and Eric O. Springsted, *Philosophy for Understanding Theology*, second edition (Louisville, KY: Westminster John Knox Press, 2007), 65–76.

elements did not become the actual body and blood of Christ because they were clearly seen to remain the elements of bread and wine even after they had been consecrated. Further, they argued that interpreting the presence of Christ in the elements in a literal sense went against the Pauline injunction that after the death, resurrection, and ascension of Christ, Christians were no tot relate to him in a physical, but rather in a spiritual, manner. Speaking of Christ, Paul writes in 2 Corinthians 5:16: "even though we once knew Christ from a human point of view, we know him no longer in that way" (NRSV). To those who held to a spiritual interpretation of the presence of Christ in the Eucharistic elements, this suggested that the understanding of the presence of Christ in these elements should follow the Pauline injunction—these elements are the body and blood of Christ in a spiritual rather than in a physical sense. However, this proposal was rejected and those who argued against a literal understanding of the presence of Christ in the Eucharistic elements were persecuted. Berenger, for example, was forced to recant.

The widespread belief among the faithful that these elements became the actual body and blood of Christ contributed to the development of the cult of the Host or devotion to the Eucharistic bread. The elevation of the Host during Mass became a theophanic moment which many Christians craved. Christians were known to move from church to church on the same day just to behold as many elevations of the Host as possible, beseeching the priest to hold up the Host a little longer so that they may see their Maker. The increasing importance of the Host led to the development, in the thirteenth century, of the Feast of Corpus Christi (the Feast of the body of Christ). During this Feast, there was a public procession of the Host within a particular community. As the historian David Chidester puts it, "By celebrating the Host, therefore, the annual procession of the Feast of Corpus Christi marked out a community—a social body—under the protection of the body of Christ."[23] Here, the Host was seen as having protective powers because it was the very presence of Christ in a community.

In fact, stories abound of miracles performed by the Host. Some talked of the effectiveness of the Host in raising the dead while others saw it as being capable of making beer taste better.[24] One of the stories tells of how a woman who kept many bees that were unproductive and which died in great numbers took the bread (the Lord's Body) home and placed it in

23. Chidester, *Christianity*, 213.
24. Bynum, *Christian Materiality*, 169–72.

one of the hives. What happened next was brought about by "the marvelous power of God" working through this Eucharistic element. The bees, "recognizing the might of their Creator, built for their sweetest Guest, out of their sweetest honeycombs, a tiny chapel of marvelous workmanship, wherein they set up an altar of the same material and laid thereon this most holy Body: and God blessed their labours."[25] In other words, the bees became productive due to the presence of the body of Christ in their midst. In other stories people took the Eucharistic bread with them as protection when they travelled or kept them at home for protection. In a context where the quests for spiritual and material well-being were critical quotidian concerns, salvation and protection were intimate concepts tied to a materialist view of Christianity. Material well-being was closely tied to spiritual reality because earthly security was based on being in right relationship with the supernatural. People could only better cultivate a right relationship with the supernatural through constant and close interaction with material things, such as the Eucharistic elements of bread and wine.

A material object that would rock the foundations of the church itself was the letter of indulgence that was embedded in the penitentiary system, one of the significant sacraments. The penitentiary system, from which our current prison system took its name, was a means of grace that was intended to continuously renew the Christian and restore their relationship with God. It developed out of the realization that Christians are sinners and in order for them to maintain their relationship with God they needed a means of continuous repentance. According to this system, Christians confessed their sins to priests and the priests, as representatives of Christ on earth, absolved them of their sins. Being absolved from sins was, however, contingent on performing some acts that were like punishment or payment for the sins one had committed. Acts of penance depended on the gravity of the sin. Sometimes Christians were asked to pray the rosary, fight in the Crusades, or conduct pilgrimages, as acts of Penance. This system, however, evolved to a point where letters were written, by the Pope or a bishop, and sold to those who could buy them for the forgiveness of sins. Some of the letters covered not only the sins one had committed but also future sins. Others covered the sins not only of those who were alive but also those who had died. These letters, therefore, became a means for the church to make money and manifested a grave abuse of the penitentiary

---

25. G. G. Coulton, *Life in the Middle Ages*, 70–72.

system.²⁶ Letters of indulgences were therefore material not only in the sense that they stood for a visible means by which divine forgiveness was transmitted to Christians but also because they were connected to an old debate in the church—the debate about the place of material possessions in the Christian life. In fact, the money generated from the sale of indulgences was not so much for the benefit of the entire church as it was sometimes for the benefit of some corrupt church officials. Thus, the debate about the sale of indulgences should be placed within the context of the debate about whether or not the church or church leaders should focus on amassing material possessions.

The debate about whether or not the church should be concerned about increasing its material possession could itself be seen as a debate about how the church could be seen as a conduit of God's presence in the world. The core of this debate could be summarized as follows: in order to be an effective mediator of divine life in the world, does the church need to possess earthly power as represented by material possessions? Here we move from a limited understanding of material things as represented by specific objects used in Christian devotion, such as statues, relics, or the Host, to a broader understanding of material things that includes political and economic power.

Debates about the corrupting influence of economic and political power on the church were a regular part of medieval Christian life but it was especially demonstrated in the debate among the followers of St. Francis of Assisi (c. 1182–1226). St. Francis, who was himself from a rich background, had taught that Christian spirituality was contingent on being poor. Like Jesus Christ whose influence on the world did not depend on his economic or political power, Francis taught that the Christian life did not depend on the accumulation of wealth but rather on abandoning oneself at the mercy of divine providence. Thus, his followers, like himself, were to live by begging and they were not to own property. However, this was to change soon after the death of St. Francis as some in his movement began to seek a more settled and secure life that could be obtained only through property ownership while others insisted on following the way of poverty that St. Francis had urged on his followers. These groups were

---

26. For more on the evolution of indulgences in medieval England, see R. N. Swanson, *Indulgences in Late Medieval England: Passports to Paradise* (Cambridge: Cambridge University Press, 2007). For more on Roman Catholic teaching on indulgence, see the article on "Indulgences" on *New Advent* at the following link: http://www.newadvent.org/cathen/07783a.htm. Accessed on August 1, 2013.

God and Matter in Medieval Theology

known as observant or spiritual Franciscans and conventional Franciscans. In this debate, the Pope was on the side of conventional Franciscans who favored property ownership because the Pope was deeply immersed in the economic and political intrigues of the time.[27] The defeat of the Franciscan group that favored poverty as the highest spiritual ideal was a declaration that material things, in this case wealth and political power, were the major ways by which divine life is manifested in the world. The recognition of the necessity of possessing wealth and political power demonstrated that a poor and powerless church could not effectively represent God in the world. Thus, according to the medieval catholic church, the grace of God was not only mediated through material things such as the Eucharist but also through the material possessions of the church that gave it economic and political power to influence the lives of people. Those who challenged some of the ways the church related to material things were seen as heretics and persecuted for their troubles.

The defeat of the observant or spiritual Franciscans, however, did not mean the end of the challenge to the materialism of the medieval church. A significant figure who followed in the footsteps of the observant Franciscans was the English scholar, John Wyclif (c. 1320–1384).[28] Wyclif's theology on material possession was based on the doctrine of creation. Since God is the creator of everything, Wyclif taught, God is to be understood as the only true owner of everything. Even humans themselves belong to God because God made them and at creation God did not ask them to own what has been created but rather to take care of these things. According to Wyclif, dominion (*dominium*) over everything ultimately belongs to God and human relationship to all material things should be guided by this critical understanding of God as creator and true owner of all. Adam and Eve understood this before the fall because they did not own anything in the Garden of Eden. In the Garden of Eden, there was no master-servant relationship and everything was seen as belonging to God, the true owner of all. After the fall, however, sin brought about the illusion of property ownership and people began to forget that they were not the true owners of material things, having themselves been created. Forgetting that they are themselves creatures who cannot properly own other creatures, human

---

27. Steven Ozment, *The Age of Reform*, 98–115.

28. Much of the reflection in this section is drawn from Stephen Lahey, "Wyclif and Lollardy," in *The Medieval Theologians: An Introduction to Theology in the Middle Ages*, ed. G. R. Evans (Oxford: Blackwell, 2001), 334–54.

beings began to desire to own and control other things and even people for their own benefit. However, to claim ownership over any part of God's creation is illusory because a creature cannot be the owner of other created things. When creatures, like human beings, begin to claim total ownership and control of what has been created, it creates the condition where God is no longer regarded as the rightful owner of all and thus sets the stage for the dethroning of God. From this perspective, property ownership could be seen as standing at the root of atheism. Property ownership stands at the root of atheism because it focuses human attention on controlling material things, making them forget that their entire attention has to be focused on God who is the creator of all material things, including humans themselves.

According to Wyclif, the proper way to relate to things is through *evangelical dominium*, where people live together and share things in love as Christ did with the Twelve and as the early church did. This attitude toward material things demonstrates that the role of the church is not so much to accumulate earthly wealth and power as it is to care for the spiritual needs of the people of God. When the church is so focused on property ownership and the accumulation of power, as obtained throughout the Middle Ages, the church is acting contrary to what it should be doing.

Practicing evangelical dominion, according to Wyclif, requires redemption through Christ because the fall of Eve and Adam vitiated human capacity to practice evangelical dominion. Redemption enables Christians to relate to things in ways that make clear that God, not humans, is the true owner of these things. Because focusing on the accumulation of wealth and power undermines the high standards that are to be expected of the church and sullies the name of God, the church should be concerned with spiritual things, the care of souls, rather than ,material or temporal things. While the church is concerned with spiritual things, the king is to be concerned with the management of material things. In this scheme of things, the king should himself be a Christian who recognizes God as the true owner of these things. This recognition would enable the king to manage temporal affairs diligently, seeing his role as managing the affairs of God. In fact, for Wyclif, the king could not be just if he did not participate in the justice of God through redemption. However, the standard of morality that applies to the church does not seem to apply to the king because the king may go to war to protect what God has placed under him but it is out of order for the church to go to war. In fact, Wyclif's view that the church should be concerned about spiritual matters while the king should be concerned about temporal matters led him to argue that the king could strip the church of its property so that the corruption brought upon the English church through the focus on the accumulation of material possessions and power may be abated.

Even though Wyclif's thought developed in a context where national monarchs were beginning to challenge the power of the church in medieval Europe, his thought stands in line with a strand of thinking in the Middle Ages that increasingly began to see spiritual and temporal affairs as somehow distinct but related. As we enter the early modern period, it would increasingly be argued that the church should properly be concerned with spiritual things while the king should be properly concerned with temporal things. We see this in Luther's so-called two-kingdom ethic in which the state and the church perform different functions but are both under God.[29] The tendency to separate the spiritual and the material could therefore be seen to be at the root of the current dominant view of the separation between church and state, a separation that is not what was originally intended by arguments against the materialism and corruption of the church. While the point was originally to call upon the church to eschew a focus on the material and the temporal, in our time calling for such separation seems to be to increase human control over their own affairs, removing God from the equation. Thus, the fact that God is ultimately the owner of all, including humans themselves, have fallen by the way side. This is probably a consequence which Wyclif and others who espoused a view like his did not anticipate. Perhaps a reflection on the possible consequences of his theological construction might have alerted him to this possibility.

Be that as it may, while the question of the corrupting influence of material possession on the church was hotly debated, these debates affected the perception not only of material things in general but also specific material things. Some groups tended to reject all material things while others rejected only some material things. Those who rejected the materialism of the church were often designated as heretics.[30] Some groups, such as the Waldensians, tended to practice asceticism in order to stave off the ill-

---

29. See Scott Hendrix, "Luther," in *The Cambridge Companion to Reformation Theology*, eds., David Bagchi and David C. Steinmetz (Cambridge: Cambridge University Press, 2004), 49–50.

30. See Pelikan, *The Growth of Medieval Theology*, 229–42; John H. Arnold, *Belief and Unbelief in Medieval Europe*, 191–207; Euan Cameron, "The Waldenses," in *The Medieval Theologians*, 269–86; Gerhard Rottenwöhrer, "Dualism" in *The Medieval Theologians*, 287–302.

effects of greed in the church. Another group or a cluster of groups, was the Carthars, who developed a theology and cosmology which was Gnostic or Manichaean in character, prizing spiritual things while seeing material things as evil. This theology completely undercut much of the material objects in the life of the church and even the belief in the resurrection of the body and so was perceived as significantly outside the teachings of the catholic church. This view of the Carthars' was an extreme manifestation of the struggles which medieval Christians experienced with material things. Other groups, such as the Lollards who significantly borrowed from the views of John Wyclif, rejected certain materialistic beliefs, such as the cult of the saints, pilgrimages, image-worship, and transubstantiation. For the Lollards, these beliefs were thought to be both unscriptural and corrupting and therefore ought be discontinued. They saw the elements of the Eucharist as not turning into the body and blood of Christ, as the church taught, but rather as representing the body of Christ. Thus, while much of the debate among theologians in the Middle Ages did not dispute the presence of Christ in the Eucharist, some Lollards denied the presence of Christ in the elements and held that "the Eucharist was but a memorial of Christ's passion."[31] Other dissenters even challenged the propriety of using the cross in worship and constructing church buildings, insisting that these things were not needful to Christian piety.

While some of those who challenged the materialism of the church were clearly labeled heretics and driven out of the official church, there were those who challenged the materialism of the church in very irenic ways and so stayed within the ambit of the official church. Such was the case with the movement known as the *Devotio Moderna* which was started by the Dutchman, Gerhard Groote (1340–1384). Thus, he and his followers adhered to the traditional understanding of the Eucharist but "diminished the importance of saints, relics, and rituals of pilgrimage" in their worship. They concentrated on living simple Christian lives in communities where all were supposed to be imitators of Christ and thus saintly. It is therefore little wonder that Thomas a Kempis (c. 1380–1471), an important medieval mystic who wrote the classic work known as *Imitation of Christ*, came from this movement. The goal was to imitate Christ through the study of the Bible and mystical writings rather than focusing on relics and pilgrimages. Although they were theologically unsophisticated, theirs was a movement that contributed in shaping Western Christianity as we know it today. With

31. Lahey, "Wyclif and Lollardy."

them, we see the interiorization of faith and the emphasis on morality rather than a focus on objects that mediate the power of God.

An important figure who also challenged medieval materialistic piety was the influential Renaissance humanist theologian, Desiderius Erasmus of Rotterdam (c. 1466–1535). Erasmus, like the *Devotio Moderna* movement, deemphasized materialistic Christianity through his perception of Christianity as a faith that calls for the cultivation of inner piety by concentrating on the examination and exposition of the word of God (the biblical text). Like Justin Martyr of the early centuries of Christianity, Erasmus saw the faith as a philosophy, the philosophy of Christ or *philosophia Christi*. This *philosophia Christi* focused on the person of Christ as narrated in the Bible and urged Christians to emulate Christ through a concentration on the spiritual rather than placing other material objects in the place of Christ. His focus on the person of Christ as narrated in the Bible led him to press for better means to convey the message of the text. That is why he developed a Greek New Testament and called for a reading of the text that has the power to transform lives. For him, therefore, the theologian was also a rhetorician who uses words to convince people of the importance of the gospel. For him, Christians were not to rely on "external forms of worship" such as "pilgrimages, the veneration of saints, and the observance of rites," which were "merely crutches to help the weaker brethren," but rather on "prayer and devotion."[32]

It was however the challenge against the selling of indulgences that made it possible for many of these dissenting voices to gain the official status which they have attained in our own time. Luther's rejection of indulgences brought many of the arguments against the materialism of the medieval church to the fore and facilitated the process by which many medieval heretical positions would find a home in Protestantism. Luther was therefore an embodiment of the heretical positions that had gone before and a rejection of his positions was also a rejection of all other positions that had previously been declared heretical. In spite of the rejection of Luther's positions, the tide against medieval materialism could not be abated but continued with the rise of Western iconoclasts who orchestrated the destruction of images. Much of the use of images in worship would closely come to be associated with Roman Catholicism and some Protestant groups would reject the use of all material objects in their worship. While groups that

---

32. Erika Rummel, "The Theology of Erasmus," in *The Cambridge Companion to Reformation Theology*, 36.

eschew church buildings, such as the Quakers, are sometimes presented as having their origins in the Reformation, it is important to see that they had medieval forerunners. The question about the place of material things in the life of faith would nevertheless remain a complex one. However, with the problematizing of material things in the Middle Ages, the road to the interiorization and the rationalization of the Christian faith had begun to be paved. The rationalistic faith that developed during the later Middle Ages, stretching to our own time, should therefore come as no surprise.[33] The question that ought to be asked now is whether or not this move to a rationalistic faith, especially in the churches of the West, constructed or is constructing piety in salutary ways. Perhaps one's response to this question would depend on whether or not one is in favor of the problematizing of the materialistic faith of the Middle Ages. We shall have more to say about this in chapter five.

Conclusion

The debate about the place of material things in the Christian life could be seen as revolving around two questions: one, whether or not Christians should prize material things, and two, whether or not material objects may have positive or adverse effect on the nature of Christian piety. In the first place, the question is about whether or not Christians ought to prize material things. In the Middle Ages, like in our time, the quest for wealth and power were often distracting to a clergy that was supposed to be paragons of Christian virtue. The quest for power and wealth often exposed the clergy as concerned with something far less than the worship and honor of God on which they were supposed to focus. In the debate about poverty, for example, we see that the position of the church seemed to be that one of the ways in which God is manifested in the world is through power and wealth. Thus, it seems appropriate for the church and members of the clergy to be opulent because without such opulence they may not have the power to influence the world. One of the consequences of the debate about the church's relation to material possession is that, by placing the state over the church, the church came to be increasingly removed from the center of power and wealth so that in our time the church seems to be marginal. This notwithstanding, gaining wealth and power continues to be a persistent temptation

---

33. For the religious roots of the modern world see Michael Allen Gillespie, *The Theological Origins of Modernity* (Chicago: The University of Chicago Press, 2008).

to the church and it still does not appear that it is clear how the church ought to address this matter. Even in our own time, the church sometimes cozies up to centers of power and wealth because it seems that the church needs these things in order to be influential in the world. Chasing wealth and power is a perennial temptation which Christians would need to guard against by gaining better understanding of material things. Theologically speaking, Christians should not shun material things because these things may be a means of divine manifestation in the world. In fact, there is no other way in which Christians can conceive salutary events, given that we ourselves are material objects. However, these material things could also be extremely estranging. Perhaps the development of Christian wisdom in our time should be demonstrated through our awareness of when and how material things have become estranging. This is because we seem to find it difficult to figure out when these material things have become estranging rather than empowering. A piety that is based on procuring power and wealth, the medieval debates seem to suggest, stands on shallow ground.

The second part of the debates deals with the place of specific material objects in the construction of Christian piety. That is, how does God use specific material objects such as the saints, the Eucharist, and pilgrimage sites, in the development of Christian piety? Does God even use these objects in sustaining Christian piety? Is there a danger that these material objects could themselves be construed as inherently divine so that they, rather than God, may become the focus of Christian worship? This question is especially poignant when it comes to the argument about the real presence. The notion of transubstantiation, as discussed above, seems to imply that material objects (bread and wine) actually become divine. If material objects actually become divine, it should come as no surprise that there should be devotion to these objects. And this is what people often did, as demonstrated by the devotion to the Host. The classic argument often made to counter the claim that people worship these objects is to insist that the worship is not due to the object but to that which these objects represent or point to, that is, that these objects point beyond themselves to someone greater. However, in addition to the fact that in the Eucharistic debates the official position was that the Eucharist was Christ himself rather than a representation of Christ, Bynum has recently argued that, for most people, the material objects common in medieval Christian worship were perceived to have a power of their own rather than standing for, or pointing to, something greater. That is, those who practiced devotion to the

Host, for example, did not see the Host as pointing to the power of Christ who is greater than the Host. "People behaved," Bynum writes, "as if images [objects] were what they represented."[34] Thus, where people tend to see the power of God as manifested in particular objects, it is not hard for them to start seeing the objects themselves as locus of power rather than seeing God as the locus of all power. The questions about the place of the material in the construction of Christian piety, as we will see in the next chapter, do not only apply to the debates about material things in medieval Christianity but also has relevance for contemporary African Christianity. It speaks to the question of the kind of faith which is cultivated in Christians and whether this faith is theologically sound and anthropologically salutary.

---

34. Bynum, *Christian Materiality*, 125.

CHAPTER 4

Assessing the Theology of Inculturation

THE BASIC FRAMEWORK THAT legitimizes the theology of inculturation is the view that, as the Christian faith moves from one context to another, it is often reshaped so that it may make sense in new contexts. If, in its missionary enterprise, the faith insists on maintaining idioms which people outside its original context do not understand, these people would hardly assent to the message of the gospel. It is thought that even if people in different contexts somehow assent to the message of the gospel without a good understanding of what the gospel is about, they would hardly be grounded in it and so their faith may be somehow superficial. The basic idea here is that the Christian faith is like a language that developed in a particular context and is thus not spoken universally. It is a local language that has to be made universal as the faith travels from place to place. In order for people everywhere to speak this local 'language' fluently, they do not simply need to learn only the grammar of the Christian 'language'; rather, the Christian 'language' needs to be translated into the different local 'languages' which people already speak so that they may understand the faith in their own local cultures. Proclaiming the gospel in a new context is therefore akin to teaching a person a foreign language by translating words, ideas, and practices of that foreign language into the 'language' which the person being taught already knows. For example, in order to teach the Christian faith to a person from Babungo, Cameroon, the Christian faith needs to be translated into the Babungo language or worldview if the Babungo person is to understand the faith better and make it her or his own. Understanding the

Christian 'language' in terms of the 'language' which people already speak, it is believed, helps people make the faith their own rather than seeing it as a foreign element in their midst.[1] As is well known, the Christian faith developed in Jewish and Greco-Roman contexts and then moved on into other contexts such as the Asian, African, and Euro-American. As the faith moves from place to place it therefore does not remain the same; it takes on local colors as some elements of the faith are translated into local idioms so that Christians in varied local contexts may better appreciate and practice it. In this process, both local cultures and the Christian faith undergo change.[2] Inculturation is therefore a method of Christian missions.

As a method of Christian missions, the theological framework for the theology of inculturation is the Christian idea of the incarnation that tells the story of God's relation with and concern for the world. The Christian faith teaches that God is not a material object and so, except for theophanies, God could not interact with humans as if God were a material object. However, according to the Christian narrative, in order for God to rectify the estrangement which humans had incurred through the fall of Adam and Eve, God had to become human. In Jesus Christ, therefore, God became human and came to live with humans in order to teach them how they should live with God. Thus, in Jesus Christ God became that which is not essentially God—human—in order to enable humans to know how life with God should be lived, thus helping them to fully experience their maker. In a sense, therefore, God inculturated God's self in the human context in order to enable humans to understand how to live with God. The incarnation is therefore a method of divine inculturation in which God did

---

1. For inculturation as translation, see Lamin Sanneh, *Translating the Message: The Missionary Impact on Culture*, second edition (Maryknoll, New York: Orbis Books, 2009). For a different appraisal of the relation between the Christian 'language' and other 'languages,' see John Milbank, *The Word Made Strange: Theology, Language, Culture* (Oxford: Blackwell Publishers, 1997). For the difficulty of translating the Christian message from one language to another, see Jim Harries, *Communication in Mission and Development: Relating to the Church in Africa* (Eugene, Oregon: Wipf and Stock, 2013).

2. For an in-depth study of the nature of inculturation with specific reference to Africa see Laurenti Magesa, *Anatomy of Inculturation: Transforming the Church in Africa* (Maryknoll, New York: Orbis Books, 2004). Speaking of inculturation from the perspective of Bible reading in Africa, one scholar describes it as "the attempt to root the biblical message in the different contexts where it is received" ("l'effort d'enraciner le message biblique dans les divers lieux où il est accueilli"). See André Kabasele Mukenge, "Les Lecture Africaines de la Bible à l'aube du troisième millenaire," in *Cultural Readings of the Bible in Africa*, ed. André KaLoba-basele Mukenge, Jean-Claude Loba-Mkole, and Dieudonné P. Aroga Bessong (Yaoundé, Cameroon: Édition Clé, 2007), 23.

Assessing the Theology of Inculturation

not lose divinity but took up humanity, bringing together two 'languages'—the human and the divine—in order to enable humans to better understand their place in divine life. Inculturation as a method of Christian missions demonstrates that such missions are, in the final analysis, the mission of God.

As intimated above, this divine inculturation in the human context was however done in a particular Jewish context. As the gospel moves from the Jewish context to other contexts, those who become Christians in these different contexts have to think about the Christian faith in terms of how God in Jesus Christ could be or is incarnated in their own contexts. A central question that is posed here is how the incarnation of God in Jesus Christ in a Jewish context can be understood in contexts that are different from the initial Jewish context. What about this incarnation needs to stay the same even in different contexts and what about it needs to be reinterpreted for better understanding in different contexts? Inspiration for addressing these questions is found in the Bible itself, as Magesa has shown.[3] A classic example of this is depicted when the first Jewish Christians struggled with the question of whether or not non-Jewish Christians needed to practice the faith in the same way as Jewish Christians (Acts 15). It was recognized at this early stage in the development of the faith that non-Jewish Christians did not have to practice the faith in the same way as Jewish Christians. Thus, it would appear that an important justification for the theology of inculturation is not only a theological one but also a practical one—the better comprehension and practice of the Christian faith in different contexts.

Seen from the above perspective, the theology of inculturation is a significant method of constructing Christian piety and the question that needs to be raised is what kind of piety this method of doing theology is constructing. One main problem with this method of doing theology, however, comes from the question of how to translate the faith into another context in a way that its original contents and practices do not suffer distortions that may make the faith unrecognizable. Thus, the thorniest question for the theology of inculturation has to do with how the faith may change in different contexts but somehow remain the same. This question arises because Christians often seem to assume that the faith has a core, even though situating this core is often a matter of debate.[4] The theology of in-

---

3. Magesa, *Anatomy of Inculturation*.

4. See Lamin Sanneh, *Whose Religion is Christianity? The Gospel Beyond the West* (Grand Rapids, MI: Eerdmans, 2003).

cutlturation therefore seems to deal with the classic question of the relation between Christianity and culture: how, if at all, should particular cultures affect the transmission of the Christian faith?[5] This is the question which the theology of inculturation in Africa, like inculturation everywhere, is supposed to address.

However, when the Christian faith came to Africa during the modern missionary movement, the central question was not simply that of the relation between Christianity and African cultures.[6] At the center of the evolution of the theology of inculturation in Africa was the question of African identity, that is, what it means to be an African and a Christian. This question of identity arose because African theologians who resorted to the theology of inculturation felt that their African identity had been assaulted both by the Christianity that was brought to Africa by Western missionaries and by colonialism.[7] The theology of inculturation continues to be practiced from the perspective of the marginalization of Africans, especially sub-Saharan Africans, in the global cultural, social, political and economic systems. Looking at the definitions and descriptions of the theology of inculturation in Africa, one would see an evolution. From its beginnings it dealt largely with the question of African cultural identity but now, as a result of severe criticisms, the definition has been broadened to include the issue of Africa's place in the global political economy.[8] Thus, while the theology of inculturation and the theology of liberation were seen as distinct modes of doing theology in Africa, it has now come to be acknowledged that the theology of inculturation also encompasses the element of liberation.[9] The theology of inculturation encompasses liberation, first,

---

5. See Andrew Walls, *The Missionary Movement in Christian History: Studies in the Transmission of Faith* (Maryknoll, New York: Orbis Books, 1996) and H. Richarch Niebuhr, *Christ and Culture* (New York, NY: HarperCollins, 1951).

6. See Andrew Walls, *The Cross-Cultural Process in Christian History* (Maryknoll, New York: Orbis Books, 2002), 177–214.

7. See Kwameh Bediako, *Theology and Identity: The Impact of Culture Upon Christian Thought in the Second Century and in Modern Africa* (Eugene, Oregon: Wipf and Stock, 2011), chapter 6.

8. For part of this debate, see Simeon O. Ilesanmi, "Inculturation and Liberation: Christian Social Ethics and the African Theology Project," *Annual of the Society of Christian Ethics* (January 1995): 49–73; Luke Lungile Pato, "Indigenization and Liberation: A Challenge to Theology in the Southern African Context," *Journal of Theology for Southern Africa* 99 (November 1997): 40–46. Also see Emmanuel Martey, *African Theology: Inculturation and Liberation* (Maryknoll, New York: Orbis Books, 1993).

9. For more of this, see Laurenti Magesa, "A Theological Journey," *Exchange*, vol.

because it is an attempt to reposition and valorize an African culture that had been maligned by Western philosophers, missionaries and colonialists. Revalorizing maligned African cultures was a means of recreating the self-image of Africans and so enable them rise up from under the weight of inferiority that the debasing of their ancestral cultures had heaped upon them. Second, the theology of inculturation encompasses liberation because it was aimed at lifting up the voices of an oppressed people and advocating for their full participation in a global political economy that has often marginalized them. See from this perspective, even Black Theology in South Africa was a form of inculturation theology.

From the above, it can therefore be seen that African theology of inculturation developed in a situation of conflict. Even though we may say that the theology of incultation as a whole began in a situation of conflict (like the primordial conflict between God and humans that necessitated the incarnation in order to seek a resolution and the conflict in the early church about whether or not non-Jewish Christians needed to take up some Jewish practices in order to be fully Christians) the conflict that led to the development of the theology of inculturation in Africa was quite toxic because it was couched in the social construct of racism and the dominant framework of imperialism. In this context, in order to justify colonialism, black Africans were depicted as belonging to the lowest racial stock whose cultures were generally below Western cultures that were seen as the ideal. Thus, non-Christian Africa was compared to the Christian West and found wanting. Non-Christian Africa was described as without religion and without God and as made up of people who needed to be civilized by the Christian West. Terms like primitive, savage, animism, fetish, polytheism, and the like, were used to describe Africans and their worldviews, and these terms indicated the lower manifestations of the higher forms of religious life that were represented by Western Christianity.[10] Early African theology of inculturation therefore focused on demonstrating that these Western characterizations of African traditional religious worldviews were not accurate representations of what Africans believe. It was intended to show that African religious

---

32 no. 1 (2003): 43–53.

10. For depictions of African religions by the West, see Afe Adogame et al., eds., *European Traditions in the Study of Religions in Africa* (Wiesbaden: Harrassowitz Verlag, 2004).

beliefs were in many ways similar or sometimes even superior to the Western Christian traditions that had been brought to Africa.[11]

From the above, therefore, it can be seen that African theology of inculturation has been simultaneously reactive and proactive, appropriating elements of African traditional religious cultures to talk back to Christianity, but also crafting an African Christian theology at the same time. This dual function of African inculturation theology is different from what a theology of inculturation should ideally be about. As we saw above, the theology of inculturation should ideally be about how to make the Christian faith make sense in new contexts. It should be about the connection between Christianity and the local cultures into which Christianity has been transmitted. In the African context, however, the theology of inculturation came to be, in part, a means of pushing back against manifestations of Western Christianity and its derogation of Africa dignity.

This background meant that African theologians would be doing double duty—reclaiming Africa's pre-Christian traditional religions on the one hand and working out how the Christian faith may or may not be connected to these pre-Christian traditions.[12] For example, the pre-Christian African understanding of God was sometimes compared with the Christian understanding of God in a bid to see how the African conception of God measures up to the Christian conception of God and vice versa.[13] In all this, the impetus sometimes seemed to be to demonstrate that the African conception of God was in no wise inferior to the Christian conception of God. The question sometimes appeared to be not so much about how the Christian idea of God may be made to fit in the African context but rather about how Africans may continue to worship the God or gods of their ancestors but from a Christian perspective.[14] Thus, the point appeared to be

11. Even though he was a Christian, Gabriel Setiloane, for example, argued that the idea of God in African Traditional Religion is superior to the idea of God in the Western Christianity that was brought to Africa. See Mogomme Alpheus Masoga, "A Critical Dialogue with Gabriel Molehe Setiloane: The Unfinished Business of the African Divinity Question," Unpublished, http://uir.unisa.ac.za/bitstream/handle/10500/6624/Masoga.pdf?sequence=1. Accessed online on August 1, 2013.

12. For a recent example of this see, Laurenti Magesa, *What is Not Sacred?: African Spirituality* (Maryknoll, New York: Orbis Books, 2013).

13. See Bolaji Idowu, *Olódùmarè: God in Yoruba Beliefs* (London: Longman, 1962); John Mbiti, *Concepts of God in Africa* (London: SPCK, 1970). Masoga, "A Critical Dialogue with Gabriel Molehe Setiloane."

14. For example, see Elochukwu Eugene Uzukwu, *God, Spirit, and Human Wholeness*.

Assessing the Theology of Inculturation

not so much about how Africans should be Christianized but rather about how Christianity should be Africanized. The emphasis was sometimes placed not on Christianizing Africans because being a Christian seemed to carry the sting of de-Africanization and de-Africanization was a bad thing because it spelt deracination and capitulation to Western machinations. African theologians seemed to have felt that they needed to prove their Africanness by bringing elements of African traditional religious cultures and Christianity together. Thus, the goal was sometimes not just to make Africans better understand and practice the Christian faith but rather to push back against the undignified ways in which Western Christians had treated, and even continue to treat, Africans. A good case may be made that some forms of inculturation theology are not so much intended to inform African Christians about the Christian faith but rather to inform Western Christians about African Traditional Religions.[15] In a sense, African theology of inculturation was not entirely meant to educate Africans but rather to educate the West about the nature of African religious worldview. Thus it is that the question of inculturation in Africa has been problematic not only because it is complex to contextualize elements of the Christian faith in any context but also because it originated in a context of acrimony between African Christian theologians and the West and even between African Christian and non-Christian scholars.[16] Any evaluation of the ways in which the Christian faith has been inculturated in Africa should bear this complex context in mind. This context has made the theology of inculturation in Africa to be not just a form of contextual theology but also a means of redefining the place of Africa, especially sub-Saharan Africa, in the world.[17] Keeping this context in mind, this chapter addresses three broad areas of inculturation: worship, ethics, and what is commonly described as the African spiritualized worldview. It shall be argued that while the theology of inculturation has much to contribute in contextualizing Christianity in Africa, it also leaves much to be desired. Engaging the spiritualized cosmology, it will be argued, is the most pressing issue for the theology of

---

15. For examples, read the following works and ask yourself who the audience is: Bolaji Idowu, *African Traditional Religion: A Definition* (London: SPCK, 1973) and John Mbiti, *African Religions and Philosophy* (London: Heinemann, 1969).

16. See Okot p'Bitek and Kwasi Wiredu, *Decolonizing African Religions: A Short History of African Religions in Western Scholarship* (New York: Diasporic Africa Press, 2011).

17. For more on the theology of inculturation as contextual theology, see T. Derrick Mashau and Martha T. Frederiks, "Coming of Age in African Theology," *Exchange* 37 (2008): 109–23.

Theology as Construction of Piety

inculturation because this cosmology is the heart of African understanding of how life should be lived. It will be shown that the question of bringing together the Christian faith and the African spiritualized worldview needs to be recalibrated in order to enable Africans to effectively deal with the challenges of the modern world.

Worship and the Theology of Inculturation

The inculturation of Christian worship in particular contexts is a universal endeavor. We have already encountered this in the recalibration of the place of worship in Christian ethics in Chapter One and it is a process that has been going on in American Protestantism, especially with the recent tendency to move from "traditional" to "contemporary" or "blended" worship services, among others.[18] It is also found in churches around the world.[19] Like the process of inculturation as a whole, inculturating Christian worship in the African context seems to be a combative affair, especially as manifested in the Roman Catholic tradition after the Second Vatican Council (1962–1965). It seems to be combative because this inculturation of worship may be seen as rooted both in the history of asserting the African identity in the modern world and a desire to better comprehend the Christian faith.[20] In this section, we shall discuss elements of the inculturation of Christian worship in Africa such as the experiential nature

---

18. See Constance M. Cherry, *The Worship Architect: A Blueprint for Designing Culturally Relevant and Biblically Faithful Services* (Grand Rapids, MI: Baker Academic, 2010); Marva Dawn, *Reaching Out Without Dumbing Down: A Theology of Worship for this Urgent Time* (Grand Rapids, MI: Eerdmans, 1995); Robert E. Webber, *Blended Worship* (Hendrickson Publishers, 1996); Robert E. Webber, *Planning Blended Worship* (Nashville, TN: Abingdon Press, 1998); Robb Redman, *The Great Worship Awakening: Singing a New Song in the Postmodern Church* (San Francisco, CA: Jossey-Bass, 2002).

19. See, for examples, Paul M Collins, *Christian Inculturation in India* (Aldershot, England: Ashgate Publishing Limited, 2007); Kurt D. Selles, "Protestant Worship with Chinese Characteristics: Reflections on a Chinese Worship Service," *Exchange* 41 (2012): 1–18.

20. See Elochukwu Uzukwu, *Liturgy: Truly Christian, Truly African* (Eldoret, Kenya: Gaba Publications, 1982); Uzukwu, *Worship as Body Language: Introduction to Christian Worship, an African Orientation* (Collegeville, MN: Liturgical Press, 1997); Joseph G. Healy, "Inculturation of Liturgy and Worship in Africa," *Worship* 60 (1986): 412–23; Asamoah-Gyadu, *Contemporary Pentecostal Christianity: Interpretations from an African Context* (Eugene, Oregon: Wipf and Stock, 2013), 17–33.

Assessing the Theology of Inculturation

of African worship, the elements used in the Eucharist, worship art, and marriage rites.

The claim that African worship is experiential is replete in the literature that deals with the nature of worship in Africa. As experiential, African worship involves the whole person in movements and gestures that include drumming, singing, clapping, dancing, and ecstatic activities. The Nigerian theologian, Elochukwu Uzukwu, who is arguably the premier African sacramental theologian, has described these movements as "body language" which is ethnic in character. He has therefore called for the Roman Catholic Church in Africa to be immersed in African forms of worship rather than being saddled with worship forms that emanate from Greco-Roman and Latin traditions.[21] In fact, this experiential worship has been cited as a significant reason why many Africans left, and are living, some historic mission churches to join the Pentecostal churches. The worship experience in Pentecostal services are said to have drawn from the pre-Christian African worship style in which followers of particular gods experience these gods in a bodily manner, such as through possessions and trances. This worship experience does not only create significant intimacy between the worshipper and the god/spirit, but is also therapeutic in character because it is aimed at healing the personal and communal bodies.[22] The cerebral worship services that are sometimes characterized by reading from texts and singing from hymn books do not appear to cut it for many Africans as they seek a worship experience that is spontaneous, ecstatic, and therapeutic. Worship services that involve total bodily and spiritual engagement have been instituted in some Roman Catholic churches, especially as seen in Yaoundé, Cameroon and the Democratic Republic of Congo, and may be found in many Protestant churches across Africa today, especially those with Pentecostal/charismatic leanings.[23]

Considering that contemporary African Pentecostalism is characterized by experiential worship and orality and that the Azusa Street revival that led to the development of American Pentecostalism was led by an African American, some have postulated African experiential and oral worship as the genesis of contemporary Pentecostalism.[24] However, if Harvey

---

21. Uzukwu, *Worship as Body Language*.

22. See Susan J. Rasmussen, "Spirit Possession in Africa," in *The Wiley-Blackwell Companion to African Religions*, ed. Elias Bongmba, 184–97.

23. Healy, "Inculturation of Liturgy and Worship in Africa," 184–97.

24. See Walter J. Hollenweger, *Pentecostalism: Origins and Development Worldwide*

Cox is correct that the rise of Pentecostalism bespeaks the rejuvenation of a primal spirituality characterized by universal ecstatic speech, trance, dance, healing, etc., then it would appear that experiential worship is not essentially an African way of worship.[25] This should give us pause as we attempt to characterize what is African and what is not. Such pause does not mean that we may not claim as African a form of worship that is clearly seen to be widespread in the continent but rather that we should not pigeonhole Africans as characterized only by one way of worship. Even though the experiential form of worship is appealing to many Africans, there are many others for whom such worship may not be appealing. Thus, while it is important to reclaim this form of worship in African Christianity, it is also necessary to note that not all Africans may want to worship in this way. We must come to see that there are many ways of worshiping God and the experiential mode of worship is not better that the cerebral one. We should therefore avoid the temptation of presenting the experiential form of worship as the best form of worship in Africa simply because it is rooted in what is seen to be African spirituality and the way many Africans seem to worship. Inculturating the worship experience in Africa should not simply be based on opposing what is seen as Western form of worship to an African form of worship. Such a view of the matter promotes essentialism that is not supported by the evidence on the ground. We need to take a sober look at the various forms of worship in the continent and evaluate whether these forms of worship cultivate helpful piety among its practitioners. Not all churches in Africa would like to worship in the experiential mode of the Living Streams Ministries International in Ghana, as described by Asamoah-Gyadu.[26] There appears to be a mode of thinking in the field of African Christianity that tradition, or what the majority of people do, is necessarily the right way to go. We may need to realize that this may sometimes not be the case; we need to subject every form of worship to rigorous theological evaluation in terms of the kind of piety they cultivate.

Such theological evaluation may be directed at experiential worship services that hardly include the celebration of the Eucharist or Holy Communion. The Eucharist has been a central part of Christian worship from the beginnings of the church because it celebrates an event that stands at the heart of the life of the church—the life, death, and resurrection of our

---

(Peabody, MA: Hendrickson Publishers, 1997), 18–24.

25. Cox, *Fire From Heaven*, 82.

26. Asamoah-Gyadu, *Contemporary Pentecostal Christianity*, 21–22.

Lord Jesus Christ and how this procures the salvation of the world. However, celebration of the Eucharist is hardly central to the worship of many of the churches that practice experiential worship—as if the Eucharist is peripheral to the life of the church. In stressing experiential worship as African, does the Eucharist have to be excised or relegated to the periphery? In excising or marginalizing the Eucharist from regular worship, however, some of these churches that claim to be practicing an African form of worship are actually practicing the form of worship of Protestant churches in the West that sparingly celebrate the Eucharist.[27] Given that communal meal is important in the African context, perhaps celebration of the Eucharist need to be more important in African churches. African Roman Catholic churches however take the celebration of the Eucharist seriously, even though many rural churches go for long periods of time without celebrating the Eucharist because of lack of resident priests. In these churches, however, experiential worship is practiced within the framework of the celebration of the Eucharist.

Some African Roman Catholic theologians have however raised questions about the elements that are used in the celebration of the Eucharist. The questions arise from the use of bread and wine in the celebration of the Eucharist. Problematizing these elements, some African theologians hold that bread and wine are Mediterranean and Western foods not commonly grown or consumed by many Africans. Raising questions about the provenance of bread and wine has led Uzukwu to do a study of the provenance of some of the common foods found in Africa.[28] While recognizing that some foods which are thought to be indigenous, such as corn or cassava, actually originate from outside the continent, Uzukwu insists that the food that is used in the Eucharist should be food that is locally produced and commonly consumed rather than imported and less commonly consumed. The wheat used in making bread is not grown in many African countries and the grapes used in making wine grow only in a few African countries. This means that the elements that are used in the Eucharist are not common African meals and they are often imported; this marginalizes not only African staple foods but also Africa's economies. In order not to continue this marginalization of the continent around the Eucharistic table, Uzukwu suggests that locally grown food and locally brewed drinks should be used

27. Asamoah-Gyadu, *Contemporary Pentecostal Christianity*, 145–59.
28. Uzukwu Eugene, "Food and Drink in Africa, and the Eucharist," Afer XXII (1980): 370–98.

instead. However, attempts to use locally produced food and drink in the Eucharist does not appear to have gone down well with the Roman Catholic hierarchy as Bishop Dupont of Chad, who celebrated the Eucharist using local elements, was relieved of his duty in the 1970s.[29] So far, it does not appear that the use of African produced food and drinks in the Eucharist is a widespread phenomenon.

However, the fact that the use of indigenous foods and drinks in the Eucharist does not appear to be widespread in the continent should not mean that such a practice would be out of order. In evaluating this issue, it is important to keep two things in mind. First, the elements used in the Eucharist should not be seen as carved in stone. As Uzukwu has argued, the fact that Christ used bread and wine in the supper from which the Eucharist derives does not mean that bread and wine are the only elements that should be used in celebrating the Eucharist. Christ used bread and wine because those were the common foods used in such celebrations in the context in which he grew up. If he grew up in a context where rice and bear were commonly used, he would have used rice and beer. His use of bread and wine was therefore contextual and should not be made universal. What seems critical is that Christ had a meal with his followers on the day before his death and it is that meal that is celebrated in the Eucharist. The elements used in that meal should not be seen as the only elements that must be used in all places at all times. Rejecting African foods from the Eucharistic table does not only miss the central point of the Eucharist but also seems to portray African produced food and drink as unworthy of cultivating relationship with God. The second thing that should be borne in mind is that many Africans are now used to foods and drinks that are not locally produced or indigenous to the continent. Bread, for example, is commonly consumed in many African cities. In the modern world, African diet has come to be quite complex as some Africans do not eat only that which could be seen as locally produced or indigenous. Thus, bread and wine may not appear to be as foreign to Africans as may seem to be the case. Even though elements used in the production of bread and wine may be imported in many African countries, such may be seen as what it means to be part of the modern world which Christianity has contributed in creating. Just as Africans have come to appropriate the Christian faith which is not indigenous to the continent (even though some may like to think that it is indigenous) so too are Africans also putting up with some of

29. Uzukwu, "Food and Drink," 170.

its idiosyncrasies. Putting up with some of the idiosyncrasies of the faith, however, does not mean that Africans should not be free to determine what to use in the celebration of the Eucharist. Rather, it means that Africans should be free to use bread and wine if they so desire and some other food and drink if they so desire.

A further critical question in the inculturation of worship in Africa is the use of art. Speaking of the variety of African liturgical art in the Roman Catholic tradition, Uzukwu writes: "African artists are beginning to speak their communities' faith through images. The painting of Mary and the Child Jesus dominating the sanctuary in the cathedral of Yaoundé, the carvings and paintings in the cathedral of Kinshasa, the wood-carved Stations of the Cross in the Visitation Sisters' chapel in Loango, Congo, the varieties in vestment designs found all over Africa, testify to a burgeoning of African liturgical art."[30] In spite of this burgeoning in African art, an art form that has raised significant controversy is the painting of Jesus Christ as black. The complaint here seems to be that painting Christ black may confuse Africans about the skin color of the historical Jesus. The issue about confusing the skin color of the historical Jesus was apparently not raised when Christ was painted for centuries as having white pigmentation. In fact, the image of Christ that still hangs on the wall of many African Christian homes today is that of a white Christ. Many, if not all, of the films about Christ still being shown in Africa today are films that portray him as white. Scenes from films portraying Jesus as white are often superimposed on gospel music videos used in spreading the gospel, especially in sub-Saharan Africa.[31] The portrayal of Jesus Christ as white, however, places significant distortions in the African conception of the historical Jesus. Historically, Christ was more likely brown than white or black. Thus, portraying him as black or white may lead to similar confusion. Questions do not need to be raised only when Jesus is painted black; similar questions need to be raised when he is painted white.

Given that the Christian faith seeks to take the local color of every context in which it finds itself, it is therefore necessary for Christ to be painted in the color of the inhabitants of each place where the faith finds

---

30. Uzukwu, *Liturgy: Truly African, Truly Christian* (Eldoret: Spearhead, 1982, 35, cited in Healey, "Inculturation of Liturgy and Worship in Africa," 422.

31. Damaris Seleina Parsitau, "Gospel Music in Africa," in *The Wiley-Blackwell Companion to African Religions*, 489–502; Ogbu Kalu, "Holy Praiseco: Negotiating Sacred and Popular Music and Dance in African Pentecostalism," *Pneuma* 32 (2010): 16–40.

itself.³² This should be especially so in Africa where people have been evangelized through the use of images of a white Christ, giving the erroneous impression that Christ was white. The tendency to paint Christ black in the African context apparently began in the early eighteenth century when the Congolese girl, Kimpa Vita, taught that Christ and his disciples were black.³³ She was burnt at the stake for heresy by European missionaries. Contemporary artists are beginning to paint Christ black, especially as seen in the portrayal of Christ in the Cameroon context in the "Life of Jesus Mafa" paintings.³⁴ While it is important to state that Jesus was neither black nor white, the color of his skin has come to carry racial undertones when it is easily thought that he was white but his blackness is problematized. The blackness of Jesus, as his depiction in any other color, needs to be normalized so as to thoroughly contextualize him in the African context. This is not to say that Africans should believe that Jesus was black—that would be just as false as believing that he was white. It is rather to enable Africans to begin to think Jesus in terms of the black skin so that we may reach a point where it would be recognized that even though Jesus is not black, portraying him as a black person may be a way of comprehending him better in the African context. In order for this to happen, Africans do not only need to paint or carve Jesus as black, they also need to produce and popularize films in which Jesus is portrayed as black. Doing this is the point at which successful inculturation needs to be underwritten by economic fortitude. This goes into the heart of the main argument of this book, namely that the theology of inculturation needs to be recalibrated to foster Africa's economic power in the modern world. Successful inculturation therefore needs to be seen as tied to economic strength.

A final area in the inculturation of Christian worship in Africa deals with rites, especially the rite of marriage. The main issue concerning marriage and African Christianity has to do with just how marriage should be conducted. This issue has generated heated debates especially in the Roman Catholic tradition where marriage is considered a sacrament and

---

32. See, for example, the images of Christ on the front cover of Philip Jenkins, *The Next Christendom: The Coming of Global Christianity* (Oxford: Oxford University Press, 2011).

33. Elizabeth Isichei, *A History of Christianity in Africa: From Antiquity to Present* (Grand Rapids, MI: Eerdmans, 1995), 66; Adrian Hastings, *The Church in Africa, 1450-1950* (Oxford: Oxford University Press, 1996), 104-7.

34. Healey, "Inculturation of Liturgy," 422; for the paintings see "Vie de Jesus Mafa," at: http://www.jesusmafa.com/?lang=en, accessed on July 9th, 2013.

thus significant for salvation. African marriages that are not conducted following the Roman Catholic tradition are considered null and void by that tradition. This has led to talk about the regularizing of Christian marriage in Africa.[35] Calling for the regularizing of Christian marriage in Africa sometimes imply that marriages properly constituted in the African traditional systems are irregular and can only be made regular by the church. Thus, a Christian whose marriage is not sanctioned by the church, even if such a marriage has been regularly conducted in the African traditional system, is, for the Roman Catholic tradition, not in good standing in the church. Thus, people whose marriages have been properly constituted according to African traditions are not allowed to participate in the Eucharist. By rejecting marriages that have been properly conducted in the African traditional system, the church seems to be saying that God does not sanction such marriages, thus calling properly constituted African marriages into question.

Calling into question properly constituted African marriages has been especially occasioned by the coming together of three systems in the continent: the colonial state, the Christian faith, and African traditional religious cultures. This combination has led to a situation where Africans sometimes have to get married three times in order to be considered properly married—traditionally, in the courts, and in the church. However, in two of these systems, the colonial state and the church, marriage is seen as a punctiliar affair, that is, as materializing at a particular point in time when a particular rite is performed. For the African traditional system, however, marriage is a process made up of stages. In some cases, the process is completed only after the couple has been living together and even had children. However, the conception of marriage as a process does not matter to the church if the couple has not been married in church. Thus, even though a couple may be regarded as married in a particular African community, they may not be regarded as married by the church.

Furthermore, it is often easier for couples to get married traditionally than in the church because church weddings are often associated with the educated and wealthy elite who have the financial resources to perform them. Thus, scholars are now calling for the church to rethink its attitude toward properly constituted traditional marriages. Considering that the

---

35. For more on this, see Adrian Hastings, *African Catholicism: Essays in Discovery* (London: SCM Press, 1989). For a history of Christian engagement with African marriages, see Adrian Hastings, "The Church's Response to African Marriage," *African Ecclesiastical Review* XIII .3 (1971): 193–203.

cumbersome process of getting married already appears to be preventing some people from getting married at all, the church needs to figure out how to make the process less cumbersome and taxing.[36] The church also needs to recognize that, while marriage is an important Christian institution, there is no theological backing for any specific way of performing a marriage rite. Thus, a specific way of conducting marriage should not be imposed on African Christians. The church therefore needs to recognize marriages that have been properly constituted in African traditional contexts.

Other areas of marriage that are debated in Africa include polygamy and homosexuality/same-sex marriage. However, these issues will not be addressed at this point because the questions raised about them are not so much about ritual as they are about ethics. Questions about polygamy and homosexuality/same-sex marriage deal with whether these types of relationships are right or wrong and good or bad. These are ethical questions and will be addressed under the inculturation of Christian ethics below.

Inculturation of Christian Ethics in Africa

A critical question in the inculturation of Christian ethics in Africa has to do with how the ethical system of African traditional religious cultures may be related to Christian ethical traditions—should African ethical systems take priority over Christian ethical systems or vice versa, or should they be harmonized? In order to adequately respond to these questions, we need to pose the question of the provenance and telos of African traditional religious ethics and Christian ethics? Inquiring into the provenance and telos of the two ethical systems will help us understand how they may be related to each other.

While Christian ethics is very diverse,[37] it may be seen to be bipolar in terms of bringing together two important visions, the human or creaturely and the divine. Christian ethics is aimed at human or creaturely well-being

---

36. For the decline of church weddings in Africa and the reasons why, see Lazar Arasu and George Kainikunnel, "The Church in Africa and the Issue of Christian Marriage," *Afer* (August 1996): 229–34.

37. For the diversity in Christian ethics, see Gene Outka, "Christian Ethics?" in *The Blackwell Companion to Religious Ethics*, ed. William Schweiker (Oxford: Blackwell, 2005), 197–203; Vigen Guroian, "Differentiation in Christian Ethics," in *The Blackwell Companion to Religious Ethics*, 214–26; Jean Porter, "Trajectories in Christian Ethics," in *The Blackwell Companion to Religious Ethics*, 227–36.

Assessing the Theology of Inculturation

but it places this within the context of divine life so that creaturely well-being is ultimately realized when God will be all in all (*First Corinthians* 15:28). Christian ethics is therefore seen as beginning with God and ending in God. This is not to say that the human imagination is not important in crafting Christian ethics. For Christian ethics, however, human imagination, especially when it moves towards the good, is situated within the divine imagination so that human life is formed by God and directed toward its fullness with God in the new heaven and the new earth (Revelation 21). Thus, we may say that Christian ethics involves God and creation but with creation ultimately finding its place in God. From this perspective, Christian ethics is theocentric in the sense that it focuses on what God has done and what God will do to ultimately resolve the divine-creaturely drama in divine life. This view of Christian ethics should not be construed as undermining the importance of human happiness in this life (as insistence on the hereafter in Christian life has often seemed to do); rather, it points out that human happiness in this life is placed within the broader framework of eternal divine life, including the life to come. Within this framework, the life, death, and resurrection of Jesus Christ is often thought to be central, given that it is the event of Jesus Christ that is foundational in the birth of the Christian faith.

The question of the provenance of African traditional ethics is still being debated. While philosophers generally seem to think that African traditional ethics has its origins in the human imagination, scholars of African Traditional Religions seem to place its genesis in God.[38] Even though scholars do not appear to agree on the origins of African traditional ethics, they seem to agree about its telos—ensuring human well-being. It is therefore generally acknowledged that African traditional ethics in anthropocentric not in the sense of negating the spiritual realm but rather in the sense of having human well-being as its ultimate vision. As Bujo has put it, "life is the highest principle of ethical conduct,"[39] "life in its widest sense is what functions as the hinge for the elaboration of ethical norms. Everything that contributes to maintaining, strengthening, and perfecting individual

---

38. For more on this debate, see Barry Hallen, "African Ethics?" in *The Blackwell Companion to Religious Ethics*, 407–12; Segun Gbadegesin, "Origins of African Ethics," in *The Blackwell Companion to Religious Ethics*, 413–22; Magesa, *African Religion*, 35–76; John Mbiti, *Introduction to African Religion* (London: Heinemann, 1991), 171–79.

39. Bénézet Bujo, *Foundations of an African Ethic: Beyond the Universal Claims of Western Morality*, trans. Brian McNeil (New York: Crossroad Publishing, 2001), 3.

as well as communal life is good and right."⁴⁰ According to Bujo, therefore, African traditional ethics is focused on cultivating fullness of life that is both human and cosmic but ultimately has its foundation in God.⁴¹ Even though Bujo says that God is the ultimate foundation of African ethics so that African ethics is anthropocentric, cosmic, and theocentric, he goes on to construct his ethical reflection within the framework of the well-being of the human community.⁴² Within this framework, the life of the community is the measure of morality. Here, the transcendent is made immanent within the life of the community because it is in the life of the community that all dimensions of life—the seen and the unseen, the past, present and future—converge. In fact, the past and the future resolve in the present because the present is the arena in which the cosmic drama is enacted. Thus it is that Bujo has evolved a four-dimensional ethic that includes the living, the dead, the not-yet born, and God, but which resolves in the life of the community.⁴³ In this, therefore, Bujo and most scholars of African ethics are agreed: African ethics is focused on cultivating the well-being of individuals in a community. This well-being is often conceived in terms of individual and communal health, peace, and prosperity. In traditional Africa such health, peace, and prosperity include having many children, livestock, long life-span, and other markers of comfortable living. Experiencing such health, peace, and prosperity in the modern world is what Magesa seems to refer to as "abundant life."⁴⁴ When African Christians describe Jesus as giver of abundant life (John 10:10), the African understanding of well-being is what they seem to have in mind.⁴⁵ It is a vision of life in which the spiritual and the material realms work together for the benefit of life here in the world, both now and in the future. The goal seems to be that, through the cooperation of the physical and the spiritual worlds, creaturely life may continue to be healthy and prosperous.

---

40. Bénézet Bujo, "Differentiations in African Ethics," in *The Blackwell Companion to Religious Ethics*, 428.

41. Bujo, "Differentiations in African Ethics," 425–26; Bujo, *African Theology in Its Social Context*, trans. John O'Donohue, M. Afr. (Maryknoll, NY: Orbis Books, 1992), 17–18.

42. Bujo, *Foundations of an African Ethic*, 1–2.

43. Bujo, "Differentiations in African Ethics," 424.

44. Magesa, *African Religion: The Moral Traditions of Abundant life*.

45. Diane B. Stinton, *Jesus of Africa: Voices of Contemporary African Christology* (Maryknoll, NY: Orbis Books, 2004), 54–80.

Assessing the Theology of Inculturation

However, when the Christian faith talks of life, are these the dimensions of life that are meant or does the Christian faith mean something different? Without a doubt when the Christian faith talks of life, it includes the dimensions of individual and communal well-being described in the African Traditional Religions. Life in the Christian vision includes health, longevity, children, wealth, individual and communal peace both in the present and in the future. In fact, these are central to what God promised Abraham when God asked Abraham to start a new life with God and this vision of life is also common in the Psalms, especially where the Psalms continuously point out how dead people do not praise God (see Psalms. 6, 88 and 115). Also, this understanding of life is part of what Jesus was concerned about when he walked the earth. This can be seen in his healing ministry, which included feeding the hungry, raising the dead, and healing the sick. Just as African traditional religious systems endeavor to make individuals and communities to be in sync with the physical and spiritual realms for their well-being, so too does the Christian faith endeavor to make humans to be in sync with the spiritual and the physical realms for their well-being. It is therefore unfortunate that Christianity has sometimes been historically interpreted as being far more concerned about the spiritual realm than the material realm. This is especially so in the case of the understanding of salvation, especially in some evangelical Christian circles. In these circles, salvation has come to be understood largely as the need to go to heaven after death so that the idea that people ought to live decent lives in this world is sometimes seen as an inconvenient extra to a Christian view of salvation. This evangelical understanding of Christian salvation has led to a situation where salvation has come to be conceived as a "fabulous ghost," something that people hear about but which they hardly ever see.[46] It is for this reason that severe poverty, injustices, illness, and even death have come to be compatible with a Christian understanding of salvation. Strictly speaking, these things are antithetical to a Christian understanding of salvation because they negate the vision of ultimate well-being situated in God through Jesus Christ. If there is one thing which the Christian faith may learn from the African understanding of salvation, it is the view that salvation ought to be manifested in decent human life in this world. Jesus Christ demonstrated in his earthly ministry that salvation is not divorced

---

46. Gerrit Brand, *Speaking of a Fabulous Ghost: In Search of Theological Criteria, with Special Reference to the Debate on Salvation in African Christian Theology* (Frankfurt am Main: Peter Lang, 2002).

from our quality of life here in the world. To overcome the divorce between material well-being and salvation, Christians have been called upon to see salvation as holistic in nature, including both the physical and the spiritual. Thus, in recent times Christians have started talking about salvation as dealing with the whole person, communities, and the rest of creation, rather than just with the spiritual dimension.[47] However, the apparent comfort which Christians still maintain in the face of widespread suffering in both the Majority and Minority worlds shows that Christians still have a lot to learn about the material implications of the Christian understanding of salvation.

Stressing the importance of present well-being in the Christian understanding of salvation, as is being done especially by African Pentecostal/Charismatic Christianity, has led to the critique that such an emphasis does not take seriously the place of suffering in Christian life. It is pointed out that the suffering of Christ speaks to the place of suffering in the Christian life.[48] This critique, however, fails to see that suffering, even in the life of Christ, is an aberration; it is not the way things are supposed to be. The death of Christ was murder caused by those who felt threatened by his preaching and the reign of God which he made manifest during his earthly ministry. Thus, we should not see suffering as a normal part of life but rather as an aberration, a challenge to the manifestation of the life of God in the world. Christians must therefore never learn to be comfortable with suffering because normalizing suffering may make us to be insensitive to the suffering of others, vitiating our eschatological vision of peace in the process.

In spite of the importance of material well-being in the Christian understanding of salvation, the Christian faith also teaches that salvation is not exhausted in the present. Christians look forward for ultimate fulfillment in a city whose architect and builder is God (Heb 11:10). Thus, in the Christian salvific scheme, the well-being of individuals and communities is critical but such good is not exhausted in the present. Everything does not revolve around the life of the community or creation but is pulled forward, so to speak, into the future life of God. This tension is captured in the notions of "realized" and "consequent" eschatology where realized

---

47. Howard A. Snyder, *Salvation Means Creation Healed: The Ecology of Sin and Grace: Overcoming the Divorce Between Earth and Heaven* (Eugene, OR: Wipf and Stock, 2011).

48. See Asamoah-Gyadu, *Contemporary Pentecostal Christianity*, 105–20.

eschatology stands for the elements of Christian salvation that are already a reality in this life and consequent eschatology stands for those elements that will only be experienced in the future.[49] The difference between realized and consequent eschatology should however not be pressed too far because they do not simply represent two different moments but rather are intricately interconnected. Elements of realized eschatology are found in consequent eschatology and vice versa. This notwithstanding, the difference between the Christian telos and the telos of African traditional worldview should be clear: the African traditional view seems to revolve around the life of the community or cosmos, as Bujo and others have argued. The Christian view takes the life of the community and cosmos quite seriously but gathers up the present life into the future life of God. In fact, one can say that for Christianity it is the future that draws the present toward approximating perfection. That is, in the story of Christian eschatology, the present often falls short because it does not adequately approximate our future life in God.

Pointing out this difference is not to say that African Traditional Religions do not have a vision of the future. In African Traditional Religions there are visions of the future in which persons pass over to the spirit world of the ancestors in death.[50] However, even this future vision does not narrate a history in which all is ultimately resolved in God, as in the Christian narrative, but is rather replayed in the life of the community as ancestors become participants in the community in the cycle of life, connecting the community with the spiritual realm for ultimate communal well-being now and in the future. Thus, it seems that the vision of the Christian faith is similar to but also different from that of African Traditional Religions. It is similar in that it stresses the importance of bringing together the spiritual and the material for the well-being of creation in the present and the future but different in that the Christian faith has a vision of everything finding its ultimate place in a future life with God.[51] Thus, there is a theocentric and futuristic dimension to the Christian faith that does not appear to obtain

---

49. The division of Christian salvation into the already and the not yet appears to have been introduced into recent Christian theology by George Eldon Ladd. See George Eldon Ladd, *A Theology of the New Testament*, revised edition (Grand Rapids, MI: Eerdmans, 1993), 61–65.

50. See Chirevo V. Kwenda, "Affliction and Healing: Salvation in African Religion," *Journal of Theology of Southern Africa* 103 (March 1999): 1–12.

51. Jurgen Moltmann, *The Coming of God: Christian Eschatology*, trans. Margaret Kohl (Minneapolis, MN: Fortress Press, 2004).

Theology as Construction of Piety

in African Traditional Religions. When Uzukwu says that "the intention of God for religions, including the Christian religion, is the healing service for humans," he is correct, but that is not the whole story.[52] Uzukwu's depiction of the matter does not take into consideration the futuristic dimensions of Christian eschatology and so he locates Christian salvific discourse mainly within the dimension of African traditional religious vision.

Insisting on the difference between African Traditional Religions and Christianity is not to demonstrate that one is right and the other is wrong or that one is good and the other is bad. It is rather to point out that both religions have different dimensions that should be mined for their potential salutary implications for life in Africa. Resolving Christianity into African Traditional Religions or vice versa may lead us to forget important dynamics that may be appropriated for the construction of salutary piety in the continent. Inculturating Christian ethics ,or any other dimension of the Christian faith in Africa, therefore, does not mean that African Traditional Religions need to be made to look like Christianity or vice versa.[53] Rather, it means that African Christians need to figure out how elements of the Christian faith may or may not fit in various African contexts. Because of the differences that obtain between the two faiths, ethics from a Christian perspective would be similar to but also different from ethics from an African traditional religious perspective. Ethics from a Christian perspective would therefore need to rely extensively on the Christian narrative than would ethics from an African Traditional religious perspective.[54] Connections should be made when African traditional ethics appear to coincide with Christian ethics. For example, the African communal ethic known as *Ubuntu* has been demonstrated to have shaped the thought of Archbishop Desmond Tutu of South Africa who brought Ubuntu together with the Christian idea of forgiveness in his effort to lead the Truth and Reconciliation Commission in South Africa.[55] Thus, there are instances where African ethics go together with Christian ethics and vice versa. However, there are also instances where they diverge. A key area of such divergence

---

52. Uzukwu, *God, Spirit, and Human Wholeness*, 210.

53. For a critique of the presentation of African Traditional Religion in Christian garb, see p'Bitek and Wiredu, *Decolonizing African Religions*.

54. See Paulinus Ikechukwu Odozor, "An African Moral Theology of Inculturation: Methodological Considerations," Theological Studies 69 (2008): 583–609.

55. See Michael Jesse Battle, *Reconciliation: The Ubuntu Theology of Desmond Tutu* (Cleveland, OH: Pilgrim Press, 1997); Desmond Tutu, *No Future Without Forgiveness* (New York, NY: DoubleDay, 1999).

Assessing the Theology of Inculturation

can be seen in Bujo's discussion of the place of marriage and procreation in sustaining the multidimensional African community.[56]

Since, according to Bujo, the community is the measure of all ethical reflections and actions, ensuring the survival and flourishing of community is essential to African spirituality. African community, it should be remembered, has four dimensions: the living, the dead, the yet to be born, and God. However, communities often emerge through marriage and procreation. According to Bujo, community emerges from the interaction among a *monad* (individual), a *dyad* (male and female) and a *triad* (male, female, and progeny that combine to make communities or plurality). Within this framework procreation is critical and marriage serves as the context for procreating and thus ensuring the future of the community. A tremendous and awesome responsibility is thus placed on the living—they are responsible for bringing forth the yet to be born so as to ensure the survival of the living and the dead. In this scheme of things the life of the dead, or what John Mbiti calls the living-dead, is not placed in a Christian theological context in which the dead are expected to spend eternity with God; rather, the life of the dead is sustained through *anamnesis*, the memory accorded the dead by the living. In this eschatology, there is a mixture of what one might call African ancestral eschatology with a Christian theological anthropology. The accent is however placed on African ancestral eschatology in which the continuation of the life of the dead depend not so much on God as it does on the living. The dead are interested in the survival and flourishing of the living because without a living community to remember the dead, the life of the dead will evaporate. The living are also very interested in procreation because the living are the potential dead and without a living community to remember them when they are dead, they too would go out of existence. In short, this African ancestral eschatology seems to be saying that our life after death depends on whether we procreate or not.

This view would have been less controversial if it simply stated that humans need to procreate because the survival of every human community depends on it. However, the point here is not just about the survival of physical human community but also the survival of the spiritual ancestral life. At a very basic level, therefore, those who do not procreate may never become ancestors. We use "may" here because it is possible for those who

---

56. See Bénézet Bujo, "Vatican II and the Challenge of Marriage and Family in Africa." I have addressed the issues raised in this section in David T. Ngong, "Christianity as Fertility Religion."

113

do not procreate to be made ancestors in traditional African societies. But these are often people who are seen to have made significant contributions to their communities even if they may not have had children. However, African societies have not often treated people who do not procreate kindly because of the centrality of anamnestic ancestral eschatology in these communities. That people who do not bear children are marginalized in African societies is echoed by one of the most influential scholars of African Traditional Religions, John Mbiti, when he writes:

> marriage and procreation in African communities are a unity: without procreation marriage is incomplete. . . . A person who, therefore, has no descendants quenches the fire of life, and becomes forever dead since his line of physical continuation is blocked if he does not get married and bear children. . . . Unfortunate, therefore, is the man or woman who has nobody to 'remember' him (her), after physical death. To lack someone close who keeps the departed in their personal immortality is the worst misfortune and punishment that any person could suffer. To die without getting married and without children is to be completely cut off from the human society, to become disconnected, to become an outcast and to lose all links with mankind.[57]

This ancestral eschatology has caused tremendous grief to countless men and women in Africa, one of whom is an important African theologian, the Ghanaian Mercy Amba Oduyoye. In a very revealing article, she grieves the spite with which she was treated by her in-laws because she was unable to conceive a child.[58] In spite of the fact that she has raised many of the children in her extended family to adulthood, she was still treated with scorn because she could not have her own child. She writes of awkward conversations with people who simply assumed that as a married woman she should have children. She reports of embracing biblical stories of women and men who had children even when they were past their childbearing age, in hopes that she, too, might have children even as she got older. She writes of how Christian men who were friends of her husband's proposed to make her pregnant if her husband was the problem (that is, the infertile one). She underwent both traditional and Western medical treatments,

---

57. Mbiti, *African Religions and Philosophy*, 133-34.

58. For Oduyoye's story, see Mercy Amba Oduyoye, "A Coming Home to Myself: The Childless Woman in the West African Space," in *Liberating Eschatology: Essays in Honor of Letty M. Russell*, ed. Margaret A. Farley and Serene Jones (Louisville, Kentucky: Westminster John Knox Press, 1999), 105-20.

some of them in very humiliating circumstances, before finally accepting her lot as an infertile woman destined to be remembered in other ways. If she were the one who was infertile, such was ground for her husband to get married to a second wife so as to have a child by her. Oduyoye even talks of men, some of them pastors, who had children out of wedlock because their wives could not conceive. Since these men were not allowed to marry a second wife because of their position in the church, they preferred to have children out of wedlock. She mused how the marital vow and the injunction against adultery do not mean much if there aren't children in some African Christian marriages. In this context, the important issue seems to be not so much faithfulness and companionship in marriage but rather the ability to procreate. In all her struggles, both church and society in Nigeria and Ghana, the two African countries where she lives and works, hardly had a soothing word for her.

Oduyoye's forlornness in the African Christian scene led her to symbolically disavow her marital status by opting to reclaim her maiden name. This symbolic move was preceded by her request to divorce her husband, given that she could not be the kind of wife society wanted her to be. A successful marriage, according to this African anthropological eschatology, is one teaming with children. Oduyoye's marital experience as a childless wife made her to feel that nothing else mattered in this African universe. Thus, she symbolically disavowed her marital status by reclaiming her maiden name, Amba Ewudziwa, the name she was given on the eighth day after she was born. This is how, she says, she "would like to come home to herself" as a childless wife, a "woman alone," in the West African space.[59] Oduyoye's disavowal of her marital status because it offers her no fulfillment as a childless wife is a stinging indictment of the African anthropological eschatology and the African church that uncritically espouses it. In addition to symbolically disavowing her marital status as a coping mechanism against the "child factor" in the West African space, Oduyoye also draws from her Christian spirituality characterized by a deep prayer life and the recognition of various spiritual gifts. She makes the following recommendation for African theology:

> For me childlessness in the West African space has been a challenge—to my womanhood, my humanity, and my faith. . . . It is for the church to acknowledge and raise up the diversity of God's gifts and to celebrate all the ways of bringing forth life. My concern

---

59. Oduyoye, "A Coming Home to Myself," 107.

is for a theology of procreation that responds to this challenge, a theology and eschatology that will speak to both those who reproduce themselves biologically and those who do not, a theology that embraces forms of fruitfulness, biological and beyond.[60]

African theology has, so far, not heeded her call for there is a dearth of theological treatment of infertility in African theology. The ancestral eschatology that is based on procreation has rather been carried over into the burgeoning Pentecostal churches where infertility is interpreted as a curse that needs to be broken. Infertile couples are made to see infertility as an evil which can only be relieved through having their own children. Even adoption, they are told, is no substitute for having their own children.[61] In all this, central questions that keep coming to mind are: where is Christian theology in this eschatology? Does the human journey into divine life ultimately depend on human beings? Is African ancestral eschatology a sufficient Christian theological eschatology? If theology is the construction of piety, what kind of piety is being constructed in African Christians who are being conditioned by this ancestral eschatology? Is it not a kind of piety that may lead people to treat others in unwholesome ways, thus even threatening the overall well-being of communities?

A related context in which Bujo's treatment of African marriage is situated is that of the relation among the monad, the dyad, and the triad that leads to plurality. The monad is the individual person who is an incomplete version of the notion of *Ubuntu* (I am because you are; you are because I am).[62] Since the monad is the incomplete version of the notion of Ubuntu, part of the being of the monad is found by finding the other, particularly the other of the opposite sex. In this case, part of the being of the male is found by finding a female and vice versa. By finding each other, the two unite to produce a third, the triad. It is the various connections among the monad, the dyad and the triad that form the multitude or plurality of the community. The main point here is that a person is incomplete if they remain a monad or single. They are still incomplete even if they become a dyad by finding each other of the opposite sex but without conceiving a

60. Oduyoye, "A Coming Home to Myself," 119.

61. Kwabena Asamoah-Gyadu, "Broken Calabashes and Covenants of Fruitfulness: Cursing Barrenness in Contemporary African Christianity," *Journal of Religion in Africa* 37 no 4 (2007): 437–60.

62. For more on the notion of Ubuntu, see the essays in Ronald Nicolson, ed. *Persons in Community: African Ethics in a Global Culture* (Scottsville, South Africa: University of Kwazulu-Natal Press, 2008).

Assessing the Theology of Inculturation

triad. Completion comes only if they procreate and thus form a triad that gives rise to the plurality of community. Thus, both the childless, single person and the childless couple are equally unwelcome in the community because they contravene the procreation requirement.[63]

In fact, as we have seen above, the community allows for polygamy (more precisely—polygyny) where there is childlessness in a marriage. It is important to point out that what is allowed for is polygyny because it appears that in most African societies only men are allowed to marry more than one wife; women are not allowed to marry more than one husband (polyandry). Polygyny is sometimes allowed apparently because of the common but mistaken assumption that women are often the infertile ones in cases where couples are unable to have children. Be that as it may, polygyny (polygamy) is practiced in part to address the issue of procreation crucial to the ancestral eschatology.[64] The question of polygamy in Africa has been quite controversial because Western Christian missionaries often rejected it, prescribing monogamy as the proper Christian form of marriage. When Western Christian missionaries came to Africa, men who converted to the faith but had many wives were sometimes asked to divorce the others and keep just one. Asking African men to divorce their wives and be left with just one became controversial in inculturation theology because repudiating polygamy was interpreted as repudiating a respected African tradition. However, as women began having a say in the matter, they have begun to challenge this tradition, pointing out that it is against the interests of African women.[65] Some African churches currently discourage the practice while others do not.

The question of polygamy cannot be adjudicated based on the claim that it is unchristian while monogamy is a Christian practice. Part of the reason for this is that there is biblical warrant for both forms of marriage and there is no clear biblical sanction of one over the other. In fact, in spite of the prevalence of polygamy in the Bible, there is no one in the biblical narrative who is condemned for being a polygamist. The issue can also not be adjudicated by claiming that polygamy is African tradition while

---

63. Bujo, *Foundations of an African Ethic*, 34–36.

64. For more on why polygyny may be practiced, see Ester Boserup, "The Economics of Polygamy," in *Perspectives on Africa: A Reader in Culture, History, and Representation*, eds. Roy Richard Grinker, Stephen C. Lubkemann, and Christopher B. Steiner, second edition (Malden, MA: Blackwell, 1997), 389–98.

65. See Mercy Amba Oduyoye, *Introducing African Women's Theology* (Cleveland, OH: The Pilgrim Press, 2001.

monogamy is Western or unAfrican. There is both the practice of monogamy and polygamy in African traditional societies. However, the question of whether or not polygamy should be sanctioned on the basis of childlessness in marriage needs to be addressed. To marry a second wife because the first one is unable to conceive, even if we grant that it is the woman's fault, is problematic. It is a patriarchal tendency because the purpose is often to promote the name of the man not the name of the woman. This chauvinistic act marginalizes women in many ways and it is not quite clear how the practice honors God. In some patriarchal African contexts, men may take second wives even if the first one has only female children. The purpose, in this case, is to have a male child or male children because male children are the ones who could be heirs in some African societies. Thus, it seems clear that patriarchy significantly contributes to the practice of polygamy.

It is important to note that polygamy is now being challenged by some women and the church needs to listen to their voices. However, in cases where women choose to be involved in polygamy, their choices should also be respected. The church should however reject polygamy in cases where it is clear that the woman does not want to be involved in a polygamous marriage but is rather being forced by her family to do so. The question of polygamy in the African church is therefore complex and should be addressed on a case by case basis rather than postulating monogamy as the ideal Christian marriage or polygamy as a traditional African practice. Practicing polygamy on the basis of the African ancestral eschatology may be backed by traditional African worldviews but not by the Christian faith. It should however be noted that polygamy is declining in contemporary Africa.[66]

A related question has to do with how to conceptualize celibacy within the context of African community. Since it is the case that monads are by nature incomplete versions of the Ubuntu, are celibates therefore subhuman? This question becomes urgent when we consider that celibates are not only those who will never become a dyad by meeting members of the opposite sex but are also those who have taken vows to never procreate and so will never form a triad, unless they break their vows. The question becomes even more urgent when we take into consideration the fact of African ancestral eschatology. Who will remember these people when they

---

66. See James Fenske, *African Polygamy: Past and Present*, CSAE Working Paper, WPS 2012-20, Oxford Center for the Study of African Economies, November 28, 2012, 1–30, accessed on August 6, 2013.

die, given that they have no offspring to keep their memory alive? Bujo sees this as a challenge to the Roman Catholic Church that enjoins celibacy on priests and discusses this issue in the context of whether or not priests should be allowed to get married.[67] However, it is important to note that the celibate life is not unknown in traditional Africa, especially when such celibacy was imposed on a person by a god.[68] Even more, a trajectory that is addressing the issue of celibacy is that the community as a whole tends to make ancestors of celibates, as it happened in Cameroon in the case of the late African theologian, Jean-Marc Éla, who died in 2008.[69] Considering that he was a Roman Catholic priest who did not have offspring to remember him and that he was perceived as someone who had lived a life that made significant contributions to his people, his village community made him an ancestor. This shows that it is possible to make someone an ancestor in African anthropological eschatology even if that person does not have a child. However, this method of making someone an ancestor is centered on human achievement, albeit an achievement different from biological procreation. This eschatology, notwithstanding, is still significantly different from a Christian theological eschatology. It appears to make no place for grace and it is reserved only for the well placed in a community. Martin Luther would have described this as salvation by works.

A final question which the ancestral eschatology raises is that of the place of homosexuality/same-sex marriage in traditional African communities. Homosexuality, as Bujo sees it, is effectively ruled out by the nature of Ubuntu. In fact, Bujo sees homosexuality as "a sexist discrimination against part of the human race," a practice which "shows an unwillingness to accept the enrichment that comes from heterogeneity."[70] Homosexuals, like infertile people, kill the creative impulse that generates the community of both the living and the dead. Homosexuals, in the African scheme of things, will never form a dyad because they will never meet the opposite sex. Because they will never form a dyad, it follows that they will also never form a triad and a plurality. Thus, homosexuality/same sex marriage is rejected in Africa not only on biblical or theological grounds but also on the

---

67. Bujo, *Foundations of an African Ethic*, 7.

68. See Aylward Shorter, *Celibacy and African Culture* (Nairobi: Paulines Publication, 1998).

69. See David T. Ngong, "The Theologian as Missionary," *Journal of Theology for Southern Africa* 136 (2010): 1–19.

70. Bujo, *Foundations of an African Ethic*, 6.

Theology as Construction of Piety

ground of African anthropology which finds its ultimate end in ancestral eschatology. In spite of this rejection of homosexuality/same sex marriage, Bujo acknowledges that there have been homosexuals in Africa.[71] One must hasten to add that there continues to be homosexuals in Africa.[72] Thus, the pressing question that needs to be raised is how to treat homosexuals in contemporary Africa? The widespread homophobia in much of Africa is well known. In some cases, homosexuals have been brutally beaten and some have even been killed while others have sought asylum in foreign lands. Is this the fate which African Christian theologians expect to befall homosexuals in our continent? Does portraying homosexuals as enemies of a holistic life not put their lives in more danger? Why would African theologians want to be seen as people who have taken up the cudgel against homosexuals?[73] More importantly, where is God in all this?

A Christian theological eschatology is an eschatology that is not based on procreation, notwithstanding the claim in 1Timothy 2:15 that women will be saved through procreation. Christian eschatology is based on the life, death, and resurrection of Christ and how this singular event draws wayward human beings into the triune divine life. Taking the life of Jesus Christ seriously, it becomes clear that our life with God does not finally rest on the offspring we bear but on our single-minded desire to dwell in the life of God. As far as we know, Jesus Christ himself did not have any children and we remember him today not because of his biological offspring but because he draws us into the life of the triune God. In fact, some African theologians, such as Charles Nyamity and Bujo, have even described Jesus Christ as ancestor.[74] That Jesus is the proto-ancestor of some Africans is

---

71. Bujo, *Foundations of an African Ethic*, 6.

72. For more on this, see Marc Epprecht, *Unspoken Facts: A History of Homosexualities in Africa* (Harare, Zimbabwe: GALZ, 2008); Neville Hoad, *African Intimacies: Race, Homosexuality and Globalization* (Minneapolis, MN: University of Minnesota Press, 2006).

73. See Colin Stewart, *From Wrongs to Gay Rights* (Laguna Nigel, CA: P. C. Haddiwiggle Publishing Company, 2013); Adriaan S. Van Klinken and Masiiwa Ragies Gunda, "Taking up the Cudgel Against Gay Rights? Trends and Trajectories in African Christian Theologies on Homosexuality," *Journal of Homosexuality* 59 (2012): 114–38. Also see Marc Epprecht, "Religion and Same Sex Relations in Africa," in *The Wiley-Blackwell Companion to African Religions*, ed. Elias Kifon Bongmba (Oxford: Oxford University Press, 2012), 515–28.

74. See Ludovic Lado, "The Roman Catholic Church and African Religions: A Problematic Encounter," *The Way* vol. 45 no. 3 (July 2006): 7–21, especially p. 14. Available online at: http://www.theway.org.uk/453Lado.pdf. Accessed on August 1, 2013. Also see

Assessing the Theology of Inculturation

clearly not based on any claim that these Africans are his biological offspring. It is rather a declaration that these Africans have come to accept Jesus Christ as their savior. Accepting a childless person as an ancestor and savior of Africans should serve to redefine what it means to be an ancestor in African Christian theology because Jesus Christ does not fit the ordinary definition of an ancestor in Africa. The life, death, and resurrection of Jesus Christ ought to transform the anthropological eschatology of African Traditional Religions that seem to inform some forms of African Christian theology today. African Christian eschatology ought to be a theocentric eschatology that takes up the human into divine life, valorizing the biological in the spiritual life of God. This view of salvation is one that takes up the material into divine life so that all material forms of life are transformed in God. In this scheme of things, having children is a good thing but it is ultimately not decisive for the Christian life with God. As Christians, our goal is to participate, now and eternally, in the life of God rather than to become ancestors. Becoming an ancestor is a worthy goal that needs to be pursued by Africans who cherish that goal. However, African Christians should be enabled to come to the realization that becoming an ancestor is not the critical issue in a Christian eschatology; participating eternally in divine life is the goal. In this case, the continuation of life is not based on human memory but on divine memory. And divine memory is not based on whether or not people have offspring. This Christian eschatological perspective, rather than an ancestral eschatology, should be the foundation for African Christian ethics. Ancestral eschatology may be used in African traditional religious ethics but it should not form the foundation of a Christian ethic because it is different from the Christian eschatological vision.

Inculturation, African Spiritualized Cosmology, and the Needs of the People

A final area to be addressed with respect to inculturating the Christian faith in Africa is the African spiritualized cosmology. What is described as the African spiritualized cosmology is the belief that in the African traditional contexts, the physical and the spiritual realms are not strictly separated but rather interact. This view is captured in the now (in)famous claim of Mbiti's, namely that "Africans are notoriously religious." According to Mbiti, for Africans, "[r]eligion permeates all departments of life so fully that it is not

---

Robert J. Schreiter, ed., *Faces of Jesus in Africa* (Maryknoll, NY: Orbis Books, 1991).

easy or possible always to isolate it."[75] Here, the spiritual and the physical often mingle so that it is sometimes not quite clear where the physical ends and the spiritual begins. Here, spiritual realities affect the material universe and vice versa. This is captured in the idea of the African community discussed above, were the living, the dead, the yet to be born and God form a single community. This spiritualized cosmology is therefore at the heart of African worldviews.

Especially important in this cosmology is the nature of causality. While some things are clearly seen to have physical causation, others are seen to have both physical and spiritual causations.[76] The spiritual world is therefore believed to have real power over the physical world and so humans need to be in sync with the spiritual world if they are to experience overall well-being. For example, where ancestors are unhappy with the living because the living seems to have forgotten the dead, the living may be afflicted with one difficulty or another to remind them of their duty toward the dead. Also, some people are believed to possess spiritual power which can be used to heal or harm others and are thus seen as conduits into the spiritual world. In this context, individual and collective well-being does not only depend on physical activities but also on human relations to the spiritual world. Individuals sometimes become rich or poor not just because of hard work but also because of the nature of their connection to the spiritual realm. Health is obtained not just through physical activities but through tapping into the spiritual realm.

African inculturation theologians argue that upon coming to Africa, the Christian faith should have been directed at addressing this spiritualized cosmology because Africans experience their lives within this cosmology. However, Western Christian missionaries, infected by the Enlightenment imagination that had driven the spiritual from the world, insisted on forcing this Enlightenment imagination on Africans. Thus, rather than addressing the felt needs of Africans in this context, Western missionaries were busy describing Africa as the dark continent, a place inhabited by superstitious people. The failure of Western missionaries is then obvious as Africans who became Christians had one foot in the church and the other in traditional African spiritual practices. Thus it was that when an African faced a life-threatening circumstance, they would consult the spirit mediums to find

---

75. Mbiti, *African Religions and Philosophy*, 1.

76. See E. E. Evans-Pritchard, *Witchcraft, Oracles, and Magic Among the Azande* (Oxford: Oxford University Press, 1937).

out the cause of their troubles rather than talk it through with their pastors or priests. This made African Christians to have divided loyalties and this divided loyalty can still be seen in some mission founded churches, such as the Methodist, Presbyterian, Baptist, or Roman Catholic, as they still do not address this spiritualized cosmology effectively.

However, the narrative goes, there emerged some indigenous churches in Africa that took this spiritualized cosmology seriously. These prophet-healing indigenous churches took the African spiritualized cosmology seriously by presenting Jesus Christ as the Savior whose power is stronger than all malevolent spiritual powers in the African cosmology. The power of Jesus Christ is therefore presented as more than enough to help African Christians overcome the wiles of evil spiritual forces and so Africans do not need to rely on harnessing the spiritual forces in the African universe to enhance their well-being; all they needed to do is rely on Jesus Christ for such help. With this new preaching of the prophet-healing churches Africans began to see that the Christian faith addressed their felt needs and so they started flocking to these new African Initiated Churches (AICs). Further, Pentecostal/Charismatic Christianity emerged in Africa and also took this spiritualized cosmology seriously, addressing it through the power of the Spirit of Jesus Christ. The Pentecostal/Charismatic churches came to see the AICs as somehow still too cozy with elements of the African traditional contexts and so many Africans started leaving these AICs and flocking into these Pentecostal churches that are seen to address this spiritualized cosmology. Recognizing that many Africans are flocking into Pentecostal churches, many mission founded churches are now becoming Pentecostal in order to stem the tide of diminishing church membership. Thus, we now talk of the Pentecostalization of African Christianity because many African churches are becoming Pentecostal or charismatic in character. These Pentecostal or charismatic churches are therefore seen to be attractive because they are addressing the felt needs of Africans, felt needs that are often perceived as having spiritual provenance.[77]

Because this spiritualized cosmology is central to African worldviews and is critical to current African theology of inculturation, especially as

---

77. For More on this narrative of African Christianity, see Kofi Appiah-Kubi, "Indigenous African Christian Churches: Signs of Authenticity," in *African Theology En Route*, ed. Kofi Appiah-Kubi and Sergio Torres (Maryknoll, NY: Orbis Books, 1979), 120; Asonzeh Ukah, "African Christianities: Features, Promises, and Problems" *Working Paper* 79, 1–18, http://www.ifeas.uni-mainz.de/Dateien/AP79.pdf, accessed on August 1, 2013.

seen in the significant growth of Pentecostalism in the continent, critically evaluating the piety which this discourse creates is central to this project. While this manner of presenting the Christian faith in Africa takes seriously the African spiritualized cosmology, a question that may be raised at this point is whether these pneumatic churches address the felt needs of the people, as it is often claimed. In order to respond to this question, it is important to first respond to another question: what are the felt needs of Africans? Within the context of the spiritualized cosmology, the felt needs of Africans are often assumed to be spiritual. Since Africans believe that the spiritual has a bearing on the physical, the best way to address their felt needs seems to be to supply a spiritual solution. Thus, if one does not have a job, for example, it may be that they are being blocked by their ancestral heritage—they would therefore need to make a complete break with their past spiritual home and be fully situated within the Christian story if they wish to overcome this crisis.[78] If people are barren, they would need to be exorcised of the spirit or spirits blocking them. Thus, because of their spiritual imagination, it seems that the felt needs of Africans should always be located in the spiritual realm. But what if the felt needs of Africans is not spiritual at all but is rather physical? What if the felt needs of Africans can be addressed not only from a spiritual perspective but also, and especially, from a physical perspective? What if the felt needs of Africans is to be able to go to the hospital when they are ill, get a good education so as to be able to have the prospects of decent lives, live in peace within their own countries so that they do not need to risk their lives migrating to other countries, as it sometimes happens? It is the submission of this book that the felt needs of Africans need to be placed within the context of the modern world and addressed within the context of the longings of Africans in this modern world. In this modern world many Africans long to live modern lives. They want to have good, clean water, food to eat when they are hungry, be able to get good education so as to be able to compete favorably with anyone around the world. Africans want to live dignified lives, taking care of their needs as they arise rather than often relying on aid from foreign countries. These are the felt needs of Africans today.

All of this is not to say that the spiritual is not important to Africans. It would be hard to deny the spirituality of Africans because that would

---

78. Birgit Meyer, "'Make a Complete Break with the Past,' Memory and Post-Colonial Modernity in Ghanaian Pentecostal Discourse," *Journal of Religion in Africa* 28.3 (August 1998): 316–49.

Assessing the Theology of Inculturation

fail to take into consideration the reality on the ground. The reality on the ground is that Africans maintain a strong connection to the spiritual world. However, as we saw above, this connection to the spiritual world is intended to ensure human flourishing in this life. That is why African Traditional Religions have been described as anthropocentric. Thus, to take African spiritualized cosmology seriously is to take the anthropocentrical slant of this cosmology seriously. If African traditional religious thought is anthropocentric, this anthropocentrism needs to be contextualized in the modern world and we need to ask what it means to live a decent life in the modern world. How does focusing on cultivating the spiritualized cosmology both in African Traditional Religions and in Christianity enhance this anthropocentric vision? How does focusing on cultivating the spiritualized cosmology construct a piety that enables Africans to flourish in the modern world in which they have been and continue to be marginalized? It may be that cultivating this spiritualized cosmology may help Africans deal with the pressing issues that they face in the modern world but this does not appear clear at this point in the history of the continent, in spite of persistent claims to the contrary.[79]

The focus of the churches that promote this spiritualized cosmology is similar to some Christian practices in Europe in the Middles Ages. As it was in the Middle Ages, contemporary African Pentecostal/charismatic churches rely on holy people, holy places, and holy things to mediate salvation as overall well-being. A famous prophet in Africa is the Nigerian Televangelist called T. B. Joshua. People flock to him from far and wide for healing and recently there was a stampede in Accra in which some people died in the process of struggling to get holy water from him during one of his events in Ghana.[80] It is reported that in these churches the Eucharist is seen largely as a "miracle meal" because it is believed to have the power to perform miracles.[81] We can therefore see that there is an uncanny similarity between contemporary African Christianity and the medieval Christi-

---

79. For more on the story of Christianity and the African worldview, see Allan H. Anderson, *African Reformation: African Initiated Christianity in the Twentieth Century* (Trenton, NJ: Africa World Press, 2001); Ogbu Kalu, *African Pentecostalism: An Introduction* (Oxford: Oxford University Press, 2008); J. Kwabena Asamoah-Gyadu, *African Charismatics: Current Developments within Independent Indigenous Pentecostalism in Ghana* (Leiden and Boston: Brill, 2005).

80. BBC News, "Ghana Stampede Kills Four at TB Joshua's Church," http://www.bbc.co.uk/news/world-africa-22595573. Accessed on August 1, 2013.

81. Asamoah-Gyadu, *Contemporary Pentecostal Christianity*, 145–59.

Theology as Construction of Piety

anity we saw in the previous chapter. While some, such as the postliberals we saw in Chapter One, may be calling for the return of medieval Christianity, it is not clear that this specific manifestation of medieval Christianity in the African context is salutary. Our modern world is a world in which science and technology have come to have significant effects in improving the lives of people. Any piety that hopes to adequately address the felt needs of contemporary African people should be placed within the context of modern science and technology and so cultivate what may be described as *interdisciplinary spirituality* or *piety*. Interdisciplinary spirituality is a form of spirituality in which faith and science work together for the well-being of human beings and the rest of creation. It is quite interesting that non-Africans have been the ones drawing the attention of African theologians to the importance of engaging science and technology in the modern world.[82] It is clear that addressing the contemporary situation in Africa needs a multifaceted approach. However, science and technology should be seen as central to this multifaceted approach and African theologians should be addressing the question of science and technology in their work. Addressing the issue of science and technology in African theological discourse should not mean uncritically embracing science and technology but rather acknowledging that they have critical roles to play as Africans look forward to constructing a dignified future and an inspiring Christian piety.[83]

Conclusion

This chapter has been concerned with the kind of piety which the theology of inculturation constructs for African Christians. We have seen that the theology of inculturation may, in some cases, construct salutary piety while, in other cases, it may not construct a very helpful piety. The theology of inculturation is supposed to help Africans navigate the contemporary world in a dignified way and this should be the case especially with reflections on the nature of African Christian worship, ethics, and engaging the African spiritualized cosmology. However, critically engaging the African spiritualized cosmology is essential to constructing a form of Christian

---

82. See M. Amaladoss, "Cross-Inculturation of Indian and African Christianity, *African Ecclesial Review* 32.3 (June 1990): 166; Paul Gifford, "Africa's Inculturation Theology: Observations of an Outsider," *Hekima Review* 38 (May 2008): 18–34.

83. See David Tonghou Ngong, *The Holy Spirit and Salvation in African Christian Theology* (New York, NY: Peter Lang, 2010).

piety that enhances Africans' dignified participation in the modern world. This is so because inculturation theology's current engagement with this cosmology does not appear to take seriously the importance of science and technology in modern African life. Merely complaining that modernity marginalizes Africans will not do; equipping Africans with the tools with which modernity marginalizes them would enable them to begin to be agents of their destinies. It is therefore critical that African theology of inculturation help in constructing an interdisciplinary spirituality or piety

CHAPTER 5

Constructing an Interdisciplinary Piety

THE DISPARATE CHAPTERS OF this book are held together by a single theme: theology is the construction of piety. Whenever theologians theologize their goal is to construct piety for good or ill. In Chapter One we addressed the question of what it means to construct piety and engaged postliberal theology to demonstrate that theologians need to probe the consequences of the piety which their theologies construct. Probing the consequences of the piety our theology constructs is important because an apparently harmless and innocent theology may have unsalutary effects on human well-being and piety. In Chapter Two we demonstrated that the debates around the doctrine of God in the early church were about the construction of piety. We indicated that the question about the place of providence in these debates confuse the fact that they were intended to construct piety. Even if we grant that the role of providence in these debates is unproblematic, it would still not discount the fact that the theological debates were intended to construct piety. We also wondered whether there might be some salutary effects to some of the positions that were condemned during these debates. In Chapter Three we saw how the materialistic Christianity of the Middle Ages was problematized and how this eventually paved the way for the interiorization and intellectualization of the Christian faith, resulting in our modern world that is characterized by the undermining of religion and the elevation of science and technology.[1] While the advent of modernity is

1. For an extensive expose of how modernity affected Christian theological discourse, see Roger E. Oslon, *The Journey of Modern Theology* (Downers Grove, IL: IVP

Constructing an Interdisciplinary Piety

generally acknowledged to have been challenging to the development of the Christian faith, it should also be acknowledged that the development of science and technology, products of the modern Christian imagination, also has salutary consequences to human beings and Christian piety. It is the position of this project that these salutary consequences should be mined in contemporary African theology, especially in the theology of inculturation. In Chapter Four, we focused on the development of the theology of inculturation and wondered about the salutary implications of the piety which this theology constructs. We saw that this form of theology has some salutary elements but also noted that it does not adequately prepare African Christians to engage the modern world, specifically with regards to the appropriation of science and technology, which are central to how the modern world turns. Because of the centrality of science and technology in the modern world, African theology of inculturation therefore needs to seriously engage them for the salutary effects they may have in the continent. Focusing on enhancing the awareness of the importance of science and technology in the construction of Christian piety in Africa means that African theology needs to develop an *interdisciplinary piety* or *spirituality*. This chapter describes interdisciplinary spirituality, discusses why and how African theology should develop it, and concludes with laying a theological foundation for this spirituality.

What is Interdisciplinary Spirituality?

As we saw in Chapter One, piety or spirituality for Christians describes their total relationship to God. Piety or spirituality does not deal only with part of the being of a Christian but with their whole person, so that Christians ought to see piety as their way of life before the triune God. Thus, piety does not involve only the soul or only the body but the whole person and its relation to God. It does not involve only the individual person but also the whole community and the cosmos. This way of understanding piety is

---

Press, 2013); James C. Livingston, *Modern Christian Thought, vol. 1: The Enlightenment and the Nineteenth Century*, second edition (Minneapolis, MN: Fortress Press, 2006); James C. Livingston et al., *Modern Christian Thought, vol. 2: The Twentieth Century*, second edition (Minneapolis, MN: Fortress Press, 2006). For the relation between modernity and the Christian faith, see Charles Taylor, *A Secular Age* (Cambridge, MA: The Belknap Press of Harvard University Press, 2007) and Michael Warner, Jonathan VanAntwerpen, and Craig Calhoun, eds., *Varieties of Secularism in a Secular Age*, reprint edition (Cambridge, MA: Harvard University Press, 2013).

holistic because it addresses the whole beings of persons and communities rather than just parts. The whole being of a Christian, in this case, involves the body and soul or whatever understanding of a person may be embraced in specific Christian anthropology. In cultivating an interdisciplinary spirituality, therefore, the spiritual and material dimensions of human beings and the rest of creation are seen as equally important. This means that the soul is not more important than the body and the body is not more important than the soul; the present is not more important than the future and vice versa. An interdisciplinary spirituality is therefore a holistic spirituality because it treats all dimensions of human beings, communities, and the cosmos as equally important.

A further dimension of interdisciplinary spirituality is that it draws inspiration from the recent call for interdisciplinarity in academia.[2] The call for interdisciplinarity in academia is based on the realization, first, that life is not broken down into different academic disciplines and, second, that the division among the various disciplines may lead to the development of tunnel visions, with everyone concentrating only on a narrow area of study, thinking that their area of study is the most important, thus failing to see that connecting with other areas may yield more fruitful results. Thus, academics have been called upon to cooperate across disciplines so that a more holistic understanding of what they are investigating may be had. In contemporary academia, focusing on just a single discipline or project, without finding out how that discipline or project connects with others, is not highly appreciated. Thus, even though academics cannot be experts in many fields, they work with experts from different fields in order to see how their work connects with or diverges from other disciplines. This gives academics a better understanding of where they fit in the whole and what they need to do to better connect to the whole or enhance the whole. Pointing out that interdisciplinary piety draws from the pursuit of interdisciplinarity in academia, however, does not mean that interdisciplinary piety should be conceived as mainly academic and elitist. Because we already indicated above that life is lived in an interdisciplinary manner, it goes without saying that an interdisciplinary piety also characterizes the faith of ordinary people. The point here is to enhance this piety through stressing the importance of science and technology in the life of faith.

---

2. See Allen R. Repko, *Interdisciplinary Research: Process and Theory*, second edition (Thousand Oaks, CA: Sage Publications, 2011), 1–48.

Constructing an Interdisciplinary Piety

From the above, it can be deduced that interdisciplinary spirituality is the form of piety that views Christian relationship with God and the world from more than just a single perspective, in this case, just a narrowly religious perspective. When Christian relationship with God and the world is seen strictly from a religious perspective, Christians are trained to think that the quality of their relationship with God is the single most important thing in determining their quality of life in the world. Thus, we often hear expressions like "Jesus is the answer," even if we do not know the question. When Christian relationship with God and the world is seen strictly from a religious perspective, Christians are urged to pray for everything—for good health, for prosperity, for visa to travel abroad, for employment, and for many other things that people need in life. This form of spirituality, like the scholar who focuses on just one discipline, may produce a tunnel vision. When Christians practice this *tunnel vision spirituality*, it produces the kind of piety which Asamoah-Gyadu describes when he discusses the nature of prayer in Ghanaian Pentecostalism—people pray to get visa to go to Europe, for employment, fertility, and others, without paying serious attention to the other dimensions that affect the possibility of obtaining these things.[3] The point here is not that people should not pray for these things—not praying would negate the very idea of interdisciplinary spirituality being urged here. Rather, the point is that while praying for employment, one should not be oblivious of the fact that the rate of employment in the local or national economy or even the skill one has, may affect one's chances of finding a job. Thinking that one is unemployed mainly because of the nature of one's spirituality, where spirituality is understood strictly as the quality of one's relation to God, may make one oblivious of the fact that the skill one may have is simply not highly marketable or that the rate of unemployment in the local or national economy is just too high. Developing a new and more marketable skill or an improvement in the rate of employment may help one procure a job. Not to put too fine a point on the matter, prayer alone may not help someone find a job or get a visa to travel. So many other things go into making each of these things happen. The story is often told of the student who neglected her studies, spent much time in church praying, thinking that God would enable her pass her exams. She took the exams and when the results were published it showed that she had failed. She did not pass the exam because she had failed to

---

3. See Asamoah-Gyadu, *Contemporary Pentecostal Christianity*, 35–57, where he discusses worship and prayer in Ghanaian Pentecostal spirituality.

see that prayer should go together with her studies rather than apart from it. An interdisciplinary spirituality will therefore not just urge prayer but also help people take seriously the other dimensions of life that affect their overall well-being and relationship with God. Thus, an interdisciplinary spirituality will not just focus on prayer for healing, for example, but will also investigate other forms of healing, such as using indigenous pharmacology or Western medicine.[4]

However, it is often suggested that those who rely on prayer for healing are often poor people who cannot afford sophisticated modern medicine. In this case, it appears that the churches help these people to get by in the absence of good medical care. When the wealthy get ill, however, they often go to sophisticated hospitals, sometimes they travel to Europe, America, India, or China, to get medical treatment. It is now customary for most African presidents and even theologians to go to Europe and America or the Middle East for medical treatment because medical care in their countries does not meet even their own expectations. Since the poor cannot afford sophisticated forms of medical care, it appears that the best option now available for them is spiritual healing. Thus, many churches in Africa now seem to be falling over each other, competing to establish healing worship services. Focusing on constructing such a narrow piety for the poor may be a classic manifestation of Karl Marx's concern about the marginalizing effects of religion.[5] In this case, the poor are taught to rely on prayer when they are ill while the rich often jet off to foreign climes to seek treatment when they are ill. An interdisciplinary spirituality will urge prayer and the construction of and accessibility to good medical facilities.[6] An interdisciplinary spirituality will teach Christians to think of their well-being as located in God but accessed through prayer and hu-

---

4. For an example of where a reflection on interdisciplinary piety would have been appropriate but not done, see Allan Anderson, "Pentecostal Approaches to Faith and Healing," *International Review of Mission* 91.363 (October 2002): 523–34. Note that the role of modern medicine is not emphasized in the article even though parts of the story takes place in a hospital.

5. John Raines, ed. *Marx on Religion* (Philadelphia, PA: Temple University Press, 2002), 167–86.

6. For an example of a theological construction aimed at fostering an interdisciplinary piety about the question of health and healing in Africa, see Deborah van den Bosch-Heij, *Spirit and Healing in Africa: A Reformed Pneumatological Perspective* (Bloemfontein, South Africa: SUN MeDIA, 2012). Also see the International Religious Health Assets Program at the University of Cape Town at: http://www.arhap.uct.ac.za/, accessed August 2, 2013.

man making (*poesis*). Interdisciplinary spirituality teaches Christians that God works through prayer and science and not only through one or the other. It is interdisciplinary because it sees God as working through more than just what is thought of as the supernatural. It is a spirituality that sees the sacred as multidimensional. In fact, in interdisciplinary spirituality, everything is sacred thus making the sacred multidimensional.[7] Thus, in interdisciplinary spirituality, the religious perspective is broadened to include science and technology and helpful appropriation of science and technology is seen as a spiritual exercise. In order to construct this type of piety, preachers need to pray for the sick *and* also make it possible for them to receive alternative medical care as appropriate. Interdisciplinary spirituality is far more demanding than what happens in church on Wednesday or Sunday because it requires Christians to offer a broader form of pastoral care that goes beyond prayer and visitations. It requires Christians to work to develop concrete environments that promote life. Interdisciplinary spirituality goes to school and enters laboratories. It builds good roads and performs irrigations. Interdisciplinary spirituality works for the creation of job opportunities. Inasmuch as the religious is depicted as strictly supernaturalistic in character, interdisciplinary spirituality regards such piety as dangerously narrow. The depiction of the religious as including both the supernaturalistic *and* that which is usually not recognized as supernatural, such as the scientific, is amendable to our understanding of interdisciplinary spirituality or piety.[8]

This book is therefore a call for African theology of inculturation, especially its latest incarnation in African Pentecostal/Charismatic Christianity, to cultivate a piety that takes the scientific seriously. This is not to say that African theology has not taken the sciences seriously. In fact, African theologians have engaged the sciences but this engagement has largely been limited to the social sciences such as politics, economics, anthropology, and sociology, among others. African theologians need to continue engaging these disciplines in spite of the recent argument by the British theologian, John Milbank, that these disciplines have secular provenance.[9] Engaging these disciplines does not only contribute in generating interdisciplin-

7. Laurenti Magesa, *What is Not Sacred?*

8. For a form of this kind of piety, see Peter L. Berger, "A Friendly Dissent from Pentecostalism," *First Things* (November 2012): 45–50. Against Berger, it should be said that this form of spirituality is not incompatible with Pentecostalism, as he seems to suggest.

9. John Milbank, *Theology and Social Theory*.

ary piety but also throws light on how societies and communities may be organized for the maximum enhancement of overall well-being.[10] However, African theologians need to go further. They need to go further to ensure that their engagement of these disciplines does not remain only among theologians but should also influence ordinary Christians. They need to go even further in engaging the natural sciences and work for the ways of thinking found in the natural sciences to influence ordinary Christians.

However, modern science has had a controversial relationship to the religious imagination and African inculturation theologians often seem to be against the modern scientific imagination. Modern science's controversial relationship to religion is due in part to the fact that the ways of thinking in modern science seem to be diametrically opposed to religion. Modern science has been described as having the following characteristics: the recognition of no other authorities but nature itself accessed through critical rationalism and empiricism; it aims to conquer nature through artificial experiments; it sees the world from a mechanistic rather than an organistic perspective; it explains natural things and events in mathematical terms and attempts to quantify qualities.[11] These characteristics of modern science seem diametrically opposed to religion, which seems to be based on the authority of traditional thought. The perception of nature as its own authority and the mechanical explanation of the world directly clash with a religious worldview that seems to have an organistic understanding of the universe. Modern science is therefore often seen as having contributed to denuding the world of the spiritual, thus resulting in the secularization of the West. Most contemporary theologians have been challenging this scientific imagination and the theology of inculturation has often positioned itself against this imagination. One may therefore wonder whether bringing together science and religion in Africa would not validate the charge that Africa is simply copying the West. Is the attempt to bring together the two disciplines in Africa not just a preoccupation of the theologian who is asking questions in which ordinary Christians are not interested? Can people not live complete and successful Christian lives without worrying about modern science and technology? Also, would bringing together science and religion in Africa not further undermine the indigenous worldviews

---

10. See Jared Diamond, *Guns, Germs, and Steel*, 433–40.

11. R. Hooykaas, "The Rise of Modern Science: When and Why?" in *The Scientific Revolution*, ed. Marcus Hellyer (Oxford: Blackwell, 2003), 21–22. Also see, David S. Landes, *The Wealth and Poverty of Nations*, 200–7.

Constructing an Interdisciplinary Piety

that some scholars and even organizations are trying to protect from being destroyed through the encroachment of Western science?[12] These and other important questions make it necessary to give good reasons why African theology of inculturation should engage modern science and technology.

To give a preliminary response to some of these questions, it must be acknowledged that science, especially the physical sciences, sees the world in ways that are sometimes different from how religion sees it. Many people have stopped believing in spiritual realities because of their scientific endeavors and part of contemporary Western theology has been preoccupied with responding to atheistic challenges to the Christian faith, especially as emanating from Sigmund Freud, Frederick Nietzsche, and Karl Marx. Scientists such as Richard Dawkins and Stephen Hawking continue to pose challenges to spiritualistic cosmologies because of their mechanistic understanding of the universe. Modern science therefore poses significant challenges to the religious imagination. These challenges, however, do not mean that religious people should retreat from engaging the sciences. The fact that an endeavor may be fraught with dangers does not mean that it should not be pursued. Those with significant life experiences tell us that most things we do in life often have both positive and negative sides. There is an African saying that the world is made up of both dark and bright sides. One is however not to follow either the dark side or the bright side but is rather to walk in the middle. This saying makes the point of the complexity of African worldview and we shall have occasion to revisit this point below. However, the point being made here is that human life cannot be free of negative elements and to think that such freedom could be had is to mistake the nature of life. Thus, it is important to acknowledge that encouraging an interdisciplinary imagination could actually be bad for religion. It could, for example, lead to atheism. However, it does not have to be so. That it does not have to be so is testified by the scientists who led what has been described as the Scientific Revolution and some contemporary scientists.[13]

---

12. For the relationship between indigenous life with modern science, see John A Grim, "Indigenous Lifeways and Knowing the World," in *The Oxford Handbook of Religion and Science*, ed. Philip Clayton (Oxford: Oxford University Press, 2008), 1–34. Also see John A. Grim, ed., *Indigenous Traditions and Ecology: The Interbeing of Cosmology and Community* (Cambridge, MA: Harvard University Press, 2001).

13. John Polkinghorne is a good example of a contemporary scientist who is also a religious person, a Christian. See his *Science and Theology* (Minneapolis, MN: Fortress Press, 1998) and *Quantum Physics and Theology* (New Haven, CT: Yale University Press, 2008).

Theology as Construction of Piety

As we are going to see below, the scientists who led the Scientific Revolution approached science from a theological perspective. Put together with contemporary scientists who are also Christians, these people show us that engaging the sciences does not necessarily lead to atheism, even though the danger is real.

Moreover, some scholars have argued that the claim that science has been responsible for the secularization of the West may not stand up to scrutiny. They have argued that sometimes people do not stop being religious because they begin to understand the world from a scientific perspective but rather because of the ethical failings of religious people, especially religious leaders.[14] Thus, the sex abuse scandal of the Roman Catholic Church and the moral failings of some evangelical leaders in America may lead some to see religious people as hypocrites and so they may stop being religious. The stance of some churches against homosexuals may lead some to see the church as bigoted and so they may not want to be a part of such bigoted organizations. Thus, it is not quite correct to lay the blame for the secularization of society at the door of science, as has hitherto been the case. While science has a role to play in the secularization of society, the moral failings of religious people is also responsible. An investigation into why people wean themselves from the religious imagination may give us a better understanding of the role of science in this but it should be recognized that the secularization of society is not entirely the fault of science, as is often claimed.

Having disposed of the argument that an interdisciplinary piety would lead to secularization, as is the case in the West, what about the argument that modern science has endangered the lives and undermined the worldviews of indigenous peoples? Again, this charge is correct. The rapacity of modern science has led not only to the endangerment of indigenous peoples but also of people all over the world. Global warming is a direct product of modern industrial societies. The destruction which modern industrial societies have meted on the environment has led some to postulate indigenous ways of seeing the world as needful for our modern world. According to these scholars, because modern science relates to the world in a mechanistic way, it cannot adequately care for the environment. Indigenous

---

14. See John Hedley Brooke, "Science and Secularization," in *The Cambridge Companion to Science and Religion*, ed. Peter Harrison (Cambridge: Cambridge University Press, 2010), 103–23. Also see David Kinnaman and Gabe Lyons, *unChristian: What a New Generation Thinks about Christianity . . . and Why It Matters* (Grand Rapids, MI: Baker Books, 2007).

worldviews, on the other hand, see the world as organic and spiritualized so that there is interdependence between humans and the cosmos. This spiritualized vision is said to be friendlier to the environment than the scientific instrumental vision that is bent on denuding and polluting the environment.[15] While some have argued that the effect which indigenous visions may have on the environment has been exaggerated, we will not pursue that argument here.[16] We are rather going to grant that indigenous peoples have a right to live their lives the way they want to and that they do not need to be patronized. However, given that indigenous peoples have for a long time been patronized by people of science, one would hope that indigenous peoples may want to learn the ways of science in order to be able to adequately check the aggression from people of science. As Grim has shown, the children of indigenous peoples are beginning to do this.[17] If some indigenous peoples choose to maintain their lifestyle without engaging modern science, that is good and fine. This work is directed at those indigenous peoples in Africa who have been incorporated into the modern world either willingly or unwillingly and who would like to be able to control their destiny in this modern world rather than being at the mercy of the people of science. Those who prefer to hold on to indigenous visions of life to the exclusion of modern science do not have to buy into the form of piety being proposed here.

Having described the nature of interdisciplinary piety and responded to some objections that may be raised against it, especially in the African context, we will now turn to giving reasons why African theology of inculturation need to appropriate the form of piety being proposed here. After we discuss why African theology of inculturation should appropriate an interdisciplinary piety we shall turn to how this should be done before giving a theological foundation for such a piety.

Why Interdisciplinary Piety?

Considering that modern science emanated from Europe and has even sponsored colonialism in Africa, it may sound strange that the interdisciplinary piety described above should be recommended for the theology of

15. Grim. "Indigenous Lifeways."
16. See Nisbert Taringa, "How Environmental Is African Traditional Religion?" *Exchange* 35.2 (2006): 191–214.
17. Grim, "Indigenous Lifeways." 21.

inculturation in Africa. Given that the theology of inculturation seems to have developed as a push back to Western influences in Africa, would it not go against the tenets of this theology to sponsor an interdisciplinary piety? This section intends to discuss some reasons why the theology of inculturation should promote an interdisciplinary piety, in spite of the fact that the other interlocutor in this piety is Western science. The first and perhaps most significant reason the theology of inculturation needs to develop an interdisciplinary piety has been noted at several points in this work—it has to do with the fact of African marginalization in the modern world. As earlier indicated, there are many reasons for the marginalization of Africa and Africans in the modern world. African theologians have discussed many of the socio-economic and political reasons for this and made various proposals as to how they may be addressed.[18] However, one of the most significant reasons for the marginalization of Africa that has been recognized but hardly addressed in African Christian theology is modern science and its offshoot, modern technology. It has been noted that when societies lacking technological sophistication encounter societies that are technologically sophisticated, the technologically less sophisticated societies "find themselves at a disadvantage vis-à-vis the [technologically sophisticated societies], and they become overwhelmed and replaced if the disadvantage is sufficiently great."[19] The powers that often lord it over Africa and Africans, such as the European and Asian powers, manipulate and often subordinate the continent not merely through politics but especially through the use of science and technology. Because they have neglected the development of science and technology, African countries often rely on these other powers when they need things that heavily rely, for their manufacture, on science and technology. When something like a famine hits parts of Africa, food is often brought in from these foreign powers that have developed mechanized methods of farming. Similar forms of drought may happen in places like Texas and Oklahoma in the United States and Kenya and Niger in Africa. However, more people often die of the consequences of drought in Kenya and Niger than they do in Texas and Oklahoma. One of the reasons for this is that through the development of science and technology in the

18. See Elias K. Bongmba, *Dialectics of Transformation in Africa* (New York, NY: Palgrave Macmillan, 2006); Emmanuel Katongole, *The Sacrifice of Africa: A Political Theology for Africa* (Grand Rapids, MI: Eerdmans, 2010); J. N. K. Mugambi, *From Liberation to Reconstruction: African Christian Theology after the Cold War* (Nairobi, Kenya: East African Educational Publishers, 1995).

19. Diamond, *Guns, Germs, and Steel*, 255. Modified.

United States, there is often enough food to sustain people during times of drought. Such a cushion does not exist in places like Kenya or Niger where what sometimes stand between many people and death from starvation is relief food from international aid agencies. Africans cannot hold a dignified place in the world when they are often seen as objects of global charity. So far, it seems that the extensive focus on supernatural solutions in inculturation theology has not done much to address the big problems which Africans face, in spite of claims to the contrary.[20] Most Africans may not be asking questions about science and technology but their lives are affected by the lack of these things. It is the role of theologians and preachers, as leaders, to bring these issues to the attention of their people. The theology of inculturation therefore needs to be recalibrated to address the development of science and technology in Africa if the overall well-being of Africans is to be enhanced.

A second reason why African theology of inculturation should encourage an interdisciplinary spirituality can be found in the nature of African traditional religious worldviews. African traditional religious worldviews have been described as systems characterized by metaphysical complexity, which do not baptize any single perspective. According to Uzukwu, the Igbo of Nigeria express this in the following way: *"ife kwulu ife akwudebe ya* ('whenever something stands, something else stands beside it')." Among the Dogon of Mali this dualistic epistemology is expressed through their cosmological myth in which humans were created in pairs.[21] Within this context of epistemological flexibility, one point of view is never the only point of view and so absolutist or totalizing perspectives are anathema. Stressing this point, the Nigerian Noble Laureate, Wole Soyinka, says that the idea of "Revelation as Infallibility is a repugnant concept in Yoruba religion."[22] This epistemological flexibility in African religious cultures is situated within the context of belief in many gods rather than just one god. According to Uzukwu and Soyinka, monotheism is pernicious because it rejects other views, claiming the rightness of only one view. From the per-

---

20. For claims of supernatural solutions to big problems, see Asamoah-Gyadu, *Contemporary Pentecostal Christianity*, 36.

21. Uzukwu, *God, Spirit, and Human Wholeness*, 12, 10.

22. Wole Soyinka, "Tolerant Gods," in Orìsà Devotion as World Religion: The Globalization of YorùbáReligious Culture, eds., Jacob Olupona and Terry Rey (Madison, WI: The University of Wisconsin Press, 2008), 35. For more on the tolerance of the African worldview, see Lamin Sanneh, *The Crown and the Turban: Muslim and West African Pluralism* (Boulder, CO: Westview Press, 1997).

spective of African traditional religious cultures, everyone is not expected to hold only one view because everyone does not have a single destiny and destinies are often tied to devotion to one deity or another. Among the Yoruba, for example, people are devoted to the deities who govern their destinies. Thus, expecting everyone to adhere to a single deity is to assume that everyone should play the same role in life. Speaking about how a Yoruba child is made an initiate of a god, Soyinka writes that it is the discerning babaláwo (priest) who, based on his perception of specific traits of a child, determines the god to which a child is to be devoted. "It does not matter that neither parent is a follower of any such deity, or that no one in the entire household or in the history of the family has ever been an initiate of the god."[23] What matters is the specific trait that the babaláwo sees in the child. Even such initiation is not final because, upon discovering new and different trait in a child, the child may be initiated into a different or additional god. There is no friction or hostility among the gods when such events take place. This African view of life is tolerant because it allows for other perspectives. Speaking about this tolerance from an African ethical perspective, Bujo states that African ethics does not aim at "absolute 'ultimate justification' but only an 'ultimate justification' until a better argument turns up."[24] Scholars such as Soyinka and Uzukwu have argued that this flexible African worldview may be appropriated to encourage peace and harmony in a modern world where devotion to various absolutes is endangering societal peace and harmony in many regions around the world. Such flexible worldview would lead people to see that their worldviews are partial and so enable them to listen to and learn from others because it is only from such interaction that we may gain a better understand of each other and the world. From this African perspective, therefore, the world cannot be known only from one perspective but from many. As Chinua Achebe puts it, "[t]he world is like a mask dancing. If you want to see it well you do not stand in one place."[25] This view of life therefore makes Africans weary of absolutes; they are always on the lookout for other helpful ways to deal with life. It is for this reason that an interdisciplinary spirituality fits the African worldview. This flexible worldview should not be used to underscore only what the world can learn from Africa but also to underscore

23. Soyinka, "Tolerant Gods," 34.
24. Bujo, *Foundations of an African Ethic*, 22.
25. Chinua Achebe, *Arrow of God*, second edition (Oxford: Heinemann Educational, 1986), 45–46.

what Africans may learn from the rest of the world. Emphasizing supernatural spirituality in the church means focusing only on one dimension of life, the narrowly spiritual dimension, and so neglecting the other (natural) dimension. Religious engagement of the sciences may be one way by which the flexibility of the African worldview may be demonstrated and human well-being enhanced.

A further reason why an interdisciplinary spirituality may be encouraged by the church in Africa is that even though traditional African worldviews are spiritualistic, they also take the natural seriously so that engaging the natural sciences is not an unthinkable leap. In his study of health and healing in Africa, David Westerlund has demonstrated that African health and healing practices involve both spiritual and natural interpretations. His study of the traditions of health and healing among the San of southern Africa, the Masaai of eastern Africa, the Sukuma of Tanzania, the Kongo of central Africa, and the Yoruba of West Africa, demonstrate the reliance on both spiritual and natural interpretations and practices of health and healing.[26] Westerlund cites the following comments on the natural healing practices among the San:

> The Bushmen certainly are acquainted with a number of very valuable medicinal plants; some of them are specifics in the cure of several diseases which have frequently baffled the skill of the most eminent medical practitioners; and it is a matter of astonishment that no effort has been made to discover such important secrets. Thus, there were able to effect certain cures in cases of snake-bite, taenia, dysentery, and calculus, besides the rapid removal of gonorrheal affections.[27]

Westerlund also states how other scholars studying health and healing practices of the San "refer to extensive knowledge about plant medicines and provide examples of natural methods and ways of curing." In spite of this extensive knowledge of medicinal practices among the San, it is quite interesting that Westerlund notes that anthropologists and scholars of religion who study the religion of the San do not often point out this method of healing. The absence of this method of healing in the work of

---

26. David Westerlund, *African Indigenous Religions and Disease Causation: From Spiritual Beings to Living Humans* (Leiden: Brill, 2006), 209–15. Also see David Westerlund, "Religion, Illness, and Healing," in *The Wiley-Blackwell Companion to African Religions*, ed. Elias Kifon Bongmba (Oxford: Wiley-Blaxkwell, 2012), 443–56.

27. Westerlund, *African Indigenous Religions*, 209, cited from S. Feierman, "Struggle for Control."

anthropologists and scholars of San religion leads Westerlund to conclude that these scholars may either not be interested in this method of healing or the knowledge and skills in the natural and biological aspects of San medicine have deteriorated over time so that they may not be prominent among the San in recent history.[28] Among the Masaai, Westerlund points out, natural causes of diseases are of paramount importance and herbal medicine is significant. Among the Sukuma and the Kongo, only less serious afflictions are often seen to have natural causes. Among the Yoruba, there is extensive practice of herbal medicine and diseases are also seen to have natural causes. It is worth noting that, among these groups, spiritual causation of ill-health exists side by side with natural causation. It is rather unfortunate that contemporary African religious studies, especially as demonstrated in the theology of inculturation and Pentecostalism, have focused mainly on the spiritual causation and cure of illnesses in African traditional societies. The focus on spiritual causality and treatment of illnesses has contributed in giving the erroneous impression that the dominant thought form among African peoples is spiritual. Thus it is that many Christians and churches have tended to promote the spiritualized cosmology to the detriment of natural interpretations. I am aware that there are many churches that focus on natural practices in health and healing, such as found among some mission churches that have established some of the best hospitals in some African countries. However, the natural interpretations of health and healing seem to be currently falling into disrepute as spiritual healing seems to be coming to the fore in churches all over the continent. It is claimed that churches are growing because they provide spiritual healing and those that do not emphasize spiritual healing are declining. For anyone interested in the promotion of what is here described as interdisciplinary piety, this one-sided interpretation of health and healing in the church is a distressing development. However, from the above, it goes without saying that interdisciplinary piety closely approximates the African traditional religious worldviews.

    A final reason why inculturation theology should encourage an interdisciplinary spirituality is that science and technology flourish in cultures that make it possible for such flourishing to take place. The development of science and technology is therefore a cultural phenomenon. Thus, where a culture clings to spiritual interpretations to the virtual exclusion of the natural, the scientific and the technological become marginal. Of course

---

28. Westerlund, *African Indigenous Religions*, 209.

churches may not be held responsible for developing science and technology in Africa but they may contribute in creating the environment or atmosphere in which these things may flourish. While there are many elements that need to be put in place if science and technology are to flourish in a particular context, scholars have pointed out that the communication and reception of scientific and technological ideas play key parts in the growth of science and technology in a culture. Where people are not encouraged to pay attention to science and technology it may be difficult for science and technology to stick in that context.[29] Thus, science and technology may not grow where people cling to narrowly spiritual visions of life. So when Landes says that the answer to some of the health problems of pre-industrial Europe was "found, not in changed religious belief or doctrine, but in industrial innovation," he is only partly correct.[30] He is only partly correct because the industrial innovation did not arise in a vacuum; it arose in a context of changed religious beliefs. With the advent of the Scientific Revolution that would contribute to the Industrial Revolution, religious beliefs did not remain the same.[31] In fact, for those who actively participated in this event, their religious beliefs would have to be modified as popularly held beliefs would be challenged. It is this modification of religious beliefs in Africa, to seriously account for the scientific, that is being called for here. With such a modification of beliefs, churches would become sites for the creation of a culture that would press for the development of science and technology. How the churches may become sites for the creation of such a culture is what we turn to in the next section.

Tilling the Scientific Soil

Science and technology are social and cultural phenomena because they develop in specific social and cultural contexts under certain conditions. Thomas Kuhn brought home this fact when he used the concept of paradigm to argue about how change in worldview occurs in the sciences.[32]

---

29. For the importance of reception to the development of science and technology, see Diamond, *Guns, Gems, and Steel*, 253–54.

30. Landes, *The Wealth and Poverty of Nations*, xviii.

31. For the role of the Scientific Revolution in the Industrial Revolution, see Margaret C. Jacob, "The Cultural Origins of the First Industrial Revolution," in *The Scientific Revolution*, 196–215.

32. Thomas S. Kuhn, *The Structure of Scientific Revolutions*, third edition (Chicago

Theology as Construction of Piety

According to Kuhn, science is done within communities and changes in particular worldviews within scientific communities do not come easily. Kuhn describes the way science is ordinarily practiced within scientific communities as "normal science," pointing out that this science is based on commitments about, and perceptions of, the world that are hard to relinquish. These commitments, Kuhn points out, are not always based on a particular science but are also social and thus could be arbitrary.[33] That scientific worldviews are sometimes defended on social and cultural grounds could be seen in some debates during the Scientific Revolution. For example, the claim of Copernicus and Galileo, that the earth revolves around the sun rather than the other way around, was strenuously rejected by some not because meticulous investigation had proven the contrary but rather because the perception of the world by Copernicus and Galileo was based on mathematics and astronomy, disciplines that were held to be below the disciplines that should form the foundation of human knowledge (science). The disciplines that were supposed to form the foundation of human knowledge both of God and the world were, first, theology, and then natural philosophy. Theology was held to be the queen of the sciences, where the sciences were seen as means to legitimate knowledge of God and creation. The Copernican worldview breached this social and cultural understanding of disciplines by privileging mathematical astronomy over theology and natural philosophy and so was resisted.[34] A similar dynamic took place in the process through which chemistry came to be seen as a legitimate part of modern medicine, especially in France. For a long time many held the view propounded by the Greek doctor, Galen, that illnesses develop through imbalances of some elements of the body so that illness may be cured by seeking a balance of these elements through dietary means. This view was opposed by the Paraclesians (those who followed Paracelsus, the founder of this means of healing) who held that diseases may enter the body form the outside and that illnesses may be cured using chemicals. The position of the Paracelsians was rejected in France not only because it was thought to be dangerous but also because those who practiced Paracelsian medicine were mostly Protestants while those who practiced Galenic

---

and London: The University of Chicago Press, 1996); Marcus Hellyer, "Editor's Introduction: What was the Scientific Revolution?" in *The Scientific Revolution*, 7–8.

33. Kuhn, *The Structure of Scientific Revolutions*, 4–8.

34. For the portrayal of resistance to the Copernican and Galilean cosmology as based perceptions of disciplinary boundaries, see Robert S. Westman, "The Copernicans and the Churches," in *The Scientific Revolution*, 44–71.

Constructing an Interdisciplinary Piety

medicine were mostly Catholic. The politics of the Reformation entered the debates. Further, the faculty of medicine at the University of Paris had established itself as the sole authority to license medical practitioners in France, thus controlling medical practice there. The debate between the Galenists and the Paracelsians was as much a power struggle as it was a scientific struggle. In the end, chemical medicine came to be seen as legitimate medicine and we are the better for it today.[35]

Given that the development of science and technology is as much social and cultural as it is scientific, the social and cultural ground needs to be prepared if science and technology are to take root. In fact, the dissemination of science and technology is very similar to the dissemination of religion in that both have worldviews to communicate; both need missionaries to propagate their views; both look for the best ways to disseminate their views; and both need resources to help communicate their messages. An interesting point to note is that religions seem to have been far more successful at propagating their views in Africa than the sciences. That is partly why religious interpretations of events seem to be dominating natural ones. In order to develop interdisciplinary spirituality, the churches need to be involved in tilling the soil for the growth of science and technology.

The similarity between spreading a religion and spreading science and technology could be seen through a study of the dissemination of the science behind Robert Boyle's air-pump.[36] Boyle's air-pump is an instrument that was made in order to investigate the nature of air. The instrument was made in the 1660s and through his experiments, Boyle thought that he could demonstrate that air could compress and expand; but he had to convince not only those around him about this but also the wider public. Steven Shaping uses expressions such as "scientific popularization," "popularization of science," and "the creation of a scientific public" to describe the process by which new scientific and technological ideas are communicated to the masses.[37] In order to create this scientific public, Shapin avers, Boyle needed three things: *a material technology* (the air-pump), *a literary technology* (the means by which the facts discovered through the air-pump might be disseminated), and a *social technology* (governing the relations among

---

35. For more about this debate, see Allen G. Debus, "The Chemical Philosophy and the Scientific Revolution," in *The Scientific Revolution*, 157–77.

36. This discussion in this section has benefitted the insights of Steven Shapin, "Pump and Circumstance: Robert Boyle's Literary Technology," in The Scientific Revolution, 72–100.

37. Shapin, "Pump and Circumstance," 74.

Theology as Construction of Piety

scientists and the public as they attempt to communicate the facts of their experiments).[38] Thus, in his attempt to popularize science, Boyle could be described as a missionary with a message about which he was convinced (the air-pump and its experiment), the means of communication he would use (the literary technology), and the appropriate or ethical means of communicating the message (the social technology). In fact, Boyle thought of his relations to other scientists and the public as a Christian missionary might do. Writing about how to engage those who disagree with him, Boyle stated:

> And as for the (very much too common) practice of many, who write, as if they thought railing at a man's person, or wrangling about his words, necessary to the confutation of his opinions; besides that I think such a quarrelsome and injurious way of writing does very much misbecome both a philosopher and a Christian, methinks it is unwise, as it is provoking. For if I civilly endeavour to reason a man out of his opinions, I make myself but one work to do, namely, to convince his understanding; but, if in a bitter or exasperating way I oppose his errors, I increase the difficulties I would surmount, and have as well his affections against me as his judgment: and it is very uneasy to make a proselyte of him, that is not only a dissenter from us, but an enemy to us.[39]

Here we see that Boyle even thought of the would-be convert to the scientific way as a proselyte, a term that is often used in cross-cultural and religious communications. In his mission to convince others of his position, he does not only see himself as a scientist but also a Christian and imagines his mission of scientific literacy as Christian mission. He also points out that potential converts should be engaged carefully rather than brashly, eschewing ad hominem or name calling in debates because one makes enemies when they engage in ad hominem. Thus, Boyle thought that dealing in a friendly manner both with colleagues and the general public is helpful in disseminating the message of the air-pump. For Boyle, therefore, communicating the message of science needed an approachable and trusted missionary. Christian missionaries who hope to convince people of their message know that it is important to be friendly and be trusted by the people among whom they work. Here we see that the method of

---

38. Shaping, "Pump and Circumstance," 75–76. Italics in original.

39. Robert Boyle, "Proëmial Essay," 312, cited in Shaping, "Pump and Circumstance," 95.

communicating science and religion is similar. Boyle's advice in communicating science could be seen in how religion has been communicated in Africa. Those missionaries who came to Africa and condemned various African cultures only succeeded in raising the ire of Africans. But those who came and demonstrated more understanding, such as Bengt Sundkler and Placide Tempels, have had a lasting effect in the development of African Christian thought.

Apart from social technology, Boyle also needed a literary technology in order to communicate his message. Among the literary technology he appropriated, we have drawings and description of the pump and the processes to follow in order to independently carry out the experiment. Drawings of the air-pump were included in the writings of Boyle and published so that his science could spread far and wide. Boyle was also invited to demonstrate his experiment by the Royal Society, an organization that aimed at disseminating such information. Those who were present at the demonstrations at the Royal Society could also bear witness to the message wherever they went. Writing down the scientific information to be disseminated can be compared to the pamphlets and books which Christians write in order to communicate the gospel. The Royal Society could be compared to mission organizations or churches that send out and support missionaries. Given that science and religion have similar ways of communicating ideas, one may wonder why religion seems to have had such success in communicating itself than science. Could it be due to the fact that scientists do not see themselves as missionaries? Could it be due to the fact that it is far more expensive to communicate science than it is to communicate religion so that science ends up being communicated to the rich while religion is communicated to the poor? Is science, then, the religion of the rich?

This notwithstanding, African church leaders ought to begin to see themselves not only as responsible for the communication of the Christian faith but also for the communication of science in Africa. This vision of African theologians and preachers may raise many questions: would a focus on communicating science not marginalize the communication of the gospel? Would communicating science not be a classic example of using the message of the church to fund other visions, thus marginalizing the vision of the gospel? The church's contribution in creating a scientific public does not fall outside the mission of the church; it is in fact central to the mission of the church given that the good news which the church preaches addresses both the issues which people suffer in this life and the life to come. The church's message about the life to come will not have much credibility if the church does not take a central role in addressing the things which people suffer in this life. Since science and technology significantly contribute in addressing the things which people suffer in this life, it would not be out of order for the church to focus in promoting science and technology. In fact, in some ways, the churches have been doing this. One of the most significant ways in which the churches have been contributing in creating a scientific public is through the establishment of schools all over Africa, even though a significant purpose of mission schools was to enable Africans read the Bible for themselves. Some churches, including Pentecostal churches, have even established universities. Universities are significant sites for the creation of a scientific public. However, these schools and universities are still very weak in the creation not only of scientists but also of a scientific public. A conference recentl organized by the International Center for Theoretical Physics at the University of Yaoundé 1, Cameroon, brought together scientists from all over Africa (from Egypt to South Africa) to discuss the state of science in Africa.[40] The representatives from various African countries at this conference were encouraged to discuss success stories from their various countries. However, the general sentiment bespoke the lack of serious engagement of the natural sciences in most African countries. Thus, establishing schools is a good first step but actually equipping these schools to study and disseminate science, will go a long way.

Churches could also contribute in creating a scientific public through promoting mechanized farming in many African communities. Considering that churches are some of the largest and perhaps most well-endowed organizations in Africa, they could buy tractors, fertilizers, and other modern farming equipment and make these available to small scale farmers whose method of production is still largely very labor intensive. Churches may also help in irrigation projects. Helping to mechanize farming will not only increase yield but also reduce labor intensive farming and the strain this has on the human body. Churches could endow centers for the engagement of religion, science and technology in schools and universities. Churches could also organize science days in which they invite experts on specific scientific issues to come and talk to Christians. A physicist may

---

40. For the International Center for Theoretical Physics, see http://www.ictp.it/, accessed on August 31, 2013. For the conference organized in Yaoundé, Cameroon, see, http://www.youtube.com/user/ICTPchannel, accessed on August 31, 2013.

be invited to address some issues about the physical make-up of the world about which people may generally not be aware. Churches may encourage invention and innovation by creating prizes. Even more, churches may work to encourage the conducting of autopsies when people die in order to find out the natural causes of death. In Cameroon, for example, the cause of death is often not known and this leaves room for widespread rumor about the cause of a particular person's death. Conducting autopsies to consider cause of death does not mean that people are going to believe the naturalistic explanation of cause of death. However, it will provide additional explanation to contest the sometimes preferred spiritual interpretation of cause of death. Further, churches should preach about the importance of the development of science and technology from the pulpit. From the pulpit, churches ought to be urging governments to focus on the promotion of science and technology. This ought to be made an essential political struggle in our time. However, a very significant way in which the church may contribute in developing an interdisciplinary spirituality in Africa is to rethink how the Bible is read in order to begin to raise questions that may lead to the development of science and technology. We address this matter in the next section where we discuss the theological foundation for an interdisciplinary spirituality.

Theological Foundations for Interdisciplinary Spirituality

The theological foundation for interdisciplinary spirituality is based in a theology of nature rather than natural theology. Natural theology is based on the assumption that the existence of God can be deduced from observation of nature while a theology of nature meditates on the place of scientific investigation in the life of God. A theology of nature is new or being recovered inasmuch as it developed to address the separation between science and theology, a separation that hardly occurred in much of the history of the world in general and in much of Christian history.[41] During the beginnings of the development of modern science in Western Europe there was no firm separation of science from theology. Science was in fact seen as a

---

41. See John Hedley Brooke, *Science and Religion: Some Historical Perspectives* (Cambridge: Cambridge University Press, 1991); Philip Clayton, "Theology and the Physical Sciences," in *The Modern Theologians: An Introduction to Christian Theology Since 1918*, ed., David F. Ford (Oxford: Blackwell, 2006), 342–44.

theological enterprise so that the natural philosopher or scientist was, in a sense, a theologian.

We do theology of nature (science) today in order to account for how God works in the world and how belief in God may be seen as compatible with science. Theology of science is in part needful because of reductionistic naturalism or materialism. Reductionistic naturalism or materialism is the view that no metaphysical entities exist because only material things exist. This view seems to be in sync with the method of scientific investigation because the scientific method does not assume God. When scientists conduct investigations, they do not assume that the result of their investigation is influenced by God or any spiritual reality. Even though God was used to fill the gaps in the work of natural philosophers such as Isaac Newton, this is no longer the case in contemporary scientific investigations. The fact that God is not assumed in scientific investigations is known as *methodological naturalism*. It is a method of scientific investigation in which scientists do their work as if God does not exist. An implication of this is that science can be done both by people who believe in God and people who do not believe in God. However, the method to be used by both of them is based on the assumption that God does not influence the outcome of their work. Thus, chemists who manufacture drugs simply want to know the specific combination of chemicals that will result in a specific outcome if used in a specific way under specific circumstances. Such combination should be able to work on the basis of their chemical constitution alone rather than on the basis of belief in God or any other spiritual entity. A chemist may therefore believe in God but their work is based on putting together chemicals to make certain drugs, not on demonstrating whether or not and how God works through the chemicals. A Chemist may believe in God but their faith should be their private affair that should have no effect on the method of investigation in chemistry. Questions of ethics may come into play in scientific investigation but ethical questions are not methodological questions. Methodological naturalism is therefore not incompatible with the Christian faith because it does not require a scientist not to believe in God but only that a scientist follows the scientific method.[42]

For theologians, however, the question about how God works through these apparently natural processes remains. Does explaining and

---

42. For more on this, see James K. A. Smith, "Is There Room for Surprise Natural World? Naturalism, the Supernatural, and Pentecostal Spirituality," in *Science and the Spirit: A Pentecostal Engagement with the Sciences*, eds. James K. A. Smith and Amos Yong (Bloomington and Indianapolis, IN: Indiana University Press, 2010), 41–42.

Constructing an Interdisciplinary Piety

understanding things through natural processes not make God superfluous? As stated earlier, it is possible that natural explanations of things and events may make God superfluous for some people. But it needs not be so. From a Christian perspective, God has an intimate connection to creation not only as creator but also as redeemer. God's connection to creation is especially demonstrated in the Christian notion of incarnation in which God takes material form (human) in Jesus Christ in order to restore divine-human relationship. Through the incarnation, therefore, God is intimately connected to the world so that nothing that is done in the world is outside the reach of God. From a Christian perspective God influences the outcome of salutary scientific investigations even if scientists do not acknowledge this. From a Christian perspective, even when some people do not believe in God, it does not mean that God is not with them; there is nowhere where people can go to remove themselves from the presence of God. Inasmuch as anything exists, that thing exists in God. Thus, atheistic scientists may not believe in God but it does not mean that they, their work, or the outcome of their work are outside the realm of God. That God is with the atheist is based on the Christian view of God as having taken up the material into divine life through Jesus Christ; it is not based on the belief of the atheist but on what Christians believe. Thus, even though scientific investigation may not assume God, it does not mean that God is not working through the matter which science investigates. The knowledge to investigate and transform matter for the benefit of the world is, from a Christian perspective, the gift of God intended for the mission of God in the world. It is the Spirit of God that enlightens all, whether they be Christian or not. Thus, scientists whose investigations have salutary effects in the world are being used by God to effect God's salvific vision for the world. Salutary human art (*poesis* or making) is therefore a manifestation of divine art. God therefore does not work only through miracles but also through science and technology. Thus, a theological foundation for an interdisciplinary piety is located in the Trinitarian life of God who creates all things and wishes to bring all things into fullness in divine life. Through Jesus Christ God takes on matter and so sanctifies material things so that an investigation into the working of nature is an investigation into the mysteries of God in the world. Through the Spirit, God enlightens all and gives them the capacity to peer into the mysteries of God in nature.

That scientific investigation is a means of unveiling the intention of God for the world was, during the Scientific Revelation, situated in the doctrine of revelation where God's intension for the world was seen as revealed through the Bible and Nature. Because God was revealed through Nature and the Bible it was therefore possible to know the work of God in the world through God's two books, the Book of Scripture and the Book of Nature. While the Book of Scripture reveals how God works in the life of Israel and through Christ for our salvation, the Book of Nature tells us about how God works through nature for the betterment of human beings and the rest of creation.[43] Thus, we know God's activity better not only by reading the Scripture but also by reading nature. The scientist was therefore seen as one whose experiments attempted to decipher the work of God in nature for the purpose of understanding God better so as to enhance faith in God. The scientist, as we have seen above, was also a missionary and a theologian.[44] In this way, therefore, the investigation of nature (science) was seen as a spiritual exercise rather than as severed from the Christian life in God. This view of things is therefore similar to the African worldview in which the spiritual and the material are intricately connected.[45] The view of divine activity as also revealed through scientific investigation is therefore a critical theological foundation of an interdisciplinary piety. An implication of this view is that we may not adequately understand God if we do not adequately understand how nature works. In fact, we may sorely misunderstand how God works in the world if we do not adequately understand nature. Could we be misunderstanding God in Africa when emphasize only the supernatural dimension of divine activity in the world?

Such misunderstanding of how God works in the world came to the fore when some of the discoveries which scientists made through reading the Book of Nature contradicted some of the things that were believed to be revealed in the Book of Scripture. For example, the Copernican worldview held that the earth revolved around the sun (heliocentrism) while it was widely believed that the Bible teaches that it was the sun that revolved around the earth (geocentrism). Reading texts such as Joshua 10:13 which states: "And the sun stood still, and the moon stopped . . ." and Psalm 93:1 which reads: "He has established the world; it shall never be moved" (NRSV), medieval theologians thought that the earth was the center of the

43. Brooke, *Science and Religion*, 72.

44. See Celia Deane-Drummond, "Theology and the Biological Sciences," in *The Modern Theologians*, 357; Steven Shapin, *The Scientific Revolution* (Chicago and London: The University of Chicago Press, 1996), 135–42; John Henry, "Religion and the Scientific Revolution," in *The Cambridge Companion to Science and Religion*, 41–44.

45. See Laurenti Magesa, *What is Not Sacred?*

Constructing an Interdisciplinary Piety

universe and did not move while the sun and the moon revolved around the earth. This belief was held until Copernicus and Galileo challenged it with their view that the sun, not the earth, is the center of the universe, and that the earth revolves around the sun. We now know that Copernicus and Galileo were right even though some Christians condemned them at the time.

During the Scientific Revolution, the dispute about the disparate findings of the Book of Nature and the Book of Scripture raised the question of how the Bible should be read. While some insisted on reading the Bible to support the geocentric worldview, those who supported the Copernican position read the Bible to support the heliocentric worldview. While those supporting the geocentric view read texts, such as the ones above, to argue that the geocentric view is the view which God wanted people to hold for all time, supporters of the heliocentric view read the same texts to argue that God used the language in the Bible in order to reflect how people understood the world at the time, not to teach timeless truths. Again, as we now know, the reading of the Bible by supporters of the Copernican view was closer to the truth than the reading adopted by opponents of that view. We now know that the sun is the center only of our solar system, which is itself a very tiny part of the Milky Way galaxy, and that the universe is made of billions upon billions of galaxies. Through reading the Book of Nature we have come to know much about the universe that was not known previously.

One other reading of the Book of Nature that challenged the reading of the Book of Scripture is Charles Darwin's discovery that species were not all created at the time of creation, as recorded in Genesis 1, but rather evolved over time through the process of natural selection. This view is known as the theory of evolution and has been very influential in the development of the biological sciences.[46] Thus, after Darwin, are we to understand humans as having been created, as the Bible says, or as having evolved, as scientists appear to have established, or as having been created through evolution? After Darwin and other scientific revolutionaries, how are we to read the Bible? Questions like these have led some Christians to recoil from engaging the sciences. These questions are especially important in the African context because of the important place which the Bible holds in African

---

46. See Nancy Morvillo, *Science and Religion: Understanding the Issues* (Oxford: Wiley-Blackwell, 2010), 139–60; Thomas Dixon, *Science and Religion: A Very Short Introduction* (Oxford: Oxford University Press, 2008), 58–80.

Theology as Construction of Piety

Christianity.[47] Developing a theological foundation for an interdisciplinary piety in Africa requires reading the Bible in ways that not only encourage expectations of the miraculous but also promote science and technology as means through which God wishes to ensure our well-being in the world even as we look forward to the New Creation, where God will wipe away all the tears we have suffered in this mortal life (Rev 21:1–5). Developing the method of reading the Bible in ways that will cultivate the interdisciplinary piety being advocated here will be the focus of a future project.

Conclusion

This book has attempted to conceptualize theology as the construction of piety, arguing that the theologies we construct have consequences. Taking a quick tour of the history of Christian theology from the early church to the Middle Ages, it demonstrated how theology is the construction of piety. It then interrogated the nature of the piety which the theology of inculturation in Africa is constructing, insisting that the theology of inculturation ought to construct an interdisciplinary piety that takes seriously the importance of science and technology in our modern world. This final chapter has attempted to describe what this interdisciplinary piety looks like. Given that the interdisciplinary piety called for here has been problematized in African theology, this chapter has given some good reasons why this piety should be encouraged, discussed some ways by which it could be encouraged, and gave some theological foundations on which this piety should be based.

---

47. Gerald O. West and Musa W. Dube, eds., *The Bible in Africa: Transactions, Trajectories, and Trends* (Leiden: Brill, 1998); Musa W. Dube Shomanah, ed., *Other Ways of Reading: African Women and the Bible* (Atlanta: Society of Biblical Literature, 2001).

Bibliography

Achebe, Chinua. *Arrow of God*, second edition. Oxford: Heinemann Educational, 1986.
Adogame, Afe, Roswith Gerloff and Klaus Hock, eds. *Christianity in Africa and the African Diaspora: The Appropriation of a Scattered Heritage*. London: Continuum, 2008.
Adogame et al., Afe, eds. *European Traditions in the Study of Religions in Africa*. Wiesbaden: Harrassowitz Verlag, 2004.
Allen, Diogenes and Eric O. Springsted. *Philosophy for Understanding Theology*. Second edition. Louisville, KY: Westminster John Knox Press, 2007.
Amaladoss, M. "Cross-Inculturation of Indian and African Christianity." *African Ecclesial Review* 32.3 (1990): 157–168.
Anatalios, Khaled. *Athanasius*. London: Routledge, 2004.
Anderson, Allan H. *African Reformation: African Initiated Christianity in the Twentieth Century*. Trenton, NJ: Africa World Press, 2001.
Anderson, Allan. "Pentecostal Approaches to Faith and Healing." *International Review of Mission* 91.363 (October 2002): 523–534.
Appiah, Kwame Anthony. *In My Father's House: Africa in the Philosophy of Culture*. Oxford: Oxford University Press, 1992.
Appiah-Kubi, Kofi. "Indigenous African Christian Churches: Signs of Authenticity." In *African Theology En Route*, eds. Kofi Appiah-Kubi and Sergio Torres, 117–125. Maryknoll, NY: Orbis Books, 1979.
Arasu, Lazar and George Kainikunnel. "The Church in Africa and the Issue of Christian Marriage." *Afer* (August 1996): 229–234.
Arnold, John H. *Belief and Unbelief in Medieval Europe*. London: Hodder Arnold, 2005.
Asamoah-Gyadu, J. Kwabena. *African Charismatics: Current Developments within Independent Indigenous Pentecostalism in Ghana*. Leiden and Boston: Brill, 2005.
Asamoah-Gyadu, J. Kwabena. "Broken Calabashes and Covenants of Fruitfulness: Cursing Barrenness in Contemporary African Christianity." *Journal of Religion in Africa* 37.4 (2007): 437–460.
Asamoah-Gyadu, J. Kwabena. *Contemporary Pentecostal Christianity: Interpretations from an African Context*. Eugene, Oregon: Wipf and Stock, 2013.
Ayres, Lewis. "On Not Three People: The Fundamental Themes of Gregory of Nyssa's Trinitarian Theology as seen in To Ablabius: On Not Three Gods." *Modern Theology* 18.4 (October 2002): 445–474.
———. *Nicaea and Its Legacy: An Approach to Fourth-Century Trinitarian Theology*. Oxford: Oxford University Press, 2004.

Theology as Construction of Piety

———. "The Trinity and the Life of the Christian: A Liturgical Catechism." *New Blackfriars* (2010): 3–17.

Barnes, Michel René. "Review of *Ambrose of Milan and the End of the "Arian"-Nicene Conflicts* by D. H. Williams." *Journal of Religion* (April 1997):293–295.

———. *The Power of God: δύναμις in Gregory of Nyssa's Trinitarian Theology*. Washington, DC: Catholic University of America Press, 2001.

Battle, Michael Jesse. *Reconciliation: The Ubuntu Theology of Desmond Tutu*. Cleveland, OH: Pilgrim Press, 1997.

BBC News. "Ghana Stampede Kills Four at TB Joshua's Church." http://www.bbc.co.uk/news/world-africa-22595573. Accessed on August 1, 2013.

Bediako, Kwame. *Theology and Identity: The Impact of Culture Upon Christian Thought in the Second Century and in Modern Africa*. Carlisle, UK: Paternoster Publishing, 1992 and 1999.

Banner, Michael. "Review of The Blackwell Companion to Christian Ethics, eds., Stanley Hauerwas and Samuel Wells." *International Journal of Systematic Theology* (January 2007): 106–109.

Behr, John. *Formation of Christian Theology: The Way to Nicaea*, vol. 1. Crestwood, New York: St. Vladimir's Seminary Press, 2001.

Berger, Peter L. and Thomas Luckmann. *The Social Construction of Reality: A Treatise in the Sociology of Knowledge*. Garden City, NY: Doubleday, 1966.

Berger, Peter L. "A Friendly Dissent from Pentecostalism." *First Things* (November 2012): 45–50.

Behr, John. *The Nicene Faith*, 2 vols. Crestwood, NY: St. Vladimir's Seminary Press, 2004.

Bernauer, James and Jeremy Carrette. "Introduction—The Enduring Problem: Foucault, Theology and Culture." In *Michel Foucault and Theology: The Politics of Religious Experience*, ed. James Bernauer and Jeremy Carrette, 1–18. Hampshire, England: Ashgate, 2002.

Bongmba, Elias K. *Dialectics of Transformation in Africa*. New York, NY: Palgrave Macmillan, 2006.

Boserup, Ester. "The Economics of Polygamy." In *Perspectives on Africa: A Reader in Culture, History, and Representation*, eds. Roy Richard Grinker, Stephen C. Lubkemann, and Christopher B. Steiner, 389–398. Second edition. Malden, MA: Blackwell, 1997.

Bosch-Heij, Deborah van den. *Spirit and Healing in Africa: A Reformed Pneumatological Perspective*. Bloemfontein, South Africa: SUN MeDIA, 2012.

Brand, Gerrit. *Speaking of a Fabulous Ghost: In Search of Theological Criteria, with Special Reference to the Debate on Salvation in African Christian Theology*. Frankfurt am Main: Peter Lang, 2002.

Brooke, John Hedley. *Science and Religion: Some Historical Perspectives*. Cambridge: Cambridge University Press, 1991.

———. "Science and Secularization." In *The Cambridge Companion to Science and Religion*, ed. Peter Harrison, 103–123. Cambridge: Cambridge University Press, 2010.

Brubaker, Leslie. *Inventing Byzantium Iconoclasm*. London, UK: Bristol Classical Press, 2012.

Bujo, Bénézet. *Foundations of an African Ethic: Beyond the Universal Claims of Western Morality*. Translated by Brian McNeil. New York: Crossroad Publishing, 2001.

Bibliography

———. "Differentiations in African Ethics." In *The Blackwell Companion to Religious Ethics*, ed. William Schweiker, 423-437. Oxford: Blackwell, 2005.
———. *African Theology in Its Social Context*. Translated by John O'Donohue. Maryknoll, NY: Orbis Books, 1992.
———. "Vatican II and the Challenge of Marriage and Family in Africa." Unpublished.
Bunyan, John. *The Pilgrim's Progress*. Wheaton, IL: Tyndale House Publishers, 1991.
Bynum, Catherine Walker. *Christian Materiality: An Essay on Religion in Late Medieval Europe*. Brooklyn, NY: Zone Books, 2011.
Cameron, Averil. *The Later Roman Empire, AD 284-430*. Cambridge, MA: Harvard University Press, 1993.
Cameron, Euan. "The Waldenses." In *The Medieval Theologians: An Introduction to Theology in the Medieval Period*, ed. G. R. Evans, 269-286. Oxford: Blackwell, 2001.
Charry, Ellen. *By the Renewing of Your Minds: The Pastoral Function of Christian Doctrine*. Oxford: Oxford University Press, 1997.
Cherry, Constance M. *The Worship Architect: A Blueprint for Designing Culturally Relevant and Biblically Faithful Services*. Grand Rapids, MI: Baker Academic, 2010.
Chidester, David. *Christianity: A Global History*. New York, NY: HarperSanFrancisco, 2000.
Chitando, Ezra. "Phenomenology of Religion and the Study of African Traditional Religions." *Method and Theory in the Study of Religion* 17 (2005): 299-316.
Clark, Clifton R. "Ogbu Kalu and Africa's Christianity: A Tribute." *Pneuma* 32 (2010): 107-120.
Clayton, Philip. "Theology and the Physical Sciences." In *The Modern Theologians: An Introduction to Christian Theology Since 1918*, ed., David F. Ford, 342-356. Oxford: Blackwell, 2006.
Coakley, Sarah. *Powers and Submissions: Spirituality, Philosophy and Gender*. Oxford: Blackwell, 2002.
Collins, Paul M. *Christian Inculturation in India*. Aldershot, England: Ashgate Publishing Limited, 2007.
Concannon, Ellen. "The Eucharist as Source of St. Cyril of Alexandria's Christology." *Pro Ecclesia* 18.3 (2009): 318-336.
Cox, Harvey. *Fire from Heaven: The Rise of Pentecostal Spirituality and the Reshaping of Religion in the Twenty-First Century*. Cambridge, MA: Da Capo Press, 2001.
———. "Response to Professor Nimi Wariboko." *Pneuma* 33 (2011): 409-416.
Coulton, G. G. *Life in the Middle Ages*. Cambridge: Cambridge University Press, 1954.
Cunningham, Mary B. and Elizabeth Theokritoff. "Who are the Orthodox Christians? A Historical Introduction." In *The Cambridge Companion to Orthodox Christian Theology*, eds. Mary B. Cunningham and Elizabeth Theokritoff, 1-20. Cambridge: Cambridge University Press, 2008.
Dawn, Marva. *Reaching Out Without Dumbing Down: A Theology of Worship for this Urgent Time*. Grand Rapids, MI: Eerdmans, 1995.
Deane-Drummond, Celia. "Theology and the Biological Sciences." In *The Modern Theologians*, ed. David F. Ford, 357-369. Oxford: Blackwell, 2006.
Debus, Allen G. "The Chemical Philosophy and the Scientific Revolution." In *The Scientific Revolution*, ed. Marcus Hellyer, 157-177. Oxford: Blackwell, 2003.
Diamond, Jared. *Guns, Germs, and Steel: The Fates of Human Society*. New York: W. W. Norton & Company, 1997.

Dixon, Thomas. *Science and Religion: A Very Short Introduction*. Oxford: Oxford University Press, 2008.

Dunn, James D. G. *The Theology of Paul the Apostle*. Grand Rapids, MI: Eerdmans, 1998.

Ekpo, Denis. "Any European Around to Help me Talk About Myself? The White Man's Burden of Black Africa's Critical Practices." *Third Text* 19.2 (March 2005): 107-124.

Elolia, Samuel K. ed. *Religion, Conflict, and Democracy in Modern Africa*. Eugene, Oregon: Pickwick Publications, 2012.

Epprecht, Marc. *Unspoken Facts: A History of Homosexualities in Africa* (Harare, Zimbabwe: GALZ, 2008).

———. "Religion and Same Sex Relations in Africa." In *The Wiley-Blackwell Companion to African Religions*, ed. Elias Kifon Bongmba, 515-528. Oxford: Oxford University Press, 2012.

Evans-Pritchard, E. E. *Witchcraft, Oracles, and Magic Among the Azande*. Oxford: Oxford University Press, 1937.

Fenske, James. "African Polygamy: Past and Present." CSAE Working Paper, WPS 2012-20, *Oxford Center for the Study of African Economies*, November 28, 2012, 1-30. Accessed on August 6, 2013.

Fodor, James. "Postliberal Theology." In *The Modern Theologians: An Introduction to Christian Theology Since 1918*, ed. David Ford, 229-248. Oxford: Blackwell, 2006.

Fortounatto, Mariamna and Mary B Cunningham. "Theology of Icon." In *The Cambridge Companion to Orthodox Christian Theology*, eds. Mary B. Cunningham and Elizabeth Theokritoff, 136-149. Cambridge: Cambridge University Press, 2008.

Foucault, Michel. "What is an Author?" In *The Foucault Reader*, ed. Paul Rabinow, 101-120. New York: Vintage Books, 2010.

———. "The Means of Correct Training." In *The Foucault Reader*, ed. Paul Rabinow, 188-205. New York: Vintage Books, 2010.

Gbadegesin, Segun. "Origins of African Ethics." In *The Blackwell Companion to Religious Ethics*, ed. William Schweiker, 413-422. Oxford: Blackwell, 2006.

Gifford, Paul ed. *The Christian Churches and the Democratization in Africa*. Leiden: Brill Academic Publishers, 1995.

Gifford, Paul. *Ghana's New Christianity: Pentecostalism in a Globalizing African Economy*. Bloomington, Indiana: Indiana University Press, 2004.

———. "Africa's Inculturation Theology: Observations of an Outsider." *Hekima Review* 38 (May 2008): 18-34.

Gillespie, Michael Allen. *The Theological Origins of Modernity*. Chicago: The University of Chicago Press, 2008.

Gornick, Mark R. *Word Made Global: Stories of African Christianity in New York City*. Grand Rapids, MI: Eerdmans, 2011.

Gregg, Robert C. and Dennis E. Groh. "The Centrality of Soteriology in Early Arianism." *Anglican Theological Review* 59.3 (1977): 260-278.

Green, Maia. "Confronting Categorical Assumptions About the Power of Religion in Africa." *Review of African Political Economy* 33.110 (2006): 635-650.

Grim, John A. ed. *Indigenous Traditions and Ecology: The Interbeing of Cosmology and Community*. Cambridge, MA: Harvard University Press, 2001.

Grim, John A. "Indigenous Lifeways and Knowing the World." In *The Oxford Handbook of Religion and Science*, ed. Philip Clayton, 1-34. Oxford: Oxford University Press, 2008.

Bibliography

Grinker, Roy Richard, Stephen C. Lubkemann, and Richard B. Steiner, eds., *Perspectives on Africa: A Reader in Culture, History, and Representation*. Oxford: Wiley-Blackwell, 2010.

Gurevich, Aron. *Medieval Popular Culture: Problems of Belief and Perception*. Translated by János M. Bak and Paul A. Hollingsworth. Cambridge: Cambridge University Press, 1988.

Guroian, Vigen. "Differentiation in Christian Ethics." In *The Blackwell Companion to Religious Ethics*, ed. William Schweiker, 214-226. Oxford: Blackwell, 2005.

Gutierrez, Gustavo. *A Theology of Liberation: History, Politics, and Salvation*. Maryknoll, NY: Orbis Books, 1973.

Gutting, Gary. "Introduction—Michel Foucault: A User's Manual." In *The Cambridge Companion to Foucault*, ed. Gary Gutting, 1-28. Cambridge: Cambridge University Press, 1994.

———. "Foucault, Michel." In *The Cambridge Dictionary of Philosophy*, ed. Robert Audi, 320-321. New York, NY: Cambridge University Press, 1995, 1999.

Hallen, Barry. "African Ethics?" In *The Blackwell Companion to Religious Ethics*, ed. William Schweiker, 406-412. Oxford: Blackwell, 2006.

Hanson, R. P. C. *The Search for the Christian Doctrine of God: The Arian Controversy* 318-381. Edinburgh: T & T Clark, 1988.

Hardy, Daniel W. "Karl Barth." In *The Modern Theologians: An Introduction to Christian Theology Since 1918*, ed. David Ford, Third Edition, 21-42. Oxford: Blackwell Publishing, 2005.

Harries, Jim. *Communication in Mission and Development: Relating to the Church in Africa*. Eugene, Oregon: Wipf and Stock, 2013.

Hastings, Adrian. "The Church's Response to African Marriage." *African Ecclesiastical Review* XIII .3 (1971): 193-203.

———. *African Catholicism: Essays in Discovery*. London: SCM Press, 1989.

———. *The Church in Africa, 1450-1950*. Oxford: Oxford University Press, 1996.

Kane, Cheikh Hamidou. *Ambiguous Adventure*. Translated by Katherine Woods. London: Heinemann, 1972.

Hauerwas, Stanley. *A Community of Character: Toward a Constructive Christian Social Ethic*. Notre Dame, IN: University of Notre Dame Press, 1981.

Hauerwas, Stanley and Samuel Wells. "Why Christian Ethics Was Invented." In *The Blackwell Companion to Christian Ethics*, eds. Stanley Hauerwas and Samuel Wells, 28-52. Oxford: Blackwell, 2004, 2006.

———. "The Gift of the Church and the Gifts God Gives It." In *The Blackwell Companion to Christian Ethics*, eds. Stanley Hauerwas and Samuel Wells, 13-27. Oxford: Blackwell, 2004, 2006.

———. "Christian Ethics as Informed Prayer." In *The Blackwell Companion to Christian Ethics*, eds. Stanley Hauerwas and Samuel Wells, 3-12. Oxford: Blackwell, 2004, 2006.

Healy, Joseph G., "Inculturation of Liturgy and Worship in Africa." *Worship* 60 (1986): 412-423.

Healy, Nicholas. "Review of *The Blackwell Companion to Christian Ethics*, eds. Stanley Hauerwas and Samuel Wells." *Studies in Christian Ethics* 19 (April 2006): 120-125.

Hellyer, Marcus. "Editor's Introduction: What was the Scientific Revolution?" In *The Scientific Revolution*, ed. Marcus Hellyer, 1-16. Oxford: Blackwell, 2003.

Hendrix, Scott. "Luther." In *The Cambridge Companion to Reformation Theology*, eds., David Bagchi and David C. Steinmetz, 39-56. Cambridge: Cambridge University Press, 2004.

Henry, John. "Religion and the Scientific Revolution." In *The Cambridge Companion to Science and Religion*, ed. Peter Harrison, 39-58. Cambridge: Cambridge University Press, 2010.

Hoad, Neville. *African Intimacies: Race, Homosexuality and Globalization*. Minneapolis, MN: University of Minnesota Press, 2006.

Hollenweger, Walter J. *Pentecostalism: Origins and Development Worldwide*. Peabody, MA: Hendrickson Publishers, 1997.

Hooykaas, R. "The Rise of Modern Science: When and Why?" In *The Scientific Revolution*, ed. Marcus Hellyer, 21-22. Oxford: Blackwell, 2003.

Idowu, Bolaji. *Olódùmarè: God in Yoruba Beliefs*. London: Longman, 1962.

———. *African Traditional Religion: A Definition*. London: SPCK, 1973.

Ilesanmi, Simeon O. "Inculturation and Liberation: Christian Social Ethics and the African Theology Project." *Annual of the Society of Christian Ethics* (January 1995): 49–73.

"Indulgences." Accessed on August 1, 2013 at *New Advent*: http://www.newadvent.org/cathen/07783a.htm.

Isichei, Elizabeth. *A History of Christianity in Africa: From Antiquity to Present*. Grand Rapids, MI: Eerdmans, 1995.

International Center for Theoretical Physics. http://www.ictp.it/. Accessed on August 31, 2013.

International Religious Health Assets Program at the University of Cape Town: http://www.arhap.uct.ac.za/. Accessed August 2, 2013.

Jacob, Margaret C. "The Cultural Origins of the First Industrial Revolution." In *The Scientific Revolution*, ed. Marcus Hellyer, 196-215. Oxford: Blackwell, 2003.

Jenkins, Philip. *The New Faces of Christianity: Believing the Bible in the Global South*. Oxford: Oxford University Press, 2006.

———. *The Next Christendom: The Coming of Global Christianity*. Oxford: Oxford University Press, 2011.

———. *Jesus Wars: How Four Patriarchs, Three Queens, and Two Emperors Decided What Christians Would Believe for the Next 1,500 Years*. New York, NY: HarperOne, 2010.

Jennings, Jr., Theodore W. *The Vocation of the Theologian*. Philadelphia, PA: Fortress, 1985.

Kalu, Ogbu. *African Pentecostalism: An Introduction*. Oxford: Oxford University Press, 2008.

———. "Holy Praiseco: Negotiating Sacred and Popular Music and Dance in African Pentecostalism." *Pneuma* 32 (2010): 16-40.

Kato, Byang H. *Theological Pitfalls in Africa*. Kisumu, Kenya: Evangel Publishing House, 1975.

Katongole, Emmanuel. "Greeting: Beyond Racial Reconciliation." In *The Blackwell Companion to Christian Ethics*, eds. Stanley Hauerwas and Samuel Wells, 68-81. Oxford: Blackwell, 2004, 2006.

———. *The Sacrifice of Africa: A Political Theology for Africa*. Grand Rapids, MI: Eerdmans, 2010.

Katz, Steven T., Shlomo Biderman and Gershon Greenberg, eds. *Wrestling with God: Jewish Theological Response During and After the Holocaust*. Oxford: Oxford University Press, 2007.

Bibliography

Kaufman, Gordon. *In Face of Mystery: A Constructive Theology*. Cambridge, MA: Harvard University Press, 1993.

Kinnaman, David and Gabe Lyons. *unChristian: What a New Generation Thinks about Christianity . . . and Why It Matters*. Grand Rapids, MI: Baker Books, 2007.

Kuhn, Thomas S. *The Structure of Scientific Revolutions*, third edition. Chicago and London: The University of Chicago Press, 1996.

Kwenda, Chirevo V. "Affliction and Healing: Salvation in African Religion." *Journal of Theology of Southern Africa* 103 (March 1999): 1–12.

Ladd, George Eldon. *A Theology of the New Testament*. Revised edition. Grand Rapids, MI: Eerdmans, 1993.

Lado, Ludovic. "The Roman Catholic Church and African Religions: A Problematic Encounter." *The Way* 45.3 (July 2006): 7–21. http://www.theway.org.uk/453Lado.pdf. Accessed on August 1, 2013.

Lahey, Stephen. "Wyclif and Lollardy." In *The Medieval Theologians: An Introduction to Theology in the Middle Ages*, ed. G. R. Evans, 334–354. Oxford: Blackwell, 2001.

Landes, David S. *The Wealth and the Poverty of Nations*. New York: W. W. Norton and Company, 1998, 1999.

Le Goff, Jacques. *Le Dieu du Moyen Âge*. Paris: Bayard, 2003.

Lindbeck, George. *The Nature of Doctrine: Religion and Theology in a Postliberal Age*. Louisville, KY: Westminster John Knox Press, 1984.

Livingston, James C. *Modern Christian Thought, vol. 1: The Enlightenment and the Nineteenth Century*. Second edition. Minneapolis, MN: Fortress Press, 2006.

Livingston, James C. et al., *Modern Christian Thought, vol. 2: The Twentieth Century*. Second edition. Minneapolis, MN: Fortress Press, 2006.

Lyman, J. Rebecca. "Heresiology: The Invention of 'heresy' and 'schism.'" In *The Cambridge History of Christianity, vol. 2: Constantine to c. 600*, eds. Augustine Casiday and Frederick W. Norris, 299–313. Cambridge: Cambridge University Press, 2007.

Magesa, Laurenti. *African Religion: The Moral Traditions of Abundant Life*. Maryknoll, NY: Orbis Books, 1997.

———. "A Theological Journey." *Exchange* 32.1 (2003): 43–53.

———. *Anatomy of Inculturation: Transforming the Church in Africa*. Maryknoll, New York: Orbis Books, 2004.

———. *What is Not Sacred? African Spirituality*. Maryknoll, New York: Orbis Books, 2013.

Maluleke, Tinyiko Sam. "Of Collapsible Coffins and Ways of Dying." *The Ecumenical Review* 54.3 (July 2002): 313–332.

Marshall, Ruth. *Political Spiritualities: The Pentecostal Revolution in Nigeria*. Chicago, IL: The University of Chicago Press, 2009.

Martey, Emmanuel. *African Theology: Inculturation and Liberation*. Maryknoll, New York: Orbis Books, 1993.

Mashau, T. Derrick and Martha T. Frederiks. "Coming of Age in African Theology." *Exchange* 37 (2008): 109–123.

Masoga, Mogomme Alpheus. "A Critical Dialogue with Gabriel Molehe Setiloane: The Unfinished Business of the African Divinity Question." Unpublished. http://uir.unisa.ac.za/bitstream/handle/10500/6624/Masoga.pdf?sequence=1. Accessed online on August 1, 2013.

Theology as Construction of Piety

Maspero, Giulio and Robert J. Woźniak, eds. *Rethinking Trinitarian Theology: Disputed Questions and Contemporary Issues in Trinitarian Theology*. London: T & T Clark, 2012.

Mbiti, John S. *African Religions and Philosophy*. New York: Praeger Publishers, 1969.

———. *Concepts of God in Africa*. London: SPCK, 1970.

———. *Introduction to African Religion*. London: Heinemann, 1991.

McIntosh, Mark A. "Theology and Spirituality." In *The Modern Theologians: An Introduction to Christian Theology Since 1918*, ed. David Ford, Third Edition, 392–407. Oxford: Blackwell Publishing, 2005.

McClendon, W. Jr. James. *Biography as Theology: How Life Stories Can Remake Today's Theology*. Philadelphia, PA: Trinity Press International, 1990.

———. *Ethics: Systematic Theology*, vol. 1. Revised edition. Nashville, TN: Abingdon, 2002.

Meyer, Birgit. "'Make a Complete Break with the Past': Memory and Post-Colonial Modernity in Ghanaian Pentecostal Discourse." *Journal of Religion in Africa* 28.3 (August 1998): 316–349.

Michael, Matthew. *Christian Theology and African Traditions*. Eugene, OR: Resource Publications, 2013.

Migliore, Daniel L. *Faith Seeking Understanding*, second edition. Grand Rapids, MI: Eerdmans, 1991, 2004.

Milbank, John. *Theology and Social Theory: Beyond Secular Reason*. Oxford, UK: Blackwell Publishers, 1990, 1993.

———. *The Word Made Strange: Theology, Language, Culture*. Oxford: Blackwell Publishers, 1997.

Moltmann, Jürgen. *Experiences in Theology: Ways and Forms of Christian Theology*. Translated by Margaret Kohl. Minneapolis, MN: Fortress Press, 2000.

———. *The Crucified God: The Cross of Christ as the Foundation and Criticism of Christian Theology*. Translated by R. A. Wilson and John Bowden. Minneapolis, MN: Fortress Press, 1993.

———. *The Coming of God: Christian Eschatology*. Translated by Margaret Kohl. Minneapolis, MN: Fortress Press, 2004.

Morvillo, Nancy. *Science and Religion: Understanding the Issues*. Oxford: Wiley-Blackwell, 2010.

Moss, Todd J. *African Development: Making Sense of the Issues and Actors*. Boulder, CO: Lynne Rienner Publishers, 2007.

Lewis S. Mudge, "Paul Ricoeur on Biblical Interpretation." In *Paul Ricoeur: Essays on Biblical Interpretation*. Edited and Translated by Lewis S. Mudge, 1–40. Philadelphia: Fortress Press, 1980).

Mugambi, J. N. K. *From Liberation to Reconstruction: African Christian Theology after the Cold War*. Nairobi, Kenya: East African Educational Publishers, 1995.

Mukenge, André Kabasele. "Les Lecture Africaines de la Bible à l'aube du troisième millenaire." In *Cultural Readings of the Bible in Africa*, ed. André KaLoba-basele Mukenge, Jean-Claude Loba-Mkole, and Dieudonné P. Aroga Bessong, 13–38. Yaoundé, Cameroon: Édition Clé, 2007.

Ngong, David Tonghou. "Left Behind" Theology Today, 59-2 (July 2002): 285–286.

———. "The Theologian as Missionary." *Journal of Theology for Southern Africa* 13 (2010): 1–19.

———. *The Holy Spirit and Salvation in African Christian Theology*. New York, NY: Peter Lang, 2010.
———. "Christianity as Fertility Religion." Unpublished.
Nicolson, Ronald, ed. *Persons in Community: African Ethics in a Global Culture*. Scottsville, South Africa: University of Kwazulu-Natal Press, 2008.
Niebuhr, H. Richarch, *Christ and Culture*. New York, NY: HarperCollins, 1951.
Oakley, Francis. *The Western Church in the Later Middle Ages*. Ithaca and London: Cornell University Press, 1979.
Odozor, Paulinus Ikechukwu. "An African Moral Theology of Inculturation: Methodological Considerations," *Theological Studies* 69 (2008): 583–609.
Oduyoye, Mercy Amba. "A Coming Home to Myself: The Childless Woman in the West African Space." In *Liberating Eschatology: Essays in Honor of Letty M. Russell*, ed. Margaret A. Farley and Serene Jones, 105–120. Louisville, Kentucky: Westminster John Knox Press, 1999.
———. *Introducing African Women's Theology*. Cleveland, OH: The Pilgrim Press, 2001.
Ogbonnaya, A. Okechukwu. *On Communitarian Divinity: An African Interpretation of the Trinity*. New York: Paragon House, 1994.
Oslon, Roger E. *The Journey of Modern Theology*. Downers Grove, IL: IVP Press, 2013.
Opoku, Kofi Asare. "African Traditional Religion: An Enduring Heritage." In *Religious Plurality in Africa: Essays in Honor of John S. Mbiti*, eds. Jacob K. Olupona and Sulayman S. Nyang, 67–82. Berlin: Mouton de Gruyter, 1993.
Outka, Gene. "Christian Ethics?" In *The Blackwell Companion to Religious Ethics*, ed. William Schweiker. Oxford: Blackwell, 2005), 197–203.
Ozment, Steven. *The Age of Reform, 1250-1550: An Intellectual and Religious History of Late Medieval and Reformation Europe*. New Haven, CT: Yale University Press, 1980.
Parsitau, Damaris Seleina. "Gospel Music in Africa." in *The Wiley-Blackwell Companion to African Religions*, ed. Elias Kifon Bongmba, 489–502. Oxford: Wiley-Blackwell, 2012.
Pato, Luke Lungile. "Indigenization and Liberation: A Challenge to Theology in the Southern African Context." *Journal of Theology for Southern Africa* 99 (November 1997): 40–46.
p'Bitek, Okot and Kwasi Wiredu. *Decolonizing African Religions: A Short History of African Religions in Western Scholarship*. New York: Diasporic Africa Press, 2011.
Pelikan, Jaroslav. *A History of the Development of Christian Doctrine, vol. 3: The Growth of Medieval Theology (600-1300)*. Chicago and London: The University of Chicago Press, 1978.
Phillips, Garry A. and Danna Nolan Fewell, "Ethics, Bible, Reading As If." In *Bible and Ethics of Reading, Semea* 77, ed. Danna Nolan Fewell and Garry A. Phillips, 1–21. Atlanta: Scholars Press, 1997.
Polkinghorne, John. *Science and Theology*. Minneapolis, MN: Fortress Press, 1998.
———. *Quantum Physics and Theology*. New Haven, CT: Yale University Press, 2008.
Porter, Jean. "Trajectories in Christian Ethics." In *The Blackwell Companion to Religious Ethics*, ed. William Schweiker, 227–236. Oxford: Blackwell, 2005.
Rabinow, Paul. "Introduction." In *The Foucault Reader*, ed. Paul Rabinow, 3–29. New York: Vintage Books.
Raines, John ed. *Marx on Religion*. Philadelphia, PA: Temple University Press, 2002.
Rasmussen, Susan J. "Spirit Possession in Africa." In *The Blackwell Companion to African Religions*, ed. Elias Bongmba, 184–197. Oxford: Blackwell, 2012.

Redman, Robb. *The Great Worship Awakening: Singing a New Song in the Postmodern Church*. San Francisco, CA: Jossey-Bass, 2002.

Repko, Allen R. *Interdisciplinary Research: Process and Theory*, second edition. Thousand Oaks, CA: Sage Publications, 2011.

Reuther, Rosemay Radford. *Sexism and God-talk: Toward a Feminist Theology*. Boston, MA: Beacon Press, 1983, 1993.

Ranger, Terrence O. ed. *Evangelical Christianity and Democracy in Africa*. Oxford: Oxford University Press, 2008.

Rottenwöhrer, Gerhard. "Dualism." In *The Medieval Theologians: An Introduction to Theology in the Medieval Period*, ed. G. R. Evans, 287–302. Oxford: Blackwell, 2001.

Rummel, Erika. 'The Theology of Erasmus." In *The Cambridge Companion to Reformation Theology*, eds., David Bagchi and David C. Steinmetz, 28–38. Cambridge: Cambridge University Press, 2004.

Sanneh, Lamin. *Translating the Message: The Missionary Impact on Culture*. Second edition. Maryknoll, New York: Orbis Books, 2009.

———. *Whose Religion is Christianity? The Gospel Beyond the West*. Grand Rapids, MI: Eerdmans, 2003.

———. *The Crown and the Turban: Muslim and West African Pluralism*. Boulder, CO: Westview Press, 1997.

Schmidt, Peter R. *The Culture and Technology of African Iron Production*. Gainesville, FL: University Press of Florida, 1996.

Schreiter, Robert J. ed. *Faces of Jesus in Africa*. Maryknoll, NY: Orbis Books, 1991.

Schüssler-Fiorenza, Elizabeth. "The Ethics of Biblical Interpretation: Decentering Biblical Scholarship." *Journal of Biblical Literature* 107.1 (1988): 3–17.

Schweiker, William. "On Religious Ethics." In *The Blackwell Companion to Religious Ethics*, ed., William Schweiker, 1–16. Oxford: Blackwell, 2006.

Selles, Kurt D. "Protestant Worship with Chinese Characteristics: Reflections on a Chinese Worship Service." *Exchange* 41 (2012): 1–18.

Snyder, Howard A. *Salvation Means Creation Healed: The Ecology of Sin and Grace: Overcoming the Divorce Between Earth and Heaven*. Eugene, OR: Wipf and Stock, 2011.

Steven Shapin, *The Scientific Revolution*. Chicago and London: The University of Chicago Press, 1996.

———. "Pump and Circumstance: Robert Boyle's Literary Technology." In *The Scientific Revolution*, ed. Marcus Hellyer, 72–100. Oxford: Blackwell, 2003.

Shomanah, Musa W. Dube ed. *Other Ways of Reading: African Women and the Bible*. Atlanta: Society of Biblical Literature, 2001.

Shorter, Aylward. *Celibacy and African Culture*. Nairobi: Paulines Publication, 1998.

Smith, James K. A. "Is There Room for Surprise Natural World? Naturalism, the Supernatural, and Pentecostal Spirituality." In *Science and the Spirit: A Pentecostal Engagement with the Sciences*, eds. James K. A. Smith and Amos Yong, 34–49. Bloomington and Indianapolis, IN: Indiana University Press, 2010.

Song, Robert. "Sharing Communion: Hunger, Food, and Genetically Modified Foods." In *The Blackwell Companion to Christian Ethics*, eds. Stanley Hauerwas and Samuel Wells, 388–400. Oxford: Blackwell, 2004, 2006.

Snoek, G. J. C. *Medieval Piety from Relics to the Eucharist: A Process of Mutual Interaction*. Leiden: Brill, 1995.

Bibliography

Soyinka, Wole. "Tolerant Gods." In *Orìsà Devotion as World Religion: The Globalization of Yorùbá Religious Culture*, eds., Jacob Olupona and Terry Rey, 31–50. Madison, WI: The University of Wisconsin Press, 2008.
Stark, Rodney. *The Triumph of Christianity: How the Jesus Movement Became the World's Largest Religion*. New York, NY: HarperOne, 2011.
Stevenson, J. *A New Eusebius*, revised by W. H. C. Frend, New Edition. London: SPCK, 1987.
———. *Creeds, Councils and Controversies: Documents Illustrating the History of the Church, AD 337–461*, New Edition. London: SPCK, 1989.
Stewart, Colin. *From Wrongs to Gay Rights*. Laguna Nigel, CA: P. C. Haddiwiggle Publishing Company, 2013.
Stinton, Diane B. *Jesus of Africa: Voices of Contemporary African Christology*. Maryknoll, NY: Orbis Books, 2004.
Swanson, R. N. *Indulgences in Late Medieval England: Passports to Paradise*. Cambridge: Cambridge University Press, 2007.
Taringa, Nisbert. "How Environmental Is African Traditional Religion?" *Exchange* 35.2 (2006): 191–214.
Taylor, Charles. *A Secular Age*. Cambridge, MA: The Belknap Press of Harvard University Press, 2007.
Taylor, Dianna. "Introduction: Power, Freedom and Subjectivity." In *Michel Foucault: Key Concepts*, ed. Dianna Taylor, 1–9. Durham, UK: ACUMEN, 2011.
Taylor, Mark Lewis. *The Theological and the Political: One the Weight of the World*. Minneapolis, MN: Fortress Press, 2011.
Tilley, Maureen A. *The Bible in Christian North Africa: The Donatist World*. Minneapolis, MN: Fortress Press, 1997.
Tillich, Paul. *Dynamics of Faith*. New York, NY: Harper, 1958.
Thiong'o, Ngugi wa. "Asia in My Life." *Chimurenga*, May 15, 2012. Accessed July 31, 2013.. http://www.chimurenga.co.za/archives/2816.
Torrance, Thomas F. "The Doctrine of the Holy Trinity According to St. Athanasius." *Anglican Theological Review* LXXI.4 (1989): 395–405.
Tours, Gregory of. *Life of the Fathers*. Translated by Edward James. Liverpool: Liverpool University Press, 1991.
Tran, Jonathan. *Foucault and Theology*. London: T & T Clark, 2011.
Tsonievsky, Elias. "The Union of the Two Natures in Christ According to the Non-Chalcedonian Churches and Orthodoxy." *Greek Orthodox Theological Review* (September 1968): 170–180.
Tutu, Desmond. *No Future Without Forgiveness*. New York, NY: DoubleDay, 1999.
Uka, Asonzeh. *A New Paradigm of Pentecostal Power: A Study of the Redeemed Christian Church of God in Nigeria*. Trenton, NJ: Africa World Press, 2008.
Ukah, Asonzeh. "African Christianities: Features, Promises, and Problems." *Working Paper* 79, 1–18. http://www.ifeas.uni-mainz.de/Dateien/AP79.pdf. Accessed on August 1, 2013.
Uzukwu, Eugene, "Food and Drink in Africa, and the Eucharist." *Afer* XXII (1980): 370–398.
Uzukwu, Elochukwu. *Liturgy: Truly Christian, Truly African*. Eldoret, Kenya: Gaba Publications, 1982.
———. *Worship as Body Language: Introduction to Christian Worship, an African Orientation*. Collegeville, MN: Liturgical Press, 1997.

Uzukwu, Elochukwu Eugene. *God, Spirit, and Human Wholeness*. Eugene, Oregon: PickwickPublications, 2012.

Van Klinken, Adriaan S. and Masiiwa Ragies Gunda. "Taking up the Cudgel Against Gay Rights? Trends and Trajectories in African Christian Theologies on Homosexuality." *Journal of Homosexuality* 59 (2012): 114–138.

"Vie de Jesus Mafa." http://www.jesusmafa.com/?lang=en. Accessed on July 9th, 2013.

Walls, Andrew. *The Missionary Movement in Christian History: Studies in the Transmission of Faith*. Maryknoll, New York: Orbis Books, 1996.

Walls, Andrew. *The Cross-Cultural Process in Christian History*. Maryknoll, New York: Orbis Books, 2002.

Walls, Andrew F. "The Cost of Discipleship: The Witness of the African Church." *Word and World* 25.4 (Fall 2005): 433–443.

Ware, Kallistos. "Eastern Christendom." In *The Oxford History of Christianity*, ed., John McManners, 131–166.Oxford: Oxford University Press, 1990.

Warner, Michael, Jonathan VanAntwerpen, and Craig Calhoun, eds. *Varieties of Secularism in a Secular Age*, reprint edition. Cambridge, MA: Harvard University Press, 2013.

Webb, Stephen H. "Review of Nicaea and Its Legacy by Lewis Ayres." *Conversations in Religion and Theology* 6.2 (2008): 134–142.

Webber, Robert E. *Blended Worship*. Hendrickson Publishers, 1996.

Webber, Robert E. *Planning Blended Worship*. Nashville, TN: Abingdon Press, 1998.

West, Gerald O. and Musa W. Dube, eds. *The Bible in Africa: Transactions, Trajectories, and Trends*. Leiden: Brill, 1998.

Westerlund, David. *African Indigenous Religions and Disease Causation: From Spiritual Beings to Living Humans*. Leiden: Brill, 2006.

———. "Religion, Illness, and Healing." In *The Wiley-Blackwell Companion to African Religions*, ed. Elias Kifon Bongmba, 443–456. Oxford: Wiley-Blaxkwell, 2012.

Westman, Robert S. "The Copernicans and the Churches." In *The Scientific Revolution*, ed. Marcus Hellyer, 44–71. Oxford: Blackwell, 2003.

Widdicombe, Peter. "Athanasius and the Making of the Doctrine of the Trinity," *Pro Ecclesia* VI.4 (Fall 1997): 456–478.

Williams, D. H. *Ambrose of Milan and the End of the "Arian"-Nicene Conflicts*. Oxford: Clarendon Press, 1995.

Williams, Rowan. *Arius: Heresy and Tradition*, revised edition. Grand Rapids, MI/ Cambridge, UK, 1987, 2001.

Williams, Rowan. *On Christian Theology*. Oxford, UK: Blackwell Publishing, 2000.

Young, Frances M. *From Nicaea to Chalcedon: A Guide to the Literature and its Background*, second edition. Grand Rapids, MI: Baker Academic, 2010.

Zalanga, Samuel. "Religion, Economic Development and Cultural Change: The Contradictory Role of Pentecostalism in Sub-Saharan Africa." *Journal of Third World Studies* XXVII (2010): 43–62.

General Index

Achebe, Chinua, 140
a Kempis, Thomas, 86
abundant life, xvii
African Pentecostalism, xvii
African Traditional Religions, xii, 11, 12, 97, 107, 109, 111, 112, 125,
ancestors, xiii, 113, 114, 120, 121, 122
Anselm of Canterbury, 8
Appiah, Anthony, xvi
Aquinas, Thomas, 8, 22, 64, 69
Arian, 53, 54
Arius, 42, 43, 44, 45, 49, 61, 66
Asamoah-Gyadu, J. Kwabena, 131
Assisi, Francis of, 82
Athanasius, 47, 48, 49, 50, 51, 56
Augustine, St., 21–22, 31, 42, 68, 69
Ayres, Lewis, 38, 39

Babungo, xii–xv, 91
Barth, Karl, 16,
Biography, xi, xvi
Book of Nature and Book of Scriptures, xxi, 152
Boyle, Robert, 145, 146, 147
Bujo, Bénézet, 107, 108, 111, 113, 119
Bunyan, John, 65
Bynum, Catherine, 64, 89, 90

Cameroon, xi–xvi, 9, 91, 119, 148, 149
Carthars, 86
celibacy, 118, 119
Chaucer, Geoffrey, 65,
Christian ethics, 20–29, 106, 107, 112
Clark, Clifton, 39
Coakley, Sarah, 39

Constantine, 41, 46
Corpenicus, Nicholaus, 144
cosmopolitan, xvii
Council of Chalcedon, 57, 67
Creed of Chalcedon, 57, 58, 58, 58, 67
Cyril (of Alexandria), 55, 56, 57, 58

Darwin, Charles, 153
demonic blockages, xviii
Diamond, Jared, xviii
Donatist, 68, 69

Éla, Jean-Marc, 119
Erasmus of Rotterdam, Desiderius, 87
eschatology/eschatological, 110, 111, 113, 116, 117, 118, 120, 121
ethics of theology, xxi, 3, 19, 20, 24, 25, 35
Eucharist, 21, 23, 27, 64, 67, 76, 77, 79, 86, 100, 101, 102, 103, 125
eudaimonia, 25, 29
Eusebius of Caesarea, 41

Fiorenza, Schüssler, 19
Foucault, Michel, xi, xxi, 3, 13–18
Franciscans, 83
Frei, Hans, 29, 31, 32
Freud, Sigmund, 12

Galilei, Galileo, 144
globalization, xiv
Gregory of Nyssa, 50, 51
Groote, Gerhard, 86

Hauerwas, Stanley, 20–29, 35

167

General Index

Healy, Nicholas, 25, 28
homosexuality/same-sex marriages, 106, 119, 120
Hume, David, 8, 41

icons/iconoclasm, 59, 60, 62, 64, 67
identity, xiii–viv,
interdisciplinary piety/spirituality, xxi, 129, 130, 131, 132, 133, 137, 140, 141, 142, 149, 151, 154

Jenkins, Philip, 31, 32

Kane, Cheikh Hamidou, xix,
Kant, Immanuel, 20–21, 23, 41
Kato, Byang, 11
Kuhn, Thomas, 143, 144

Landes, David, xviii
le Goff, Jacques, 74
Lindbeck, George, 29
Lollards, 86
Lombard, Peter, 69
Luther, Martin, 88

Magesa, Laurenti, xi, xviii, 93, 108
Maluleke, Tinyiko, 6
marriage, xv, 104, 105, 113
Marx, Karl, 12, 132
Mary (Mother of God/Virgin), 55, 57, 59, 65, 66, 71, 72, 73, 74, 77
matter/materiality, 64, 66, 78
material/materialistic, xviii, xx, xxii, 64, 65, 67, 81, 82, 83, 84, 85, 88, 110, 128
Mbiti, John, 6, 114, 121
McClendon, James, 5
Middle Ages xx, xxii, 22, 32, 63, 65, 68, 69, 71, 72, 75, 76, 78, 85, 86, 88, 125, 154
Milbank, John, 5, 133
Miracles, 67, 73, 80, 151
modern/modernity, xii, xvii, xviii, xx, 20, 21, 23, 124, 128, 129, 136, 140
Moltmann, Jürgen, xi,
monothelitic controversy, 58, 59

Moss, Todd, xviii
Nestorius, 54, 55, 57, 66
Nicaea, Council of, 38, 46, 47, 51
Nicene Creed, 51
Nicene Faith, 38, 53, 54,
Niebuhr, H Richard, 21
Nietzsche, Friedrich 12
Non-Chalcedonian churches, 57, 58

Ockham, William, 70, 71
Oduyoye, Mercy Amba, 114, 115, 116
Origen, 2, 48
Owe, xii–xv
Ozment, Steven, 67

pentecostal theology, xviii
Pentecostalism, xvi, xvii, 39, 99, 131
Pentecostal/Pentecostalization, xx, 123
piety, xx, 1, 2, 3, 4, 26, 36, 37, 64, 65, 71, 86, 90, 126, 127, 128, 129
pilgrimage, 65, 81
polygamy/polygyny, 117, 118
postliberal theology/postliberalism, 29–35
premodern, 32–35
providence, 37, 38

rationalism, xxii
Reformation, 76,
relics xxii, 73, 74, 75, 76, 86

sacraments, 67, 68, 69, 70
salvation, 64, 65, 68, 69, 70, 71, 72, 152
science(s), 23, 133, 134, 136, 137, 138, 143, 147, 148, 149
science and technology, xviii, xxi, xxii, 32, 128, 134, 135, 142, 143, 154
Scientific Revolution, 144, 153
Scotus, Duns, 70
Secular/secularization, 136
Soyinka, Wole, 139, 140
spiritual(ized) cosmology, xviii, 121, 123, 124, 125, 126

technology, xiv, 32, 33, 34
Theodosius I, 53
theological ethics, xxi, 3, 20, 35

theology of inculturation, xx, 11, 91, 92, 94, 95, 96, 104, 123, 126, 129, 138, 139
theology of nature, 149, 150
Tillich, Paul, 5
Tran, Jonathan, 18
Trinitarian theology, 38, 43, 50
Trinity, 42, 49
tunnel vision spirituality, 131
Tutu, Desmond, 112

Vita, Kimpa, 104

Ubuntu, 112, 116, 118

Uzukwu, Elochukwu, 99, 101, 103, 112, 139, 140

Waldensians, 85
Ware, Kallistos, 60
Wells, Samuel, 20–29
Westerlund, David, 141, 142
Williams, Rowan, 19, 44, 45
witchcraft, xviii
worship, 21, 23, 24, 24, 27, 98, 99, 100, 101, 132
Wyclif, John, 83, 84, 85

www.ingramcontent.com/pod-product-compliance
Lightning Source LLC
Chambersburg PA
CBHW050803160426
43192CB00010B/1628